STRUGGLE IN THE DARK

By the same author
DANGER FROM MOSCOW
FROGMAN EXTRAORDINARY
SCHOOL FOR SPIES
STALIN—THE MIRACULOUS GEORGIAN
THE TRAITOR TRADE
OUT OF THIS WORLD
HEALING HANDS
COMMANDER CRABB IS ALIVE
By Liam Nolan and J. Bernard Hutton
THE PAIN AND THE GLORY

STRUGGLE IN THE DARK

How Russian and other Iron Curtain Spies operate

by
J. Bernard Hutton

GEORGE G. HARRAP & CO. LTD
London   Toronto   Wellington   Sydney

To Harold

First published in Great Britain 1969
by GEORGE G. HARRAP & CO. LTD
182 High Holborn, London, W.C.1

© *J. Bernard Hutton* 1969
Copyright. All rights reserved
SBN 245 59486 8

Composed in Linotype Caledonia and printed at the
St Ann's Press, Park Road, Altrincham

Made in Great Britain

Preface

ESPIONAGE is as old as organized warfare and far older than civilized society. Every reader of the Bible will remember the activities of spies during the invasion of Palestine, and many will have reflected that even when weapons and tactics were primitive a commander's success often depended on his knowledge of the enemy's dispositions and strategic resources.

As centuries passed, spying activities increased and methods and tactics improved. Because it came to be recognized that organized espionage networks were far more effective than the independent efforts of individual spies, the first professional Secret Service organizations were established.

A classic example of how professional espionage worked in the sixteenth century is the following case taken from the archives of the Venetian Secret Service, considered to have been at that time the best espionage organization in the world.

In 1597 plenipotentiaries representing France and Spain met at Vervins, north-east of Paris, and finally concluded a secret agreement. The text of this treaty was written in code on parchment, which was folded, rolled up, and sealed with the signets of the Spanish negotiators. The document was then wrapped in another roll of parchment, which was again sealed. The roll was placed in a metal tube, which was soldered, and the tube was placed in a large metal container which was finally welded to a chain wrapped around the body of a reliable courier.

The courier had to travel through French and Spanish territory. He arrived at Madrid without mishap, and the Spanish Foreign Office, after examining the seals, was convinced that they were intact and that no attempt had been made to steal the secret document.

Yet by the time the courier had reached Madrid a complete and accurate copy of the treaty was being read by the Supreme Council of the Republic of Venice!

This is how it was done.

The Venetian Secret Service had leased an inn on the courier's route, and had drugged him so skilfully that he never suspected anything; they then abstracted the document, copied it, and replaced it in the containers with duplicate seals. The code was quickly deciphered by experts, and Venice, knowing of the drastic shift in Spanish policy, revised her own policy accordingly.

No-one realized what had happened until a German scholar studying Venetian archives of the sixteenth century discovered this example of ancient espionage.

The Venetian Secret Service was not the only fully organized professional intelligence organization in that era. The rulers of otherwise backward Tsarist Russia were also quick to appreciate the great advantage of well-organized professional espionage. During and after the second part of the sixteenth century, when the troops of Ivan the Terrible roamed along the Volga and conquered first Kazan and then the Tartar kingdom of Astrakhan, Tsarist intelligence was largely responsible for a great number of political, strategic, and other victories.

From the reign of Peter the Great various Russian régimes continued to develop their professional Secret Service and security-forces organizations.

Tsarist Russia boasted that it maintained the largest intelligence and secret-police organizations in the world. It also acknowledged that Britain's Secret Service had achieved the unique standard of the Venetian espionage service. From the early eighteenth century Britain's espionage and counter-espionage played a substantial rôle in strategic, political, and economic successes.

Recognition of Britain's Secret Service was acknowledged by M.V.D.[1] Lieutenant-Colonel Burlitsky, who defected to the free world. He declared:

"I believe that agents of the Western intelligence have penetrated the Government, the Army, and the Communist organizations of the Soviet Union, and probably at the highest levels.

"We were taught at the Moscow College for M.V.D. Officers that British Intelligence is particularly experienced and effective."

The *Manual of the Soviet Secret Service Orgburo* (Moscow, 1960) contains a similar statement.

France's Deuxième Bureau and Germany's Geheimdienst have also earned the highest reputations.

The only major Power without a centuries-old tradition in espionage is the United States of America. From the time that the U.S.A. came into existence spying of any description was always considered to be "alien to the principles of democracy and in-

[1] Ministerstvo Vnutrennykh Dyel = Ministry of the Interior.

dividual freedom". Indeed, the United States of America has gained experience in international intelligence only during the past fifty years. But even after U.S. espionage networks had been successfully established for over a decade there were still many influential personalities in America who considered spying of any description to be 'un-American'. In the twenties, for example, Henry Stimson, Secretary of State in the Hoover Government, declared, "Gentlemen do not read other people's letters" when he abolished the Cipher Department in his Department because of his "Let's-all-be-gentlemen" policy.

Today, of course, almost every American recognizes that no weapon vital to the maintenance of freedom should be discarded.

The many important successes of American agents working behind the Iron Curtain, and the frequent arrests and convictions of Russian and other Communist spies in the United States, and in American-controlled territories, affirm the efficiency of this, the youngest Secret Service of the main world Powers.

To the Western world the Soviet Secret Service constitutes a potential danger to the very existence of its freedom-loving peoples, because the Kremlin has vast numbers of master spies in almost every country, and controls the largest espionage network ever known.

Conservative estimates put the number of fully trained professional Soviet spies outside the Communist bloc at well over quarter of a million men and women—more than ten times the number employed by *all* the Western nations combined. In addition, the Soviet spy web in almost every free country receives active support from more than half a million Communist Party members, Red undercover agents, and fanatical fellow-travellers, bringing the total of all Communist spies to well over three-quarters of a million men and women.

Although Communism gained power in Russia only in November 1917, the Soviet Secret Service really has a much older tradition. Long before they overthrew the Tsar, Lenin and other Bolshevik leaders accepted their 'reactionary' Government's conviction that "espionage of every description is one of the most important weapons for gaining and maintaining power". Even during World War I, years before they were in power, the Bolsheviks maintained widespread clandestine espionage groups inside Tsarist Russia and abroad—in England, France, Germany, Switzerland, and many other countries.

When the Soviet Union was established the Bolshevik internal and external Secret Service was enlarged to build an organization which would clearly outclass any other intelligence service in the world. Although Lenin and his comrades maintained that "everything connected with Tsarism is reactionary and rotten", they nevertheless did not overlook the vast experience of the Tsarist Secret Service, and religiously copied Tsarist espionage methods. In fact, every *Manual of the Soviet Secret Service Orgburo* issued during the past years includes some of the same phrases as the manuals of the Tsarist service. For example: "Prevent, as far as possible, recruitment of agents who might at one time or another prove to be the wrong types because mentally and physically they may be insufficiently strong to withstand the most difficult and unforeseen situations likely to arise in their future work."

During 1966 alone Russia's special spy schools passed 1382 trainees as "fit for foreign service", and the Blakes, the Scarbecks, the Vassalls, the Stashynskys, the Wennerströms, and all the other Communist spies throughout the free world succeeded in supplying Moscow Secret Service headquarters with priceless top-secret information from the West.

Annually thousands of Russian and other Iron Curtain spies and informers are detected in America, Britain, France, West Germany, and in almost every other country, and although a considerable percentage are convicted and imprisoned, every detection of a Soviet spy, or of an espionage centre, causes only temporary dislocation of the network that covers the world. The Soviet slogan "For every single agent lost ten new and better ones must fill the temporarily created gap" still holds good, and the gap which Western counter-intelligence has torn into their espionage web is quickly repaired by dispatching replacements from Moscow, East Berlin, and other Iron Curtain spy-training centres.

In February 1965 Russia's Secret Service chief, Vladimir Semichastny, stated in his report to the Communist Party Presidium: "Moscow Secret Service headquarters receive on the average of every forty-six minutes valuable information from its foreign networks." Whether this statement is correct or whether Russia's Secret Service chief fabricated it for his Party Presidium report is, of course, impossible to establish.

Soviet Secret Service headquarters direct the operations of their master spies abroad not only from Moscow; they also maintain sub-headquarters in East Berlin, Budapest, Prague, and other Iron Curtain countries. And how this "biggest and most efficient espionage network in the world" is constituted, how Russian and other Iron Curtain spies operate in the West, is revealed in this book. It is my earnest hope that in revealing the *modus operandi* of these spies I may place people on the alert who might otherwise become the unwitting tools of those whose aim it is to crush freedom.

J. Bernard Hutton

Contents

Illustrations

Prologue

TO recruit informers for espionage Soviet master spies concentrate on those who can be blackmailed in some way, or on individuals classified as 'suitable' because of their ideologies. But Soviet espionage also uses the innocent.

The case of Miss Barbara Janet Fell, who stood trial at the Old Bailey in London in December 1962, is an illustration of how people who are anti-Communist and would not dream of doing anything to hurt their country can be recruited for Soviet espionage. The sad case of Miss Fell was given considerable publicity in the Press, but because it is a good, and fairly recent, example of how an individual can be made innocently to betray herself and her country it is worth retelling.

In 1957 Belgrade Secret Service headquarters decided to step up its activities in Britain. Its operators were split into four distinct sections—strategic, scientific, governmental, and general intelligence. Each was assigned to different master spies under orders not to communicate with each other.

The master spy whose task it was to concentrate on governmental intelligence was thirty-four-year-old Smiljan Pecjak, Press Counsellor at the Yugoslav Embassy in London. His post provided the added safeguard of diplomatic immunity.

He had already served at the Yugoslav Embassy in Paris, and was one of the best-trained spies in their entire intelligence organization.

At the age of seventeen, when Yugoslav patriots were fighting Hitler's Wehrmacht in mountain forests, Smiljan joined the guerrilla forces of General Tito (then known as the Comintern agent Josip Broz). The Communist guerrilla leader noticed the courageous and intelligent youth, and a friendship developed between them. Young Smiljan became a close associate of Tito, who was certain that this youth would make a good Communist executive.

A year later, in 1942, Smiljan was chosen to go with a delegation of eleven Yugoslav Communist guerrillas to Soviet Russia.
This was an almost impossible task, involving as it did the
crossing of vast areas of German-held territory. It was little short
of a suicide order. But Tito-Broz considered it of great political
importance that a Yugoslav guerrilla delegation should go to
Moscow as a symbol of his solidarity with the Kremlin.

After many months five of the guerrilla delegates reached
Soviet territory. For self-preservation they had been compelled
to go alone, to ensure a better chance of getting through the
Nazi-dominated territory. What happened to the remaining seven
who did not reach the Soviet Union was never discovered.

For a brief period the five surviving delegates from Yugoslavia
toured the U.S.S.R. and made innumerable propaganda speeches.
When their propaganda value was exhausted it was decided that
they should not be sent back to Yugoslavia, but be schooled in
Kuibyshev for future Communist leadership.

Smiljan passed through the University of Communism in 1944
with honours. For a few months he was attached to the Institute
611 (successor of the Comintern), but six months later was classed
as suitable for espionage training. His training as a professional
spy started in 1945 and ended in 1953. During these years he was
schooled at the two Russian spy-training centres, the Marx-
Engels School at Gorky and the Lenin Technical School at Verkhovnoye, and afterwards at the special espionage training establishment of Soyuznaya, situated between the towns of Tula and
Ryazan.

Although since 1949 Stalin's and Tito's great friendship had
turned to bitter enmity, Smiljan's espionage training in Russia was
uninterrupted. He was considered a devoted Marxist-Leninist,
and his explanation that he condemned Marshal Tito's anti-
Cominform and anti-Soviet policy was accepted.

As hostility between Soviet Russia and 'renegade' Yugoslavia
grew it became still more imperative for the Kremlin to establish
reliable master spies in Tito's country. The First Directorate at
Moscow Secret Service headquarters classified Smiljan, who was
listed under the name of Petrov, as suitable for this task, and
immediately his training at Soyuznaya ended he was briefed for
his first assignment.

Smiljan was sent to Poland, but his orders were to "escape" from
Warsaw to his native country and to make it known that he had
taken the first opportunity to return and work for his own
country. His condemnation of President Tito's anti-Cominform
and anti-Soviet policy had always been kept secret in Russia.
Moscow Secret Service headquarters now relied on Smiljan's old
guerrilla friendship with Tito to work in their favour.

The strategy worked. Smiljan's story was accepted, and he was congratulated by President Tito on his "patriotic" return. After a holiday at the Adriatic seaside resort of Dubrovnik he was given a responsible position in the Yugoslav Government, and then transferred to the Yugoslav Embassy in Paris.

When Smiljan Pecjak eventually arrived in London to become Press Counsellor at the Yugoslav Embassy his instructions from Belgrade Secret Service headquarters were to obtain as much secret information as possible from British Government sources. How he was to accomplish this was left to his own initiative and judgment.

Moscow, whom the double agent had informed of his posting and orders, was content with having an additional operator in London, and advised him to "concentrate on women in British Government posts".

It didn't take Pecjak long to learn about Miss Barbara Janet Fell, a fifty-one-year-old spinster who held a responsible position in the Central Office of Information. He arranged to meet Miss Fell—a meeting which brought tragedy to her.

The Solicitor-General, Sir Peter Rawlinson, Q.C., prosecuting Miss Fell at the Old Bailey, said that the Yugoslav Press Counsellor had "invited her to lunch, then to a party, and then their friendship developed on what might be said to be an almost traditional pattern". She believed Pecjak when he told her he loved her; she never doubted his repeated insistence that he was pro-Western, anti-German, and anti-Russian.

She was certain that the bond between them developed largely because she had succeeded in converting him to Western ideas, and she genuinely thought she would completely convert the Communist Press Counsellor to democratic thought. Foolishly she passed on to him reports from the British Ambassador in Belgrade to the Foreign Secretary about Britain's policy in Yugoslavia, and also other documents dealing with United Nations' policies.

Later, when interviewed by Detective Chief Inspector David Stratton of Scotland Yard's Special Branch, she made a statement in which she explained:

"I believed he would be responsive to guidance, and that it would be in the best interests of this country that he should be given such guidance.

"I care deeply for my country, believe in its democratic institutions and way of life, and would never do anything to hurt its interests or endanger its security."

She insisted that she never allowed Pecjak to see anything classified as secret or dealing with military matters.

The Solicitor-General pointed out at her Old Bailey trial that

Miss Fell's case bore no relation to, nor had any connection with, other spy cases, and said, "The Crown accepts that, while acting undoubtedly in an irresponsible way, she never intended acting in a manner prejudicial to the safety or interest of the State." Nevertheless, he went on, she had prejudiced the interests of the State, and her offences were serious.

Passing sentence on Miss Fell, who had pleaded guilty, Mr Justice Gorman told her:

"High office, such as you have held, has its advantages and sweets of office. But it has tremendous responsibilities.

"Every Government department and large industrial concern must have people who can be trusted. In your case your office was high and you had great responsibilities. You had a substantial salary and you were trusted.

"It would be quite unrealistic to approach this case as other than one of gravity and seriousness. The failure to live up to the responsibilities and the trust imposed in you is a very great fall."

Then the woman who had been cheated by talk of love was given a two-year prison sentence. Double agent Smiljan had safely left England with his blonde wife and two children, and returned to his own country.

Miss Fell's background? She came from a renowned family with four titled generals in her line. After graduating from Oxford she became a Fleet Street journalist, and in 1939 joined the Civil Service. Her fine record, good character, and exceptional services brought her a successful Civil Service career. Yet, though she was a most careful and conscientious Overseas Controller at the Central Office of Information, she failed to pierce the façade of the Russian-trained master spy who had chosen her as a target for extracting Government secrets.

But let us come even further up to date. Consider the happenings in Italy in March 1967, when revelations of a spy ring operating from that country were made in headlines in the Western Press.

As the ripples from the broken international Soviet spy ring spread, with arrests and deportations of suspected agents and informers by several nations, the people of the free world were shocked to discover that the extensive spy web had been working successfully in many countries of the Continent and the Mediterranean for thirteen years, supplying Moscow Secret Service headquarters with priceless N.A.T.O. and other secrets. Many people were astonished to learn that the leader of this clockwork espionage network was the attractive Italian artist-parachutist Angela Maria Rinaldi.

Let us go back to the beginning.

In 1954 Moscow Secret Service headquarters decided that the thirty-eight-year-old Angela should become the Resident Network Operator of a spy web which she was to create in Italy. She was intelligent, energetic, pretty, and pleasant, looked about fifteen years younger than her actual age, and was 'respectable'. The Soviet espionage directors believed she would succeed. They were right.

It did not take the methodical Angela long to set the machinery in motion. She was equipped by Moscow headquarters with lists of people suitable for recruitment; she went about her task skilfully, and with sufficient funds to pay her agents and informers handsomely, so that by the spring of 1954 her first network was already fully operative. Her Secret Service superiors in Moscow were pleased with the regular flow of secret information that she transmitted through her communication routes.

One of her most important agents was her husband, the Italian parachute ace Giorgio Rinaldi. He did not know that his pretty wife was almost fifteen years his senior. He believed her to be a year younger: the entry in her parachute-club membership card confirmed her 'age'.

Giorgio Rinaldi, who had access to N.A.T.O. and other air bases as a parachute ace and instructor, used ultra-modern photographic and film techniques, including miniature cameras, for taking pictures of secret bases as he flew over them to make exhibition jumps. Whenever he had the opportunity to talk with 'men in the know' he recorded every word on his concealed hair-wire recorder; he was also quick to microfilm important blueprints, documents, and plans whenever the opportunity arose.

Angela, who was nicknamed by her agents "The Tsarina", transmitted to Moscow Secret Service headquarters all the information, microfilms, and recordings she received not only from her husband, but also from all her other agents in Italy, Greece, Cyprus, Somaliland, Morocco, Spain, Portugal, Switzerland, England, Scandinavia, and other areas in Europe and Africa. Some of the information was transmitted to Moscow by means of coded high-speed radio communications; other messages were in invisible ink and reached Moscow via harmless-seeming roundabout routes. Microdot communications were affixed under postage-stamps on picture postcards or business letters, and microfilms and recordings were concealed in special innocent-looking containers.

'Dead drops', or pick-up spots, also played an important rôle, and Angela was extremely clever in choosing her 'dead drops'. Her pick-up spots at Turin Zoo, the one near the Basilica of Superga (burial-place of Italian kings), and those in and near Rome, on lonely mountainsides or in busy city centres in Switzer-

B

land, were such perfect hiding-places that no-one ever discovered
them—even by chance. And the "medieval village" in Turin's
Valentine Park which had been set up to serve as a laboratory for
processing films was a unique idea.

In 1956—two years after Angela created her first successful
spy ring in Italy—Moscow Secret Service headquarters summoned her husband Giorgio to the Soviet Union to receive training in general espionage methods. Giorgio could not travel
officially to the U.S.S.R. if Italian and Allied counter-intelligence
and security were not to be alerted, so a clandestine trip was
arranged. He flew secretly from Paris to Russia, and his journey
was, of course, not shown in his passport. At the end of the short
training course he returned to Paris by the same route, without
causing suspicion in France or Italy.

Shortly afterwards Italian security began to keep an eye on
Giorgio—when he first met a Soviet Army officer. However,
Angela was warned by her network's Control Agent of the danger,
so Giorgio stopped meeting anyone who might seem compromising. After months of frustrating round-the-clock trailing, during
which nothing was unearthed that could point to treachery,
counter-intelligence called off their activities. They were temporarily satisfied that Giorgio's meeting with the Soviet Army officer
had been a harmless encounter—no more than his casual meetings
with Allied officers and dignitaries whom he met in his capacity
as Italy's top parachutist.

During the next seven years neither Angela, her husband, nor
any of her agents and informers was suspected; a continuous
supply of important strategic secrets flowed unhindered to Moscow Secret Service headquarters.

In 1963 counter-intelligence once more began to suspect Giorgio. The Rinaldis' antique shop, which was their espionage 'cover',
appeared to be in financial difficulties, yet Giorgio seemed to
have plenty of money. Close watch was kept on him, and it was
conducted with such expertise that Angela's Control Agent failed
to notice it. Although this surveillance was fruitless, counter-
intelligence nonetheless decided to continue the watch. They
sensed that in the end they would meet with success.

Eventually security agents discovered that Giorgio had been
on a secret air trip from Paris to Russia and back. This was the
first encouraging discovery. Giorgio could, of course, have been
arrested and charged with illegal travel because his passport
failed to show his arrival in and departure from the Soviet Union,
but counter-intelligence wanted him to believe that his journey
had gone unnoticed. There was still no evidence to connect him
with espionage, but there was the possibility that, lulled into
believing he was safe, he himself would provide the required

proof. More air trips to and from the U.S.S.R. followed. Giorgio's noose was tightening.

In mid-March 1967 the spy-catchers' long wait was at last rewarded.

When Svyetlana Stalin arrived in Rome—after having defected in India and requested political asylum—Angela Rinaldi received an urgent coded high-speed radio message from her Moscow superiors asking her to use her networks to locate the "dangerous traitor" and kidnap her. Moscow's instructions were immediately put into operation: all agents and informers—including Angela, her husband, and their chauffeur-agent, Armando Girard—tried to follow Svyetlana's movements while she hid in Rome for a few days on her flight to Switzerland. And when it was discovered that the "dangerous traitor" had got away and flown to Berne Angela decided she must be located and kidnapped there.

By this time not only Giorgio but also Angela and Armando were under surveillance. Unaware of any danger, Armando Girard was arrested on the Italian-Swiss border as he was crossing over into Switzerland. He was found to be in possession of microfilm rolls of American air bases in Spain.

The next move was the arrest of Angela Maria and Giorgio Rinaldi in Turin. The scoop was fantastic. An ultra-powerful short-wave radio receiver-transmitter, code-books, and microfilms of N.A.T.O. bases in Italy and U.S. bases in other parts of Europe, together with considerable amounts of specialized espionage equipment, were seized.

Giorgio broke down and disclosed several secret 'dead drops' where Russian agents collected material left for them.

For four days counter-intelligence agents kept the 'dead drops' under secret surveillance, and on the night of March 20th, 1967, their patience was rewarded. A black Soviet Embassy car—driven by Yuryi Pavlenko, an attaché at the Soviet Embassy in Rome, with his wife, Natalia, at his side—stopped at one of the secret hiding-places at the Via Braccianese, in surburban Rome. As Pavlenko fumbled in the 'dead drop' and took a roll of microfilm out, security men pounced, and Pavlenko dashed back to his car. But two police cars pulled across the road, front and rear.

Cloaked by diplomatic immunity, the Soviet attaché was safe from arrest, and all the Italian authorities could do was to declare him *persona non grata* and expel him, together with his wife and their six-year-old son; two days after the detection the three left Rome on a Czechoslovak airliner. Angela Maria and Giorgio Rinaldi, together with Armando Girard, were officially charged with espionage, and were eventually given long-term jail sentences.

The uncovering of "The Tsarina's" espionage networks brought the following developments:

In Cyprus a Soviet Embassy attaché, Boris Petrin, and a Soviet airline employee, Nikolai Renov, were deported for complicity in the espionage. Two Cypriots were arrested and accused of spying on British and U.S. installations. One of the Cypriots, a telephonist, Vikention Boutros, handled overseas calls, including those to embassies; the other, David Shehabin, worked on the R.A.F. base at Nicosia.

In Greece a Soviet agent was arrested in Athens, and in Switzerland it was officially announced that "the possibility of arrests cannot be excluded". In Rome it was disclosed that counter-intelligence had leads to operators of Angela's international networks—in Scandinavia, France, Spain, Morocco, and elsewhere—and far-reaching arrests followed.

This unique Soviet espionage case, as fantastic as a James Bond story, is only one of the numerous cases of Communist espionage in the free world. Some of them really do merit the description of being stranger than fiction.

1

The Key to Success

SOME of the greatest spy cases of all time—even more in-
credible than the most ingenious fictional spy thrillers—belong to
World War II. They are still used by instructors at spy schools
throughout the world for acquainting intelligence cadets with the
inventiveness of ace Resident Network Operators of the past.

Take the Rote Kapelle (Red Orchestra) Network, considered
by all espionage directors and experts as a 'classic' because of its
far-reaching activities and character, and because it was perhaps
the most effective espionage web ever organized in a war.

In Germany and Nazi-occupied Europe the Allied, and particularly the Soviet, Secret Service succeeded, for a time at least,
in establishing formidable spy webs whose agents were fed with
information by "roast beef" (outside brown, inside red) German
Government officials. There is little doubt that the most effective
of these spy webs was the Red Orchestra Network, directed by
Ernst Friedrich Wollweber from—neutral Sweden.

Wollweber has been described as "the first violin of the Red
Orchestra", because he was in charge of the networks of Soviet
Secret Service agents in Nazi-occupied Europe and the Third
Reich itself. The Red Orchestra Network had at its disposal
fourteen powerful radio transmitters in the cities of Europe.
Messages were relayed every night to Moscow. About two hun-
dred agents were members of the Red Orchestra Network, but
only a handful knew the radio stations and their locations.

One of the spy centres was in Brussels, where the network was
known as the Bordo Group. It was directed by N.K.V.D. Captain
Konstantin Pavlovich Yefromov, who came to Belgium in 1939
as an engineering student. When finally detected by the Gestapo
the Bordo Group had nineteen full-time agents. But, although the
Bordo Group was smashed, the Red Orchestra Network in Belgium was not wiped out, for there was a second spy web, the
Kent Group, in Belgium, efficiently led by two Soviet Secret
Service agents, Mikhail Makharov and Pavel Danilov.

A third centre of the Red Orchestra Network was the Hilde Group, with headquarters in Amsterdam, but controlled by Yefromov from Brussels and by the Dutch Communist Maurice Wintering.

The fourth network, the Gilbert Group, had headquarters in Paris and agents in a large number of French towns. For three years the Gilbert Group sent information on the movement of Nazi troops from the West to the East.

The Rado Group in Geneva was the fifth network; the sixth was the Rössler Group in Lucerne; the seventh was in Portugal, where a radio transmitter was linked with others able to relay to Moscow.

Wollweber directed the networks by radio and by couriers from Stockholm. His agents, who hated the Hitler régime, were ready to risk their lives. Among them were Dr Arvid Harnack, a high official in the Nazi Ministry of Economic Affairs under Dr Funk; Captain Harro von Schultze-Boysen of the Luftwaffe; and Dr Adam Kuckhoff and his wife, Margarete, who translated Goebbels' speeches into English at the Nazi Propaganda Ministry. These and other intellectuals, and even some Junkers, made certain that the information came from the highest sources. Most of the members of the Red Orchestra Network inside Nazi Germany were caught and executed by the Gestapo, but for two years the Soviet Secret Service transmitters worked in the heart of enemy territory.

American and British agents also worked behind the enemy lines, and many brave men and women volunteered to be parachuted into the Continent, but the point to be stressed about the Red Orchestra Network is that is was planned long before the outbreak of war, and was complete with radio transmitters and operators even while there was still talk of "peace in our time".

Wollweber not only directed the Red Orchestra Network, but also organized a campaign of sabotage, probably unequalled in wartime, doing more damage to the Axis war effort than a fleet of submarines.

The son of a Silesian miner, Wollweber joined the German Communist Party as a youth, and grew up with it. He attracted the attention of Moscow at the end of World War I, when he organized mutinies in Hamburg. He reached Moscow, then cut off from Germany, in characteristic fashion. Signing on with a North Sea trawler, he smuggled four comrades aboard and hid them in the empty fish-tank. At sea the five Communists held up the ship with pistols and forced the captain to sail to Murmansk.

After training Wollweber was sent back to organize a worldwide system of couriers for the Comintern, as Secretary of the

International Seamen's Union. Years of service in different parts of the world followed. He became an expert in marine sabotage, and is credited with the destruction of or damage to twenty-one German, Italian, and Franco-Spanish ships carrying arms and food to the Franco forces.

From 1933 he worked at Copenhagen, ostensibly as manager of A. Salvo and Co., architects and engineers, with large offices in Denmark, all operating as private firms. For the war that was seen to be coming Wollweber was assigned the task of sabotaging Germany's sea-borne supplies. He had some dress rehearsals— the catastrophe of one of the Hitler "Strength through Joy" liners —the fire that destroyed, in 1938, the Hamburg-Amerika Line flagship *Hapag-Reliance*. And there was the sinking of the *Klaus Booge* in Hamburg harbour, the explosions aboard the *Nordeney* and *Philes*—all the work of Wollweber and his agents. This was only preparation for Wollweber's carefully planned campaign during the war years. The Soviet gave him unlimited funds.

During World War II Wollweber was under orders from Moscow not to allow any Swedish ship carrying iron ore from Luleå to reach Germany from Stockholm, Malmö, or Göteborg. Sweden was neutral, and regarded her supplies to Germany as quite legitimate, though they were, of course, a vital help to the German war effort. When several cargo-ships had been set on fire or destroyed by time bombs hidden in the hulls by Wollweber's men before they left Swedish ports, the Swedish authorities pounced on Wollweber, whom they had long suspected. But while he was in prison his agents delivered his reply: three modern destroyers of the Swedish Navy were blown up in the port of Stockholm. Shortly after Wollweber's arrest Moscow delivered a sharp protest to Stockholm, and he was eventually released.

The cargo-ships which Wollweber destroyed included the large vessels *Vaasa, Ada Gorthon, Lilje, Gustavus Adolphus, Malmö, Galeon,* and *Luleå*. He wiped out a good part of the Swedish merchant fleet, and Swedish insurance companies refused to cover ships carrying ore for Germany. To stop shipments of iron ore to Germany completely Wollweber decided to attack at the source. He sent his explosive experts to the rail junction of Krylbo, on Dalaly Lake, in Vastmansland, north-west of Stockholm. They blew up the marshalling yards with scores of goods trains carrying German tanks and ammunition from Norway to the Eastern front and raw materials from Norway and Denmark to Germany. So thorough was the sabotage that the town of Krylbo was almost wholly destroyed.

Wollweber's saboteurs did not limit their effort to Northern Europe. He planned and directed sabotage against the Italians in the Adriatic and Mediterranean, and many mysterious explosions aboard Italian, Yugoslav, and Greek ships requisitioned by the Axis Powers puzzled British Naval Intelligence, who knew nothing of Herr Wollweber at the time.

Organizing sabotage wholesale did not impair his concentrated, round-the-clock direction of the Red Orchestra Network. Together with Captain Walter Ulbricht, he even set up an additional Red Orchestra Network in Nazi Germany itself. Ulbricht had offices in the chambers of a firm of 'lawyers', and was known under the aliases of Sorensen and Urik. The new espionage centre in the Third Reich worked most efficiently.

After the War Wollweber and Ulbricht were rewarded for their "excellent work". Walter Ulbricht became Deputy Prime Minister (later the Supreme head) of the German Democratic Republic (Communist East Germany), and Ernst Friedrich Wollweber was made Secretary of State for Transport and Shipping.

In the building of Hitler's former Luftwaffe Ministry in Berlin, which the Communists rebuilt as the seat of the East German Government, Wollweber sat behind the big desk once used by Goering's deputy and, as Secretary of State for Transport and Shipping, used his skill as an agent for sabotaging Western defence in a different way. He broke laws prohibiting shipments of strategic materials to Iron Curtain countries as effectively as he had sabotaged the German ships. His high Government post was a cover for his real work—to make West Germany an arsenal for Communism.

Many masters of Ruhr industries were prepared to do business with Herr Wollweber—a little surreptitiously, perhaps, because of American and British watchfulness. In 1950 alone West German industrialists sent £24,500,000 worth of strategic materials to the Soviet Zone. During the first six months of the Korean war West German trade with Communist China also increased by 2700 per cent. Iron and steel exports from the Ruhr during 1951 to the Soviet Union, through Wollweber's good services, amounted to £833,000. In 1952 the figure almost doubled, and in 1953–54, and afterwards, the illegal trade in strategic materials between West Germany and the U.S.S.R. and Red China was in the region of £170,000,000.

By producing forged invoices and false customs declarations, by bribing customs guards, and by using devious routes through Belgium or Holland, and then by sea to Polish ports, West German industrialists shipped complete smelting and foundry plants and power stations, as well as tens of thousands of precious machine tools, to the East, where they were used to equip armament factories in Poland, Soviet Russia, and Red China. The Americans and British have tried to stop the trade, but Moscow has reason to be satisfied with Wollweber's post-War record of sabotaging Western defence efforts and supplying almost priceless industrial-strategic information of every description.

To understand how the Soviet Secret Service is able continuously to succeed and endanger the free world's existence and independence it is necessary to be familiar with the structure and tactics of Communist intelligence.

Since the early days of World War I, when the founder of the Bolshevik Secret Police and Secret Service, Feliks Edmundovich Dzhierzhinskiy, commanded but a few dozen fanatical Communist spies, the Soviet Secret Service has progressed far. Its basic principle, regardless of whether it concerns internal or international networks, has been "farsightedness in the selection of spies, to prevent, as far as possible, recruitment of agents who might at one time or another prove to be the wrong type because mentally and physically they may be insufficiently strong to withstand the most difficult and unforeseen situations likely to arise in their future work".

Comprehensive precautions are adopted to ensure that, from the very beginning, entirely suitable candidates are found. From the earliest days of Communist rule in Russia spy schools have been, and are still being, maintained, where future Soviet spies are expertly trained in every field of espionage. Yet, although the selection of spies, their training, and their successes are outstanding, Russia's espionage directors are always eager to improve organization and tactics, and the nature of the almost continuous changes in their methods will be detailed later in this book.

Apart from the exceptional and near-foolproof selection of recruits, and apart from the extraordinary structure and thoroughness of Russia's intelligence system, there is another important reason why it is so effective. This is the Soviet belief that their spies must never worry about money, and must have all the funds available to achieve the best results.

Unlike Britain, the U.S.A., and other Western countries, where there is an annual vote in Parliament for Secret Service expenditure, and where it is consequently impossible to hide large sums spent on intelligence development, Russia puts no pressure on its Secret Service to economize. On the contrary, it is encouraged to spend millions of dollars, pounds sterling, Swiss francs, and other currencies annually. Expense is no object; Soviet operators in foreign countries are allowed to spend freely—providing they show good results.

A striking example of the astronomic sums which some of their agents are permitted to spend is the case of Rudolph Rössler.

Rössler annually received from Moscow between four and five hundred *thousand* dollars! This amount comprised remuneration for his own services, his working capital for buying information, and the necessary funds for maintaining his costly and elaborate spy web.

Rössler was indeed a very important operator in the Soviet Secret Service. During World War II, working within the framework of the Red Orchestra Network, he kept Moscow headquarters supplied with accurate advance information about the location and plans of the Nazi Wehrmacht, with reports made by Nazi intelligence regarding Soviet positions and operations, and even with exact reports on the overall strategy which Hitler himself ordered or approved in top-secret conferences with trusted officers.

There is no doubt that Rössler was one of the best agents the Soviet Secret Service has ever had. He was a German editor and publisher, and pretended to be a "Liberal Catholic". Because of the enormous communication difficulties which the war between Germany and Russia imposed, the easiest way to get intelligence information out of the Third Reich was, in Rössler's opinion, to pass it on to Soviet agents in neighbouring neutral Switzerland. To cover his numerous clandestine crossings over the German-Swiss border Rössler managed to obtain employment in both the Swiss and the Nazi intelligence. The most extraordinary lesson of this story is that this unique treble agent succeeded in escaping suspicion and detection by Nazi counter-intelligence.

Another Soviet master spy whose case made headlines in the world Press—the notorious Colonel Abel—received between three hundred thousand and three-quarters of a million dollars a year for his services and for maintaining his New York and other American spy rings; and many other Russian master spies received annual funds of six-figure sums.

2

A Brilliant Master Spy

THE success of the Soviet master spy Dr Richard Sorge is of
special interest because of features rarely paralleled even in
fiction. It is no exaggeration to say that in the history of espionage it would be difficult to find a better illustration of a spy
whose individual brilliance and initiative enabled him to achieve
such spectacular results.

Sorge was born in 1895 in the oil town of Baku, on the Caspian
Sea. His father was German, an engineer employed as manager
of an oil company and married to a Russian girl. Their son
Richard stayed only a few years in the town where everything
smelled of oil and where fully veiled women walked in the narrow
streets and markets.

The Sorge family eventually returned to Germany, and Richard's father found a position in Hamburg.

With the start of World War I, Richard, then nineteen years
old, volunteered to serve in the Kaiser's Army. He was wounded
three times, but it was not until 1918 that he left the Army. He
enrolled at Kiel University, and there became a convinced
Communist.

After getting his doctor's degree in 1924 Richard went to
Moscow. He was considered to be excellent material for future
espionage duties, and in due course was sent to Soviet spy schools.
He received his first assignment from the distinguished Comintern
spy chief, Osip Pyatnitsky.

Because Sorge's father was well-to-do, Richard had private
means, and he refused to take money from the Communist Party
or the Soviet Union. He even suggested that he be sent to London
at his own expense. Pyatnitsky accepted the offer, and, supplied
with codes, names and addresses from the Central Index, and
technical espionage equipment, the new spy went to England.

Dr Richard Sorge was so successful in Britain, and later in
Scandinavia, that he was promoted in 1929 to a high post in Soviet

Military Intelligence. He maintained close contact with the Comintern and with Moscow Secret Service headquarters. He was, in fact, one of the few agents ever permitted to work for both the civilian Soviet Secret Service and Soviet Military Intelligence.

In the early thirties Richard Sorge concentrated on espionage in the Far East. He had always been particularly interested in this part of the world, and was acknowledged to be the best Soviet expert on Asia. Fluent in both Chinese and Japanese, he was, for some time, in charge of Soviet espionage in Shanghai, and visited Tokyo many times. He had many friends among prominent Chinese and Japanese politicians.

When Hitler came to power in January 1933 Dr Sorge proposed that he himself should go to the Third Reich and establish contact with leading Nazis. He had been away from Germany for almost eight years.

His proposal that he pretend to be a *Volksdeutscher*—a German living abroad—was accepted by Moscow headquarters, and it was thought that his return to the Third Reich might enable him to obtain a post in the Gestapo or in another important Nazi organization.

Proof of the esteem in which Richard Sorge was held is the fact that before the Soviet Secret Service and Military Intelligence directors issued orders for him to go to Germany his scheme was submitted direct to Stalin. Stalin approved, and signed promotion of the master spy to Lieutenant-General.

Richard Sorge returned to Germany. His statement that he was a *Volksdeutscher* who had come home to the Fatherland was accepted. He contacted the Soviet Secret Service resident director in Germany, Ignatz Reiss, and was then introduced to Dr Geissenberg, editor of the *Frankfurter Zeitung* and a German nationalist of the old school, with many friends among the Nazi leaders.

Geissenberg had no idea of Richard Sorge's mission. He was impressed with the man's brilliance, and offered him a post as a Foreign Correspondent for the *Frankfurter Zeitung*. In time he introduced Sorge to the Nazi Propaganda Minister, Dr Josef Goebbels, and to other members of the Nazi hierarchy.

Sorge must have felt that he had been born under a lucky star. The Gestapo did not discover evidence of his Communist past, and no flaw could be found in forged documents which stated that he had worked in China for a number of German firms. He was classed "reliable", and quickly joined the N.S.D.A.P.—Hitler's Nazi Party. A few months later he travelled as an accredited newspaper correspondent to Tokyo.

When Sorge next visited the Third Reich one of Admiral Canaris's agents approached him to suggest that he combine his work as Tokyo Correspondent of the *Frankfurter Zeitung* with

intelligence work for the Nazi *Nachrichtendienst* (Secret Service).
This was exactly the kind of situation Sorge had hoped would
arise. But he played it cool, expressing anxiety about his lack of
knowledge of intelligence work. Canaris's agent quickly dispelled
his doubts, and promised to advise and instruct him.

Less than a year after his return to Germany Sorge had become
an agent for the Nazi Secret Service. With the highest Nazi
credentials, he was able to establish excellent liaison with the
German Embassy in Tokyo, and he soon became friendly with
Lieutenant-Colonel Eugen Ott, a German artillery expert with the
Japanese Army. Ott even showed him secret reports he filed to
Berlin. Sorge, of course, passed all the material on to Moscow.

In his capacity as a newspaperman Richard Sorge opened a
small office in the centre of Tokyo, and engaged, as an assistant,
Ozaki Hozumi, a journalist who also happened to be a cousin
of the Japanese Prime Minister, Prince Konoye. Sorge discovered
that Hozumi had "strong progressive leanings". With careful
schooling, Sorge "developed him ideologically" into a devoted
Communist.

Lieutenant-Colonel Eugen Ott had powerful friends in Nazi
Government circles, and was promoted to German Ambassador
in Tokyo. To show how much he valued Sorge's friendship he
appointed the spy Press Attaché at the Embassy. This was a
fantastic break for Sorge. But there was also a snag: he could no
longer keep in secret touch with Moscow Secret Service headquarters from his office.

It was arranged that a Soviet Secret Service agent, Branko de
Voukelic, be sent to Tokyo as correspondent of a French illus-
trated journal, to act as cover for the espionage centre, and the
Soviet Secret Service officer Max Klausen, a radio operator, was
to act as his assistant. To give the new spy centre 'local' character
a Japanese journalist, Miyagi Yotoko, who had lived in the U.S.A.
since the end of World War I and was a secret member of the
Communist Party of America, completed the trio.

The set-up was ingenious. It was natural for the German Press
Attaché in Tokyo to mix with journalists from Paris and New
York, and no-one suspected that Yotoko or de Voukelic conveyed
the Press Attaché's material to Klausen for coded high-speed
radio transmission to Russia. To ensure that all of Klausen's radio
communications would reach Moscow (without being dependent
on favourable conditions) radio relay stations were established
in Harbin and China.

Apart from being Press Attaché of the German Embassy in
Tokyo, Richard Sorge was also a member of the Nazi Intelligence
Service. Berlin expected him to pass on any information that
might be of value to the military and political leadership of the

Third Reich, so he planted on his Nazi employers 'information' fabricated in Moscow. Some of his 'intelligence' reports to Berlin contained so much 'inside information' that Admiral Canaris and Goering, and even Himmler, repeatedly congratulated him on his excellent work.

Some of Sorge's achievements as a Soviet spy in Japan are so fantastic that had they not been discovered in official records after the occupation of Japan most people would have been inclined to dismiss them as fiction.

For instance, after the Nazi Wehrmacht had occupied the whole of the Ukraine, reached the Crimea, and begun the siege of Moscow in the late summer of 1941, Stalin feared that the Japanese would invade Siberia and force a war on two fronts. In this event the Siberian Red Army of half a million men would be unable to move to the Western front, and everything would be lost.

The only man who could supply Stalin with accurate details of what the Japanese in fact intended to do was Richard Sorge. He succeeded in obtaining the vital information from his agents in the Japanese Government. One was Ozaki Hozumi, Prince Konoye's cousin, and others were Saionji Kinkazu, a young official of the Cabinet, and Kishi Michizo and Ushiba Tomohiko, the Japanese Prime Minister's two confidential secretaries.

Through these informers Sorge secured microfilms of Cabinet minutes and of other secret Government documents. He got the microfilms to Moscow. Thus it was that Stalin knew that Japan did not intend to attack Russia, but that their war plans were directed against Great Britain and the U.S.A.

It has been established that these microfilms also contained the plans which the Japanese War Minister, General Tojo, had prepared, outlining the strategy of the Japanese General Staff for the attack on Burma and the Philippines.

When the Nazi Wehrmacht was nearing Kerch, Rostov-on-Don, and Stalingrad, in August 1941, Sorge again informed Stalin that "at a secret war council attended by the Emperor of Japan it was decided that the Japanese effort should be directed southward". Soon afterwards he reported the withdrawal of thirty Japanese divisions from Manchuria, and revealed that the Siberian frontier was guarded by only a few run-down divisions. It is therefore not surprising that Stalin paid him the highest tribute when he said, "It was Sorge who won the battle of Stalingrad, and saved our lives." Even under the Khrushchev and Kosygin-Brezhnev régimes Sorge's memory was still honoured in the Kremlin as that of a hero.

The Japanese counter-intelligence detected Richard Sorge's Soviet spy ring, and arrested Ozaki Hozumi and most of the other

members of the espionage network. But although Sorge knew his
end was near, he persisted in sending his last message to Moscow,
instead of trying to escape. On October 15th, 1941, he transmitted:

"Japan is to attack America and Britain; the danger to the
Soviet Union has passed."

Three days later he was arrested.

This brilliant Soviet master spy, who had for years obtained
vital secret information directly from highest Government sources,
had been rendered harmless and his extensive spy ring smashed.
Three years later, on November 7th, 1944, it was officially announced that he and his chief lieutenant, Ozaki Hozumi, had
been hanged.[1] Of thirty-four of Sorge's agents and informers
arrested, five died in prison; the rest served sentences from three
to fifteen years. Max Klausen, the radio operator whom Moscow
had sent to Tokyo, was the only Soviet agent freed by the Americans in October 1945.

Although the case of Dr Richard Sorge is a striking example of
how a brilliant Soviet spy obtained secrets from highest Government quarters, and of the extent to which such information played
a key rôle in Russia's strategy (and even survival), some people
may nevertheless arrive at the convenient conclusion that it is
now history, that Russian spy webs would probably no longer be
able to work successfully in the reorganized Japan of today. Such
a conclusion would be wrong. In the years since the end of World
War II, Japanese counter-intelligence have arrested several Soviet
spies and smashed a number of espionage networks.

For instance, there was the beautiful Japanese governess Kioni
who acted as a Soviet resident spy operator in Tokyo from 1955
until the summer of 1963. Only when her spy organization was
detected and its twenty-eight agents and informers arrested was
it established that this network had supplied Moscow for well
over nine years with information on Japan's defences, secret-
weapon research, science, technology, etc.

There was also the prosperous and respected export merchant
Saito who directed two parallel Soviet espionage rings that
covered virtually all Japan. It was established that they penetrated into military and research establishments, from which they
obtained information of great value to the Soviet Union.

These are only two examples of what has been going on in
Japan in recent years.

[1] Rumour has it that the official Japanese announcement about Sorge's
execution was false—that he was not killed, and that he was helped to
escape to the U.S.S.R.—and there are even eyewitnesses who claim to have
seen him after World War II. Neither official nor secret Allied or Soviet
records substantiate the rumour.

In his report to the Kremlin's Party Presidium the supreme chief of the Soviet Secret Service, Vladimir Semichastny, stated in January 1966 that the spy school of Vostochnaya, which lies about 105 miles south-east of Khabarovsk, and where spies for Japan are trained, was expected to turn out about 12 per cent more fully trained Japanese master spies in that year than ever before. (Moscow records for 1965 stated that 142 fully trained master spies for operation in Japan had passed the final examinations at Vostochnaya and were ready for operation in Japan.) He therefore confirmed that the Soviet Secret Service aims to do the same thing in Japan as it has done, and is still doing, in all other major countries of the free world—to increase drastically the number of their resident spy operators, Control Agents, and espionage networks.

Japan is a favourite hunting-ground for Soviet spies because there are so many Communists and fellow-travellers in the country. But it is also known that considerable numbers of undercover Japanese security officers infiltrate into the ranks of these organizations. Indeed, in many instances they manage to hold leading positions. Consequently Japanese counter-intelligence have managed to arrest Russian, Czechoslovak, Polish, and other Communist master spies and smash their dangerous networks. But Japan's spy-catchers are well aware that the Soviet do not for one moment relax their 'struggle in the dark'.

3

Radical Changes

THE Soviet Secret Service's frequent successes do not immunize it, or its directors, from the Kremlin's Party Presidium—the supreme body which controls everything in Russia. If the Presidium wishes to recognize some outstanding achievement the director responsible at Moscow Secret Service headquarters receives an award for "special initiative" or "special services". But if there is any serious setback in the Soviet espionage abroad the Chairman of the Committee for State Security, who is the chief of the Soviet Secret Police and the Secret Service and is accountable to the Kremlin's 'Inner Circle' for both services, is held responsible.

A striking example of how a Soviet intelligence chief can one day be a much acclaimed personality and the next day be transferred to an obscure post in the Party Secretariat is the case of Aleksandr Shelyepin, who was deposed as Chairman of the Committee for State Security in October 1961.

It was in January 1961 that trouble started for Russia's supreme Secret Service chief, when Scotland Yard's Special Branch destroyed Gordon Lonsdale's spy ring, which had been operating in England for many years. Some members of the Kremlin's 'Inner Circle' criticized the Chairman of the Committee for State Security as being responsible for the serious blow Britain's spy-catchers had struck.

Only because Shelyepin was supported by a number of Party Presidium members did he manage to survive. He was commanded to start measures to safeguard the operational groups of the Foreign Directorate, but when he passed his Kremlin orders to Moscow Secret Service headquarters he was informed that the Foreign Directorate had already carried out the reorganization on their own initiative—even before the Kremlin meeting had taken place.

Despite the reorganization, Scotland Yard's Special Branch arrested double agent George Blake, who was sentenced at the Old Bailey to forty-two years' imprisonment in May 1961.

c

This time all the members of the Party Presidium attacked "serious shortcomings in our Foreign Directorate, necessitating an immediate and far-reaching reorganization of all networks operating in the West". Shelyepin struggled to convince the Kremlin 'Inner Circle' that "Blake's arrest was the result of unforeseen and unavoidable circumstances". The Party Presidium appointed a triumvirate (consisting of Aleksei Adzhubei, Nikita Khrushchev's son-in-law; Frol Kozlov, a prominent spokesman of the Party's Central Committee; and Mikhail Suslov, the Kremlin's most dangerous doctrinaire and theoretician) to "investigate security measures in the Foreign Directorate, and make constructive suggestions for possible improvements". It was significant that the triumvirate was ordered to carry out the inquiry in secrecy, and that the supreme chief of the Soviet Secret Service was deliberately kept unaware of this.

Even as the triumvirate began their investigation Nikita Khrushchev was already considering replacing the Chairman of State Security with Vladimir Semichastny—a personal protégé who had held high posts in the Young Communist League and whose official position was, at that time, Second Secretary of Soviet Azerbaidzhan's Communist Party Central Committee. This high-ranking post was, in fact, only a cover for "special task duties" to which the Khrushchev Secretariat had assigned Semichastny. His real function was directing widespread Soviet espionage in the Middle East, and his networks operated so efficiently in Egypt, Iraq, Persia, and Turkey that it was agreed that Semischastny had the makings of a first-class espionage chief.

Although the triumvirate's inquiry into the arrest of George Blake substantiated Shelyepin's submission that "Blake's capture was the result of unforeseen and unavoidable circumstances", and that "security in the Foreign Directorate was as near perfect as possible", Shelyepin was nevertheless deposed as Chairman of the Committee for State Security at the Twenty-second Congress of the Russian Communist Party in October 1961.

As soon as Vladimir Semichastny[1] took over security he embarked on radical reorganization of the Secret Service and Secret Police. This included the transfer of former trusted officers, in minor and strictly administrative jobs, to obscure posts in remote parts of Soviet Russia. They were replaced by new executives. But Semichastny's changes did not affect the actual directors or senior officers at Moscow Secret Service headquarters. The reason was that all these men and women were fully trained, experienced specialists in international espionage, and exchanging any of them would have meant disruption of the machine.

[1] Semichastny was sacked on May 19th, 1967; his successor was Yuryi V. Andropov.

The Foreign Directorate ordered a regrouping of the majority of Russia's espionage networks throughout the free world.

Codes and lines of communications were changed; the number of Control Agents (super spies whose task it is to report to Moscow H.Q. on the activities of the spy-ring operators in foreign countries, and also to ensure fullest possible security) was substantially increased; and the Transport Department was directed to improve 'rescue' facilities for any operators who might be suspected by Western counter-intelligence.

In his December report to the Khrushchev Secretariat the new Soviet espionage chief declared:

"The reorganization of every Soviet intelligence network in all capitalist countries has been completed, and most comprehensive measures for the security and the safe working of the said organizations have been taken."

It sounded impressive, but was only a repetition of the usual reshuffle of the structure of the Foreign Directorate that takes place whenever key agents are apprehended abroad.

Despite the "drastic changes", counter-espionage in the U.S.A., Britain, West Germany, France, Finland, and many other countries continued to disrupt and damage Soviet espionage. The Kremlin's 'Inner Circle' did not blame the new broom for the continued serious dislocations in their world spy network. It would have been bad tactics to attack a recently appointed Secret Service supreme chief, so the loss of some of the really important Soviet spies abroad was explained away as having been "due to occupational risk" and "the result of unforeseen and unavoidable circumstances". Aleksandr Shelyepin, who had submitted the same explanation, could not be reinstated, so to compensate him, he was elevated to Deputy Premier and Chairman of the Party and State Control Committee.

Although the newly appointed supreme chief of the Soviet Secret Service and Secret Police took little part in the direction of Soviet spies, and merely figured as the officially recognized head, every time an outstanding espionage success was achieved the Kremlin's 'Inner Circle' attributed it to the "far-sighted and unique organizational abilities" of Nikita Khrushchev's personally picked spy chief.

In fact, Semichastny did exactly the same as each of his numerous predecessors—confined his energies to attending the regular secret or public meetings of the Party Presidium or the Central Committee, made his speeches in the Supreme Soviet, and left the actual administration of the Secret Service and Secret Police to those really expert at the job.

Russia's world espionage continued as before, maintaining its reputation as the world's most dangerous espionage service.

The Very Able Abel

4

A GRAVE error of judgment has put one of the shrewdest espionage experts in the world today at the head of Soviet Russia's organization controlling their spies in English-speaking countries.

The United States freed Colonel Rudolf Ivanovich Abel from prison and exchanged him for two Americans held by Soviet Russia. To appreciate how bad a bargain was made the career of the very able Colonel Abel should be studied.

One of the cleverest atom spy-ring operators, he worked unsuspected in New York for nine years. His career in the United States was fantastic.

Born in Moscow in 1902 and coming from a family with revolutionary sympathies, Rudolf Ivanovich began in his teens to dabble in Bolshevism. After the 1917 Revolution he joined Lenin's Party. Soviet records reveal that he was considered "a man of exceptional intelligence and unique organizational abilities" who, due to his "flexibility, unusual ingenuity, and presence of mind", was recommended for 'special' duties. He became a Russian plainclothes Secret Police officer. For successfully spying on comrades inside and outside the Party, and being "instrumental in bringing enemies of the State to justice", he was eventually chosen as a suitable recruit for service abroad. He was so outstanding a pupil at the various spy-training schools he attended that he had attained the rank of colonel by the time he had passed his final examination with honours.

In 1948 Colonel Abel arrived in Canada and entered the United States under the false identity of an American citizen named Andrew Kayotis. He went to New York, where he was to organize a spy ring. He lived in a small hotel in Manhattan, and registered under the name of "Martin Collins".

For his 'professional' career the master spy decided to use still another identity. Moscow Secret Service headquarters had supplied him with the genuine documents of a child born in New York in June 1902, but who had died two months after birth. Colonel Abel used this identity and became "Emil R. Goldfus".

In accordance with Soviet spy-school training, he did not use his hotel room as an espionage centre, fearing that a too inquisitive hotel employee might spot his special cameras and elaborate photographic equipment. Realizing also that he would require a plausible excuse for having such equipment wherever he was, he chose the cover of artist and photographer, and, using the name of Emil R. Goldfus, rented a one-room studio in Brooklyn.

For nine years Colonel Abel–Emil R. Goldfus worked skilfully and was able to obtain and transmit to Moscow—to quote the U.S. indictment—"information relating to the defence of the United States; information relating to arms, equipment, and the disposition of the United States Armed Forces; and information relating to the atomic energy programme". He also obtained "writings, photographs, negatives, maps, plans, models, notes, and instruments", which he transmitted to his superiors in Russia. Furthermore, he was under orders, in the event of war breaking out between the United States and Soviet Russia, to "engage in sabotage and transmit radio information to Moscow".

During his espionage activities in the United States, Colonel Abel transmitted intelligence information via his portable short-wave radio receiver-transmitter, and dispatched microfilms of documents, blueprints, scientific calculations, and other secret information. He worked with such care and efficiency that when he was arrested by the F.B.I. the majority of his agents and informers succeeded in escaping detection by the U.S. spy-catchers. Two of these were Morris and Lona Cohen, who later worked in another Soviet spy ring in the U.S.A. Afterwards they changed their names to Peter and Helen Kroger, eventually went to England, and in March 1961 made headlines during the Gordon Lonsdale trial at the Old Bailey.

Mr John Edgar Hoover, Director of the Federal Bureau of Investigation, United States Department of Justice, stated in February 1962:

The case of Rudolf Ivanovich Abel, Soviet citizen, is typical of the trained agent. This case originated in June of 1953, when a delivery-boy of the *Brooklyn Eagle* jingled some change in his hand and noted that one of the coins had a peculiar sound. He dropped the nickel to the floor. It fell apart, disclosing a hollow area in which was concealed a tiny photograph—a picture of a series of numbers. A detective learned of the incident from another member of the New York City Police Department whose daughter was acquainted with the newsboy. During a discussion of another investigation the detective mentioned the finding of the hollow coin to the F.B.I. agent. When the detective contacted the delivery-boy the youth handed over the coin and the photograph it contained. Both were turned over to the F.B.I., where they were subjected to close scrutiny in the laboratory.

The nickel was unique. The face of the coin was a 1948 Jefferson nickel. A tiny hole had been drilled in the 'R' of the word 'TRUST'. It was obvious that this had been done in order that a fine needle or similar sharp instrument could be inserted to force the nickel open.

The reverse side of the coin was made from a nickel minted between 1942 and 1945. It was composed of a copper-silver alloy used during World War II, when there was a shortage of nickel.

Proprietors of novelty stores were shown photographs of the hollow coin. No-one could recall selling a nickel or other coin similar to the newsboy's nickel.

"It is not suitable for a magic trick," a novelty salesman commented. "The hollowed-out area is too small to hide anything aside from a tiny piece of paper."

Efforts to decipher the micro-photograph met with failure, nor could the kind of typewriter used in preparing the code message be identified. Inasmuch as the F.B.I. laboratory maintains a reference file concerning typewriters manufactured in the United States, a foreign-made typewriter undoubtedly was involved.

The case of the hollow coin was a frustrating one. F.B.I. agents in various parts of the country submitted hollow subway tokens, 'trick' coins, and similar objects. A half-dollar, ground in such a manner that coins could be concealed in it, was forwarded to the F.B.I. Two hollow pennies were found in Washington, D.C., and were examined in the laboratory. Neither these nor any of the entire assortment of coins examined were found to have tool markings or other distinguishing features which might link them with the unique nickel.

Who had brought the hollow nickel to New York and for whom was the coded message intended? Months of determined probing by the F.B.I.'s scientists and investigative staff merely led from one blind alley to another. From 1953 to 1957 continuing efforts were made to solve the mystery of the hollow coin.

The key to the mystery was a thirty-six-year-old Lieutenant-Colonel of the Soviet State Security Service (K.G.B.). Early in May 1957 Reino Hayhanen telephoned the United States Embassy in Paris, and subsequently arrived for an interview. The Russian espionage agent told an Embassy official: "I'm an officer of the Soviet Intelligence Service. For the past five years I have been operating in the United States. Now I need your help."

After five years in the United States the espionage agent had been ordered to return to Moscow. He dreaded the thought of going back to his Communist-ruled homeland and wanted to defect.

Hayhanen was conscripted by the N.K.V.D. in 1939. He became a respected expert in Finnish intelligence matters. In 1948 he was called to Moscow by the M.G.B. for special training. Here he studied the English language and received special training in photographing documents and in encoding and decoding messages. While his M.G.B. training continued Hayhanen worked as a mechanic in the city of Valga, Estonia. Then, in the summer of 1949, he entered Finland as Eugene Nikolai Maki, an American-born labourer. (The real Eugene Maki was born in Enaville, Idaho, on May 30th, 1919, and taken to Estonia by his parents in the mid-1920s.) From July 1949 to October 1952 Hayhanen lived in Finland and established his identity as the American-born Maki—an ordinary, hard-working citizen—in preparation for a new espionage assignment. Meanwhile he married a Finnish girl who knew him only as Eugene Maki, so carefully was his Russian background concealed.

Hayhanen visited the United States Legation in Helsinki in 1951, and executed an affidavit in which he explained that his family had left the United States in 1927. "Eugene Maki" arrived at New York City on board the Queen Mary on October 21st, 1952.

Prior to leaving Finland Hayhanen was recalled to Moscow and introduced to a Soviet agent, "Mikhail", who was to serve as his espionage superior in the United States. He was instructed to go to Central Park upon his arrival in New York. Near the Tavern on the Green, he was told, he would find a signpost marked "Horse carts".

"You will let Mikhail know of your arrival by placing a red thumb-tack on this signpost," a Soviet official told him. "If you suspect that you are under surveillance place a white thumb-tack on the board."

The information which Hayhanen gave officials in Paris was immediately checked and found to be accurate. Passage was secured on an airliner, and the defecting agent was permitted to return to the United States.

Interviewing agents learned that Hayhanen had met "Mikhail", his espionage superior, only when necessary. The meeting-place was the Prospect Park subway station. Inconspicuous hiding-places—'dead drops'—were used to exchange messages and intelligence data. An iron picket fence at the end of 7th Avenue near Macombs Bridge and the base of a lamp-post in Fort Tryon Park had been used as 'dead drops'. So had a hole in a cement

step in Prospect Park. Evidence authenticating Hayhanen's statement was found in this 'dead drop', which had been filled in with
cement by a repair crew. Under the cement F.B.I. agents found
a hollowed-out bolt two inches long and a quarter-inch in diameter containing a typewritten message.

Hayhanen said that trick containers—hollow pencils, pens,
screws, batteries, and coins—had been supplied to him by the
Soviets. Some had been magnetized so that they would adhere to
metal objects. F.B.I. agents found a hollow 50-Markkaa coin
from Finland in Hayhanen's home. Like the hollow nickel, it had
a small hole bored in a letter. Acting on this information secured
from the defecting agent, the F.B.I. laboratory was successful in
decoding the micro-photograph recovered from the hollow nickel.
The message in the nickel apparently had been intended for Hayhanen. It congratulated him on his safe arrival, advised him that
he would receive three thousand dollars in local currency, and
transmitted instructions and information.

The mystery of the hollow nickel was solved, but far more
critical challenges remained. Who was "Mikhail", Hayhanen's
superior? And since "Mikhail" dropped from the scene in 1954,
who was "Mark", the Russian spy who had taken his place?

Hayhanen had gained the impression that "Mikhail" was a
Soviet diplomatic official, and F.B.I. agents began checking long
lists of possible suspects, and checking photographs of logical
candidates with the defector. When a picture of Mikhail Nikolayevich Svirin, who had served between 1952 and 1954 as First
Secretary to the Soviet United Nations Delegation in New York,
was shown to Hayhanen the former agent said, "That's the one.
There is absolutely no doubt about it. That's 'Mikhail'."

Svirin had returned to the Soviet Union in October 1956. What
of "Mark"?

According to Hayhanen, "Mark" was a colonel in the Soviet
State Security Service, and had been engaged in espionage work
since approximately 1927. He had come to the United States in
1948 or 1949, entering by illegally crossing the Canadian border.

Hayhanen, wearing a blue-and-red-striped tie and smoking a
pipe as identification symbols, had first met "Mark" at a movie
theatre in Flushing, Long Island. Thereafter they had held frequent meetings in Prospect Park, in crowded streets, and in other
inconspicuous places. They had made trips together, and "Mark"
had sent Hayhanen on trips alone. Once the latter had been
instructed to locate an American Army sergeant who had been
recruited into Soviet espionage while he was assigned to the
United States Embassy in Moscow. He could not remember the
Army sergeant's name, but recalled that the code name "Quebec"
had been used. A piece of microfilm less than an inch square in

size was recovered from a hollow piece of steel found in Hayhanen's home. This yielded the identification of "Quebec" as Sergeant Roy Rhodes. Rhodes had allowed himself to be involved in a compromising situation, and, under the threat of blackmail, had given intelligence information to the Soviets. Information concerning Rhodes' involvement in Russian espionage was transmitted to the Army. Later, following a court-martial, the soldier was given a sentence of five years' hard labour.

The search for "Mark" meanwhile continued. Hayhanen advised that in 1955 "Mark", an accomplished photographer, had taken him to a storage-room in which photo supplies were kept on the fourth or fifth floor of a building located near Clark and Fulton Streets in Brooklyn. At 252 Fulton Street F.B.I. agents found that a photographer—one Emil R. Goldfus—had been operating a studio on the fifth floor since January 1954, and had formerly rented a fifth-floor storage-room there. But Goldfus was not at his studio. In April 1957, the same month that Hayhanen had been ordered to return to Moscow and had gone only as far as Paris, Goldfus advised acquaintances that he was going south on a several-weeks vacation because of a sinus complaint. Weeks of surveillance on the photo studio paid off. Goldfus returned. Agents followed the espionage suspect to a hotel on East 28th Street, where the man was registered under the name of Martin Collins. Two days later a photograph of the suspect, taken with a hidden camera, was shown to Hayhanen.

"You've found him," the former Soviet agent exclaimed. "That's 'Mark'."

The duel with the master spy was drawing to a close.

"Mark" was arrested by the Immigration and Naturalization Service on an alien warrant based on his illegal entry into the United States and his failure to register as an alien. He was found to have numerous false papers in different names. "Mark", admitting that he was Rudolf Ivanovich Abel, Russian citizen who had come to Quebec in 1948 under the name of Andrew Kayotis, refused to discuss his intelligence activities, but the rooms he occupied were virtual museums of modern espionage equipment. This equipment included short-wave radios, cipher-pads, cameras and film for producing microdots, and trick containers, such as a hollow shaving-brush and hollow cuff-links.

Abel was sentenced to serve thirty years on conviction of conspiracy to transmit defence information to the Soviet Union. . . . Mr Hoover concluded his account and warned:

The duel with one spy has ended, but the deadly duel with Communism continues on a score of battle-grounds. . . .

An interesting Soviet Secret Service comment on the Colonel

Abel case was published in the Party Bulletin[1] and stated: "Had ex-Lieutenant-Colonel Reino Hayhanen and Co. not betrayed their country and deserted to the imperialists, the F.B.I. would never have been able to discover any of Comrade Abel's activities, and he could have continued his important work indefinitely." The same comment also says: "Colonel Rudolf Ivanovich Abel must be regarded as a hero because he admitted only what the F.B.I. was able to prove and did not turn traitor. Colonel Abel deserves to be rewarded for his patriotic services if he ever returns to his country." And Russia's top agent was, in fact, awarded the Order of Lenin and made a Hero of the Soviet Union while serving his sentence in an American prison.

Moscow Secret Service headquarters kept an eye on the prison behaviour of Colonel Abel. For, although it was considered a remote possibility, it was nevertheless imperative for the Soviet espionage directors to know whether the master spy might yield to American 'brainwashing' and expose secrets that could dangerously damage Russia's world espionage system. But, as the director of Moscow's First Directorate expected, "Colonel Abel remained true to Soviet Intelligence tradition and stayed impervious to American pressure."

From the day Colonel Abel was sentenced the Soviet Secret Service considered exchanging him for some American spy. Discreet feelers were repeatedly put out to test the chances of success, but each attempt failed because Russia did not hold an American important enough for the U.S. Government to exchange.

Then the American U-2 pilot, Francis Gary Powers, was captured near Sverdlovsk and sentenced at Moscow's Supreme Court, in the summer of 1960, to a lengthy prison term. At last the Russians had someone whom they could offer for Abel.

Further approaches were made by Moscow to Washington—at first without success. Then, by the end of 1961, negotiations developed. In February 1962 the U.S. authorities finally agreed to exchange Abel for Powers and an American student held at Berlin's crossing-point of the Glienecker Brücke.

The Foreign Directorate got back one of their most experienced master spies, invaluable for directing Soviet espionage in the English-speaking world. The price they paid was negligible: neither Powers nor the American student was of any value to Russia.

After a brief 'rehabilitation' period, during which Colonel Abel was 'brainwashed' by Russia's Secret Service experts, this man, who is without doubt one of the best spies the U.S.S.R. has ever produced, was promoted to the rank of General and honoured

[1] Moscow, December 1957.

with medals and given a substantial financial grant. His chief reward was, however, that he was appointed to the post of director of the Anglo-American Section of the Foreign Directorate at Moscow Secret Service headquarters.

From March 1962 General Rudolf Ivanovich Abel took command of all Red spies in the English-speaking world. He completely reorganized the entire Soviet espionage system, and his reorganization was naturally based on the vast practical experience he had gained during nine years' activities as a Russian master spy in the United States.

Once again all codes and links of communication were ruthlessly changed; existing spy rings regrouped; Control Agents increased; high-speed coded radio communication between Soviet master spies abroad and Moscow headquarters permitted only in cases of extreme urgency, to exclude the danger of too frequent broadcasts being intercepted by Western counter-intelligence. Strict orders were also given to "concentrate on microdot communication" which can be ingeniously affixed under postage stamps on innocent-looking letters; and Resident Network Operators in all Anglo-Saxon countries were supplied with improved methods for safely dispatching microfilms on roundabout routes to Moscow.

Under the command of Abel, Russia's spies in the English-speaking world now work in accordance with the following rule laid down in the *Manual of the Soviet Secret Service Orgburo*, Moscow, 1962:

> No individual operator or intelligence networks are permitted to maintain contact of any sort with another intelligence organization or operator, not even if such communication is carried out through perfectly safe links of go-betweens or other foolproof means. This also applies to informers and other lower-grade members of all auxiliary organizations.

General Abel thus ended the practice of resident spy operators maintaining contact with espionage organizers in Communist embassies, consulates, or other Iron Curtain institutions enjoying diplomatic privilege, because he knew from his own experience, and from the experience of other Russian master spies, that "the absolute safety of every intelligence group can be guaranteed provided each group works completely independently and unknown to any other group or operators".

To enforce the new orders all Control Agents were instructed to "keep each operator and his organization under full observation and inform Moscow headquarters whether all operators strictly comply with their directives".

General Abel also made extensive moves to increase substantially the number of student-trainees in the Soviet spy schools.

The Marx-Engels School, Gorky, and the Lenin Technical School, Verkhovnoye, had been enlarged to accommodate additional trainees. The work on extending the key spy school of Gaczyna, where spies for the English-speaking world receive their training, started in 1963.

Until January 1st, 1962, about 230 fully trained master spies—men and women of the Gordon Lonsdale type, who are to be in charge of espionage networks—had annually passed through the Soviet's top spy schools, and been sent to Western countries; on January 1st, 1968, the number had grown to 1436! General Abel's drastic increase of these already remarkable figures indicates that he is determined to adhere to the old Soviet slogan: "For every single agent lost ten new and better ones must fill the gap."

Apart from increasing the number of Soviet master spies, Abel also set out to enlarge the total of the estimated three-quarters of a million or so Red spies and informers. Here again he ordered revised precautionary measures in the recruitment of agents and informers in foreign countries.

General Abel knew from his experience in the U.S.A. that the best informers are those who betray not for money, but through idealism. He also knew that members of the constitutional Communist Parties are unsuitable as recruits for espionage networks, because of the danger that the counter-intelligence might know them and keep them under round-the-clock surveillance, and so might be led to the actual spies. So he ordered that "only activists of the Communist Parties Undercover Cadres" (men and women who claim to be anti-Communists as a cover for Fifth Column activities) were to be considered as 'ideological' recruits for working as informers and go-betweens.

A Soviet Secret Service report stated:

> This move is an effective counter-measure against the dangerous reorganization of British Security which was recommended by the Radcliffe Committee. ... The British, American, West German, and other security measures cannot inflict any harm on the work of our residenturas [Soviet Secret Service term for an espionage network operating in a foreign country] because the newly recruited informers, etc., are unknown to the counter-intelligence as they are not recognized Communists and therefore not affected by anti-Communist witch-hunts.

Although General Abel relied to a great extent on activists of the international Communist Parties' Undercover Cadres as the main force of informers and go-betweens, he nevertheless continued recruitment of the brand of informers who betray for money.

5

Danger-point Berlin

ALTHOUGH Moscow Secret Service headquarters is the supreme control centre of Soviet world espionage, in many cases the Russians also direct spy rings operated in foreign countries by other Iron Curtain states. It would be wrong, however, to assume that all directives to Soviet spies come only from Moscow.

Since Communist rule was imposed on the Baltic states, Eastern Germany, Hungary, Poland, and the rest of the Russian satellites, Moscow has taken advantage of newly acquired territories well suited as bases for all categories of Bolshevik Avant Posts—Soviet Secret Service jargon for propaganda and subversive centres near, or inside, Western countries. Having, in practice, moved her frontiers considerably nearer to the Western world, Russia was able to establish sub-headquarters almost on the doorstep of the "class-enemies" and direct her subversive actions from neighbouring lands.

Because of its unique geographical position, East Berlin became the first and most important centre point for both the Soviet Secret Service and Institute 611—the successor of the Comintern and now known as Institute 621. Institute 611 helped to provide the Secret Service with hundreds of thousands of go-betweens, informers, and sub-agents, devoted and reliable because of their Communist ideology. The Soviet Secret Service in Berlin and the Berlin headquarters of Institute 621 maintain the closest liaison with Moscow.

Soon after the end of World War II the directors of Moscow Secret Service headquarters appointed deputies to run their Berlin Residentura and to direct from this branch headquarters Soviet master spies and espionage networks in West Germany and other free-world countries.

Although Moscow headquarters remained the supreme body of Soviet world espionage, and although the Berlin sub-headquarters was ordered to work in the closed synchronization, the espionage directors in Berlin were nevertheless in full control of their own master spies and agents.

At the start no fewer than nine hundred thoroughly trained and fully experienced Soviet Secret Service officers were sent to the branch headquarters in Berlin-Karlshorst, the completely restricted Soviet area of East Berlin, where they established themselves in the former St Antonius Hospital, and converted it into their operations centre. Almost at once the new espionage directors were able to report to Moscow successes of considerable importance.

One of the first Soviet master spies whom Berlin branch headquarters sent to the Western part of Germany was Pavel Karlovich Glinka. He left Berlin-Karlshorst in the spring of 1945 with orders to organize spy rings that would penetrate American H.Q. and transmit information of military and political importance to East Berlin.

Glinka came to Russia as a young child. His father had been a smallholder in Sudetenland who only just managed to feed his hungry family, but who believed Communist propaganda that the Soviet Union provided unique opportunities for farmers. He emigrated with his family to Russia. From Moscow the Glinkas were sent to the Autonomous Volga-German Region, where the father became a collective farmer. During the "Stalin Famine" Glinka's parents and their eldest two children fell victims to the typhoid-fever epidemic and died. The only survivors of the Glinka family were the seven-year-old Pavel Karlovich and his four-year-old sister. The Glinka children were taken care of by the town council of Engels—then capital of the Autonomous Volga-German Region of the U.S.S.R.—and were brought up in Soviet children's homes.

Once in the grip of the Communist educational machine, young Pavel Karlovich grew into a fanatic of the Communist Youth League. He was a bright youth, and his activities in the organization were noted by the Party Organizer. Glinka was recommended as "suitable for special training", and accepted by the Secret Service Selection Board. He went to several spy schools, including the top school at Prakhovka. He qualified to carry out his first assignment for the Berlin branch headquarters.

Equipped with perfect identity documents of German citizens, Glinka was ordered to make Frankfurt-am-Main his operational base. To avoid arousing suspicion he made a criss-cross journey through West Germany, during which he changed his identity several times. When he was at last satisfied that no-one would realize that he had come from Berlin he went to Frankfurt-am-

Main and found suitable accommodation in a modest, respectable residential part of the city.

Like many other Soviet master spies, Glinka, who was listed at Berlin-Karlshorst as "Bremer, Herrmann", and under other pseudonyms, chose to work under the cover of a photographer, as it provided a plausible explanation of his extensive photographic equipment, and enabled him to use cameras freely without causing suspicion. Supplied by the Central Index with the names of suitable recruits for the spy ring he was expected to establish, he succeeded in setting up a considerable network.

A continuous flow of secrets began from the U.S. administration in West Germany, in Frankfurt-am-Main, to Soviet Secret Service branch headquarters at Berlin-Karlshorst. Glinka kept Russia's espionage directors well informed on American troop movements, supply-lines, strategic developments, and plans.

Glinka also organized another unit to concentrate on the British Military Government in Minden in West Germany, on the British Rhine Army, and on other important centres maintained by Britain. A third elaborate ring established by Glinka obtained secrets from industrial and scientific establishments in West Germany, and even from key Federal Government offices.

For nearly three years Glinka earned praise from Moscow and Berlin-Karlshorst branch headquarters without ever being suspected by Allied counter-intelligence or the West German police. When he was recalled to Berlin in 1948 it was not because he was in danger, but because the Berlin crisis and the air lift had begun; his directors wished to brief him personally on aspects of the new development.

Glinka reached Berlin-Karlshorst without mishap. As a reward for his excellent work he was sent to Moscow to meet the senior directors at the First Directorate.

Glinka, however, never returned to Frankfurt-am-Main, or any other West German city. Travelling to Moscow Airport on his way back to Germany, his car collided with a lorry carrying steel girders. He was killed instantly. He was given a V.I.P. funeral—and Berlin branch headquarters immediately replaced him with another Resident Operator.

According to figures published in Bonn in October 1961, there were at that time some 16,000 Red spies at work in West Germany, most of them on orders from Berlin-Karlshorst. Bonn also stated later that the number of Red spies operating in West German territories between 1962 and 1968 was considerably higher than the 1961 figure. It is estimated that at present some 45,000 Berlin-Karlshorst controlled Red master spies are at work in other Western countries.

To understand how Moscow's branch headquarters in East Berlin is able to play such a gigantic rôle in Soviet world espionage it is necessary to know the full facts of this fantastic intelligence organization.

The Berlin-Karlshorst branch headquarters of Moscow Secret Service headquarters is organized as follows:

DIVISION ONE—FOREIGN ESPIONAGE

This division directs master spies and espionage networks in West Germany and other countries of the free world. The individual Resident Operators and espionage networks engage in military, political, scientific, technical, and economic intelligence. An additional function of Division One is the subverting of anti-Soviet political organizations, political parties, societies, and trade unions.

DIVISION TWO—COUNTER-INTELLIGENCE

The classification of this division sufficiently explains its task. An additional function of Division Two is to control the activities of Red spies from other Iron Curtain countries and to organize fullest possible liaison and synchronization of individual networks belonging to different Communist Secret Service headquarters.

DIVISION THREE—CO-ORDINATION

This division's task is to co-ordinate the Soviet Secret Service with the espionage networks of all the other Iron Curtain spy webs. The practical result of this function is that Division Three controls and supports all other Communist espionage networks.

DIVISION FOUR—EMIGRATION

The function of Division Four is to carry out operative espionage and subversion against Russian refugees and their organizations in West Germany and other Western countries.

Every division naturally has a number of sections, such as the Selection Board for Recruits, the Transport Department, the Administration Bureau, etc. The size of these branch headquarters will be appreciated if it is realized that this Residentura consists of well over a thousand directing officers housed in about six hundred offices and buildings in the sealed-off Soviet area of East Berlin.

The actual Berlin-Karlshorst branch headquarters in itself forms a potential danger to the free world. But this already gigantic espionage force is further increased by a parallel Soviet network —the G.R.U., Russia's Military Intelligence Service. The Main

Department of Health   Bureau of Records and Statistics   City of New York

CERTIFICATION OF BIRTH

THIS IS TO CERTIFY that

Martin Collins

Sex *Male* was born in the City of New York on *July 2, 1897*

according to Birth Record No. *32024* filed in the *Manhattan*

Office of this Bureau on *July 15, 1897*.

In witness whereof, the seal of the Department of Health of the City of New York has been

affixed hereto this *11* day of *Apr* 19*47*

(Otto R. P. dewald)

SIGNED WASHINGTON

ACTING ASST. REGISTRAR

_____   _____   _____
Commissioner of Health   Registrar of Records   By

Warning: This certification is not valid if it has been altered in any way whatsoever or if it does not bear the raised
seal of the Department of Health.

8411 R6M 70146 ◆ 114

The doctored birth certificate which Abel used for his 'cover' name

The very able Abel

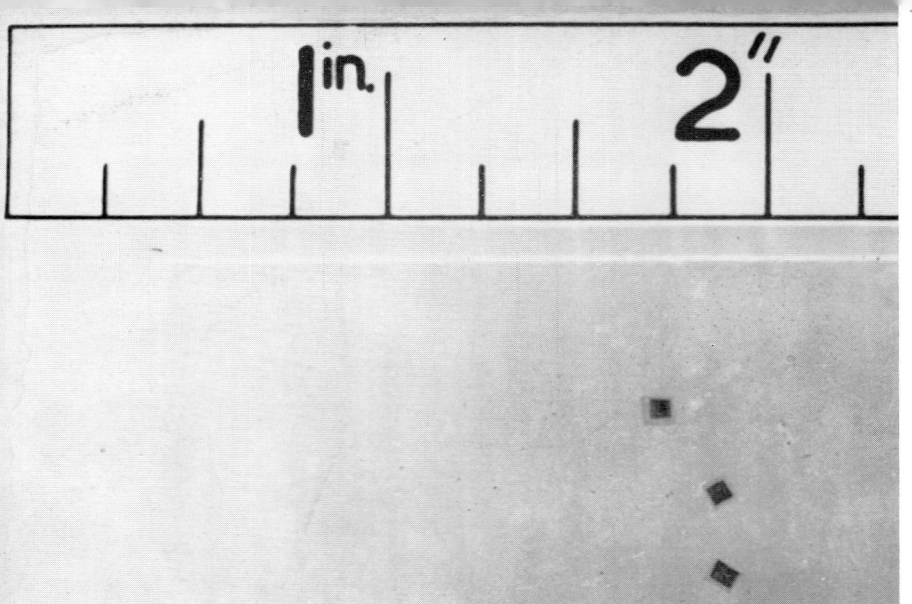

Microdots (*above*). This is what they look like and how tiny they are

Photos United Press

This is a message which has been enlarged from a microdot—no larger than a pin-head

49

Reconnaissance Directorate keeps in close touch with the Secret Service Directorate, and the two forces are more like one than two separate espionage organizations.

The East Berlin Central Branch headquarters of the Main Reconnaissance Directorate is in Wünsdorf, but it also has several departments in Berlin-Karlshorst. More than three hundred expert intelligence officers, housed in more than two hundred offices, are in charge of these departments.

The Soviet Secret Service and the Main Reconnaissance Directorates in Moscow, and their branch headquarters in Berlin, are specialized intelligence networks, which the U.S.S.R. maintains in no other country. These espionage directors also command the activities of all the operators working under the cloak of diplomatic immunity in Soviet embassies, consulates, trade missions, etc., throughout the free world. Not only Soviet Secret Service records, but also countless reports in the world Press, have revealed that these diplomatic spies are, to a very considerable extent, responsible for Western secrets of military, political, scientific, technical, and other natures reaching Russia.

D

6

Mao's New Spy Webs

WHEN speaking about Communist spies in the free world most people have in mind only the widespread Soviet Russian espionage networks. Those more familiar with Red espionage may include in this term the lesser known, but equally dangerous, intelligence world networks maintained by the six Soviet Russian satellite countries in Europe—Bulgaria, Czechoslovakia, East Germany, Hungary, Poland, and Rumania. But very few, if any, are aware of the eighth Communist world espionage system—Mao Tse-tung's well-organized and highly efficient Red Chinese Secret Service.

Until recently Communist China's espionage efforts in the Western world were not taken seriously by American and European experts. They lulled themselves with the convenient but wrong beliefs that the task of the Red Chinese Secret Service was to concentrate their intelligence attacks only on targets in Asia, and that the Red Chinese espionage force therefore did not constitute an imminent and potential danger to Western countries. So, during the past five years, this underrating of the Red Chinese espionage danger enabled Peking's master spies in America, and in most West European countries, to carry out their activities unsuspected.

The foundation-stone for a Red Chinese Secret Service, hoping to work one day as an independent and striking world espionage force, was laid nearly forty years ago. During the twenties Stalin foresaw that China would one day become a Communist country and a powerful ally of the U.S.S.R., and, adhering to Lenin's theory, "the faster efficient and effective Bolshevik intelligence cadres are established in as many capitalist countries as possible, the more rapid and the more thorough will be the development of world revolutions", he ordered that "our Chinese comrades must be trained in Secret Service work". Stalin's orders were, of course, complied with.

A spy school—Kytaiskaya—was established about seventy-five miles south of Irkutsk, near the Lake Baikal and Mongolian border, and the first Secret Service trainees were selected from those hand-picked Chinese Communists who had been sent to Russia to attend the Universities of Communism—the Lenin School and the Eastern University. Stalin's trusted Secret Service chief, Colonel Mikhail Nikolayevich Yakubovsky, was in command of the Chinese spy school, and already in the early thirties some three hundred fanatical Chinese Communists received thorough schooling in every field of espionage at Kytaiskaya.

After Mao Tse-tung became chief of the Communist Government in Kiangsi in 1934, and after the "hero of the Canton insurrection against General Chiang Kai-shek", Li Li-san, had gained still greater control of important territories in war-stricken China, the flow of Chinese Communists to Russia increased, because both Mao Tse-tung and Li Li-san realized that perfectly schooled men were needed for running the future Government and Communist Party Politburo of Red China. Those classed as suitable for Secret Service activities were sent to Colonel Yakubovsky's spy school.

When Mao Tse-tung and his comrades eventually succeeded in turning China into a Communist country, independent Red Chinese Secret Service headquarters was established in Peking. Mao Tse-tung's espionage system was organized on the same pattern as Moscow Secret Service headquarters. The directors of the various Directorates at Peking headquarters were students from Kytaiskaya who had passed through the spy school with special honours, but as they were as yet insufficiently experienced to command a world-wide espionage system, Moscow Secret Service headquarters supplied them with expert "advisers", who were, in fact, in charge of the newly created Red Chinese intelligence network.

Although a number of spy schools on the lines of Kytaiskaya were established in Red China, and although considerable numbers of trusted Chinese Communists, of both sexes, were trained annually in their own country, the original institution in the U.S.S.R., Kytaiskaya, was still used for turning out Red Chinese master spies. Only after the 'ideological' rift between Khrushchev and Mao Tse-tung deepened was the training there of Red Chinese spies stopped. But Kytaiskaya is still a key Soviet spy school. Soviet citizens of Asiatic origin are still schooled there—to provide Moscow headquarters with men and women for Russian espionage in Mao Tse-tung's Red China!

Peking's main intelligence objective is naturally Generalissimo Chiang Kai-shek's stronghold, Formosa, and substantial numbers of Red Chinese spies have been smuggled into the island.

Since the mid-fifties hundreds of Red Chinese master spies, sub-agents, and informers have been arrested in Formosa. Among them were men and women who had obtained reports, plans, blueprints, and other top-secret documents from Chiang Kai-shek's highest military circles, political and economic advisers, and from the Generalissimo's headquarters itself.

As soon as the potential danger of Red Chinese espionage was realized Nationalist China's counter-intelligence and security forces were substantially increased. Yet, although it appeared that Chiang Kai-shek's far-reaching action had curbed Red Chinese espionage in Formosa, this was not the case. Peking had succeeded during the years in smuggling still greater numbers of spies and informers into Nationalist China, and, despite the considerable number of arrests, the flow of vital top secrets to Peking headquarters steadily increased.

Nationalist China is by no means the only target of Peking intelligence. In Indonesia, for instance, Peking maintains some of the best-organized espionage networks in the Far East. The Peking headquarters' director who organized this espionage web was the Moscow-trained Wang Jen-shu—the same Wang Jen-shu who, in the revolution in 1948, led the Communist bands against both the Dutch and Indonesian authorities. He later went to Moscow for further training, and returned in the autumn of 1951 to Djakarta. His real function was to be Peking Secret Service headquarters' chief resident spy operator in Indonesia, but his official assignment was diplomatic representative of the Chinese People's Republic—a status which enabled him to be protected by diplomatic immunity.

When, in 1954, President Magyaysay liquidated the Communist Huk guerrillas who had been organized in the Philippines with direct support from Moscow and Peking, the Soviet-Red Chinese espionage network in this part of the Far East was to a great extent smashed. Who else but Wang Jen-shu should come to the rescue? This devoted disciple of Marx and Lenin quickly replaced the losses with new Russian and Red Chinese trained agents. But he did not choose a native or an Oriental as the chief resident spy operator in the Philippines: his cunning led him to choose William Joseph Pomeroy, an American citizen, born in 1920 at Rochester, New York, for he believed that this trusted man would be less suspect than any Asian.

William Joseph Pomeroy came from a respectable American family and received a good education. At the age of eighteen he joined the Young Communist League of America. During World War II he served with the U.S. Fifth Bomber Command, and took part in the liberation of the Philippines. Peace restored, he did not wish to live in the U.S.A., so he availed himself of the "G.I.

Bill of Rights", studied at the University of the Philippines, and married a Filipino girl. It was then that he joined the Communist Chinese Secret Service.

For a very considerable time the Moscow-Peking chief resident spy operator in the Philippines was able to work to the fullest satisfaction of his espionage directors and to transmit to them all the secrets he obtained through his far-flung spy rings. Eventually he was suspected, and when he fled to the Sierra Madre a price of $30,000 was put on his head.

When Pomeroy was at last captured he was charged not merely with being a Red spy, but also with several murders, arson, and kidnapping. Documents and notes found on him referred to Pedro de la Pena, a high official of the Republic's Ministry of Defence and chief of the Secret Service. De la Pena enjoyed the reputation of being an ardent anti-Communist, because he wrote bitter attacks against Soviet Russia and Red China in the paper *Free Asia*, which his 'millionaire' friend Antonio Chua Cruz owned.

Investigating William Joseph Pomeroy and all his contacts thoroughly, the Allied counter-intelligence officers discovered among other things that both Pedro de la Pena and Antonio Chua Cruz were Russian and Chinese master spies and directors of Communist espionage networks! The money which they had spent so lavishly had been extorted: from blackmail victims in Manila alone Chua Cruz had been able to squeeze over ten million pesos.

Indonesia and the Philippines are only two of the countries in the Far East where Red Chinese resident spy operators and their espionage webs are active. South Korea, Vietnam, and many other countries are also the scenes of intensified Red Chinese espionage. In all these territories blackmail is widely used to extort funds for financing Peking's agents. In fact, many cases of Red Chinese agents' blackmail are known in the U.S.A., and particularly in San Francisco.

Another target for concentrated Red Chinese espionage is Hong Kong. Since Mao Tse-tung seized power in China an immense number of Red Chinese spies and agents have been detected and arrested by British counter-intelligence and security forces. Yet, to show how efficiently Peking Secret Service headquarters direct their spies in Hong Kong, it is appropriate to record here one amazing case—a case of spying that was discovered in the late autumn of 1961.

The resident spy operator of an important Red Chinese network in Hong Kong was none other than the thirty-seven-year-old police Assistant Superintendent John Tsang, who held the position of Deputy Commandant of the Colony's Police Training School. When he had joined the Hong Kong police force in 1947 the fact that his father was a graduate of a Moscow university and that he himself had been brought up as an ardent Communist was not discovered.

The very efficient and apparently loyal police officer Tsang was considered worthy of promotion, and, in order to create a foolproof 'cover' for his espionage activities, he took every opportunity to climb as quickly as possible from rank to rank. So in 1960 he was sent to Cambridge and started a year's course in governmental administration. His fiancée, Miss Lee Suk-yin, the daughter of a wealthy Hong Kong merchant, followed him to England, and the couple were married in the university town. Three months after their return to Hong Kong, Assistant Superintendent Tsang was arrested as a Red Chinese master spy. Several high-ranking civil servants and police officers shared his fate.

For security reasons the Hong Kong authorities naturally did not release all the details about the Red Chinese espionage ring. A considerable part of the evidence was heard in camera. But it was disclosed that "this massive spy ring was engaged in sending information to Communist China. Radio messages from spies have been intercepted and tape recordings seized by the police."

It was also disclosed that fashionably dressed women in expensive cars played a leading part in the spy ring. Counter-intelligence officers, who had kept one woman under secret round-the-clock surveillance, caught her in the act of handing a Chinese messenger-boy a banknote which contained microdot messages giving the identity of a hotel frequented by a senior Hong Kong police officer. Other microfilms seized contained "secrets of vital importance to a potential enemy".

Similar revelations about Red Chinese espionage, involving high-ranking personalities, have been made during the past five years. It was always the same story—fully trained Red Chinese master spies furnished with perfect identities.

The danger from Red Chinese spies to American officials in South Vietnam was revealed in a report which a U.S. security officer in Saigon in 1967 sent to his superior. This report stated:

American officials living here are frightened of employing new housemaids—in case they are allowing spies into their homes.

Documents which have been seized by security officers in South Vietnam show that 100 girls have been trained as spies by instructors from Peking and that they have been ordered to seek work with American families. The girls, aged from seventeen to twenty, were chosen by the Red Chinese training officers for their beauty and education, particularly if they had an aptitude for English. In the same spy-training camp sixty miles north of Saigon those with long hair had it cut short to look "more presentable", and they were all deprived of their traditional Vietnamese full-length gown and long silk trousers and given simple Western dress as worn by girls in Saigon. The girl-spies were told to "pilfer documents from your employers, carry out general espionage, and assassinate your employers if you are ordered to do so".

Whether it is India or Pakistan, Korea or Laos, a large or small Far Eastern territory, the archives of practically every single Asian country contain cases of Red Chinese spies and their espionage networks detected by counter-intelligence and security officers. But the same records also contain entries about the rapidly increasing stream of new Red Chinese master spies who enter the Far Eastern countries with perfect identities and who succeed in establishing reputable 'covers'.

Up-to-date reports about Red Chinese espionage activities in America, Western Europe, Africa, Australia, and New Zealand reveal that Peking Secret Service headquarters have declared their "war without weapons" with intense force on the free world. And recent arrests of Communist spies in Germany, the Benelux countries, and many other territories of the Western world have revealed that these men and women have been in the employ of Red China.

Herr Franz Henkel, for instance, who was arrested in January 1966 while in possession of a microfilm containing N.A.T.O. defence secrets, admitted that the information had been obtained for Peking Secret Service headquarters. Mademoiselle Louise Mainard, who was arrested in March 1965 while passing on to a contact copies of highly confidential political documents, broke down and made a statement that she had been working for Red Chinese intelligence. And Kurt Gerber, who carried on him "electronic espionage equipment" when arrested in December 1965, was eventually proved to have been a Peking agent.

These cases illustrate that Peking Secret Service headquarters do not employ only Chinese nationals for espionage in Western countries. It would be too risky.

Most of the agents in the employ of the Red Chinese chief resident spy operators are fifth-columnists and fellow-travellers who are not generally known as Communists. As natives of their countries, and able to find ways and means to infiltrate into Ministries, organizations, or research centres, they find access to secret information, and can supply their Red Chinese spy chiefs with the material they require.

No-one is able to say how many Red Chinese resident spy operators and agents work in the free world. An officer of the

French Deuxième Bureau estimated the number at "hardly less than ten thousand". A Swiss counter-intelligence officer thought there were more, but an Italian security man insisted there could not be so many. But, whatever the number, they are a real and potential danger to the people of the free world.

7

Target—The World

THE picture of the Soviet and Soviet-controlled world espionage system would be incomplete if it omitted the considerable rôle that trawlers, submarines, and merchant vessels play in the continuous "war without weapons". Frequently official United States reports expose some of the activities which Russian 'fishing' trawlers, equipped with "special electronic intelligence tracking devices", carry out close to U.S. coastlines, and, according to both American and Soviet information, the Russians keep about fifty 'fishing' trawlers with "special equipment" operating in the Grand Banks fishing-grounds and vicinity—an area where naval exercises are carried out.

The United States coast and naval exercise areas are not the only target for Russian and other Iron Curtain spy ships. Soviet trawlers equipped with electronic devices regularly snoop along the Scottish coast. At least one instance is known where, in 1965, in the middle of an innocent-looking Russian 'fishing' fleet was a submarine sending and receiving frequent coded short-wave radio messages to and from Moscow. It was even disclosed that Soviet agents who were brought by the 'fishing' fleet made contact with informers on the Scottish mainland and supplied them with special equipment. This frontier violation was not detected in time, and both the shore agents as well as the 'fishing'-fleet agents succeeded in completing the operation.

The presence of Soviet trawlers near the United States, the British Isles, and other Western coastlines understandably creates great concern, especially when it is established that they are equipped with electronic devices apparently intended for espionage. No action can be taken against them, however, while they remain in international waters. So the 'fishing' vessels, with their tracking devices and various types of antennae capable of detecting electronic signals on nearly all frequencies for hundreds of miles, are able to obtain valuable information on the United

States nuclear submarine base at Holy Loch in Scotland, and also on many similar N.A.T.O. defence centres in America and other Western countries.

Sparsely populated Norway, which also is a target for Soviet espionage, decided to crack down on Red spy ships, to prevent their coming too close to those parts of the Oslo Fiord, and to areas near the ports of Kristiansand, Bergen, Stavanger, Trondheim, and the northern coastline, where the Norwegian Navy has its main bases, radar stations, and weapon-testing grounds. In June 1961 new laws were proposed to restrict movement of shipping in Norway's territorial waters, which had been, till then, an easy hunting-ground for Russian spy ships. Announcing the proposed new laws, which were planned to be effective from the autumn of 1961, the Norwegian Defence Minister, Gudmund Harlem, said:

"The ships will not be allowed to enter our waters at all unless they have a Norwegian pilot aboard, and then must sail inside new 'shipping lanes' which will be marked on all sea charts."

He explained that this measure had been taken only after years of espionage by "snoop ships" and trawlers from Russian, East German, and Polish harbours. He added that the new laws would be enforced by the Norwegian Navy, which would be strengthened by five 1800-ton frigates and five 600-ton patrol vessels, and by gunboats, torpedo-boats, and fifteen submarines—estimated to cost £6,000,000.

Although this drastic step taken by the Norwegian Government makes it impossible for Communist spy ships to photograph defence installations, etc., while sailing in territorial waters close to naval and other bases, it does not stop the Russians from gaining important Norwegian secrets by employing their specially equipped 'fishing' fleets and other vessels.

It must be remembered that these vessels are able to detect signals on nearly all frequencies for hundreds of miles, and the restriction on their movements is by no means a complete protection.

During recent years formations of Soviet submarines have been frequently detected near Western coastlines. In the autumn of 1962 it was divulged in London that "the Admiralty is concerned at the increased number of Russian submarines patrolling in packs around Britain".

Similar observations on "snooping" activities of Soviet submarine formations along coastlines of other Western countries were also made by American, West German, Spanish, French, Dutch, Belgian, and other Western experts. Some of these claim to have conclusive proof that these Soviet submarine spy patrols are equipped to enable them to detect electronic signals on almost all frequencies—as do the Russian spy trawlers.

In December 1963 the captain of a Soviet submarine, M. N. Savelyev, defected and disclosed full details of these activities, and of the equipment of the Russian underwater spy ships. This information was checked and rechecked against the statements which other Soviet naval officers had made when they escaped from their ships. The Western authorities were fully informed of the so-called "Sea Branch" of Communist world espionage, and, as a result, this information helped to improve N.A.T.O. defence installations and enemy-craft-detection devices.

The merchant navy of Russia and the other Iron Curtain countries also forms a considerable part of the Soviet Secret Service's "Sea Branch". Red cargo and passenger vessels are under orders to engage in dual activities. They use well-camouflaged electronic tracking devices and concealed antennae to carry out duties similar to those of the trawlers, and trained Secret Service officers disguised as sailors go ashore when their ships dock in foreign ports. Numerous arrests of Russian, Polish, and other Iron Curtain 'sailors' caught while engaging in espionage are sufficient confirmation of the substantial rôle that Red merchant-navy men play in Communist world espionage.

An illustration of the activities Soviet Secret Service officers carry out under the cover of Red 'sailors' is the case of Major Ivan Petrovich Lebediev. Believing that he would be facing disciplinary action for not having worked to the best of his abilities and training when his ship returned to its home port, and aware that if the Disciplinary Tribunal at Moscow Secret Service headquarters proved his negligence he would be risking long-term imprisonment or even death, he decided to seek asylum in the West. In his statement to Allied authorities he said:

> In March 1953 the State Security Selection Board passed me as suitable for Secret Police training, and I was sent to the special State Security school for home espionage at Dietskoye Selo [the former Tsarist summer residence], Leningrad. In January 1954 I passed the final examinations, was given the rank of lieutenant, and sent to Kharkov to spy on the workers of this Ukrainian industrial centre.
>
> In July 1955 I was summoned to State Security headquarters in Moscow and promoted to the rank of first lieutenant. I was given the chance to be transferred to activities abroad, and was sent to the Lenin Technical School, Verkhovnoye, for further training. . . . At the end of the twelve months' schooling I passed the exams, and, after a month's holiday at the Oktyabr Recreation Home at Kyslovodsk, the secluded Secret Service recreation home in the Caucasian mountain spa, I was sent in

September 1956 to the Reconnaissance Department at the St Antonius Hospital in Berlin-Karlshorst, which is the Berlin branch headquarters of Moscow Secret Service. My duties there were to send coded directives to field agents in West Germany and to receive from them information about their activities in political fields. During my assignment to Berlin branch headquarters I was not required to cross into West German territory because I had not been assigned to the activities of a field agent in a Western country.

At the end of my first year's service at Berlin-Karlshorst I was promoted to the rank of captain. My activities remained the same as before. In November 1958 I was recalled to Moscow headquarters and promoted to the rank of major. I was then told that the Foreign Directorate had chosen me for intelligence operations abroad, and that I should be working under the cover of a Soviet seaman. After a two months' refresher course at the Lenin Technical School, Verkhovnoye, I was sent in January 1959 to Leningrad and joined the cargo vessel *Byeloostrov*.

The statement reveals that every time the *Byeloostrov* docked in any of the numerous Western ports Lebediev went ashore and carried out espionage duties which Moscow Secret Service headquarters had ordered. But he was not the only Russian spy on the *Byeloostrov* who secretly took photographs in foreign countries, and who regularly met Soviet shore agents to whom he passed equipment, money, and specific orders, and from whom he received microfilms, documents, blueprints, and other top-secret information. During his one and a half years on the *Byeloostrov* the number of agents aboard ship was never fewer than ten, often as high as fifteen, and sometimes reached twenty.

In August 1960 he was transferred to the Polish vessel *Jaroslaw Dobrowski* commanding the other Russian and Polish spies aboard, and supervising their shore duties in foreign ports. Seven months after having taken up his position on the *Jaroslaw Dobrowski* one of his spies escaped and defected to the West. Lebediev was held responsible for not having prevented the defection, and Moscow headquarters warned him that if there were any more setbacks he would face disciplinary action. He was ordered to return to his duties on the Polish vessel.

Fourteen months later two more of his men escaped and sought asylum in the free world. Remembering Moscow headquarters' stern warning, he followed the defectors' example. In May 1962 he walked ashore in Finland and hid himself for five days—until the ship sailed. He was granted political asylum in the West.

The case of Major Lebediev is only one of the many in Western files. Although, naturally, each individual statement contains different circumstances, dates, and names, they nevertheless all corroborate the main issue—the important rôle which Russian and other Iron Curtain merchant-navy vessels play in Soviet world espionage.

Other tools of espionage are Russian long-range aircraft, equipped with cameras capable of taking perfect pictures from tremendous heights and with other sophisticated technical equipment. Sceptics who doubt that Russia could send their spy reconnaissance aircraft out on a non-stop flight to and from the U.S.A., or other far-distant countries, should read the words of the official report from the U.S. Defense Department in Washington, D.C., released on March 16th, 1963, which states:

> U.S. fighters were sent up to intercept two Russian planes which flew over Alaska.
> The fighters made radar contact with the Soviet planes—and they flew off towards Russia. They had penetrated 30 miles into American territory and stayed half an hour.
> The intrusion took place yesterday. The Russian aircraft flew between 17,000 and 34,000 feet. The U.S. fighters did not fire at them.

Soviet spy reconnaissance flights frequently take place over N.A.T.O. countries near Russia or her Red satellite neighbours, and there are regular reports of violations of United States, Canadian, South American, and other air space for the purpose of taking aerial photographs of strategic bases and tracking down radar and other defence posts.

And then there are space satellites—Russia's Sputniks and Luniks. Moscow has admitted that their enormous space-research experiments are not solely for future interplanetary travel and exploration of the solar system, but also for intelligence and military reasons. This admission came from no less an authority than the Kremlin, which declared:

> . . . Due to the epoch-making work of our foremost scientists and technicians, especially trained cosmonauts are now ready to make their journeys into outer space from where they can radio back to earth reports and pictures, thus transmitting full information of objects about which, until now, little could be learned. On their safe return to earth they submit detailed reports and photographs to document hitherto secret matters of vital interest to the defence of our country. . . .
> . . . The successful flights round the earth have proved of immense value in all fields of intelligence. With the help of special cameras and electronic devices it is now possible to obtain precise information on secret installations in any country of the world.

8

Espionage and—Murder

THE case of Bogdan Nikolayevich Stashynsky shows the various methods Moscow Secret Service headquarters use in the recruitment of their agents, and it proves that people who have not been devoted adherents of the Communist régime can be converted into reliable and trustworthy executives if sufficient pressure is brought on them.

It is a clear and official exposure and confirmation of the fact that Moscow Secret Service headquarters, in close collaboration with their Berlin-Karlshorst branch headquarters, believe that espionage combined with terror (even murder) is a justifiable means of obtaining results.

Bogdan Nikolayevich Stashynsky was born on November 4th, 1931, in the Ukrainian village of Bershovitsy, near the then Soviet-Polish frontier. The village once consisted of about a thousand poor smallholder peasants, most of them adherents of the Greek Catholic Church, as are the majority of Ukrainian nationalists. These people stubbornly opposed the Kremlin's fierce anti-religion drives and the ruthless enforcement of the collectivization of the land. Merciless terrorizing by the Secret Police reduced the population to fewer than eight hundred, but the Stashynsky family managed to survive because the father also worked as a cabinet-maker in the State-run collective, to help feed his wife and children. The Soviet administration in the area considered him a "desirable element".

When Nazi Germany opened its *Blitzkrieg* against Russia in June 1941 Bogdan was a schoolboy. His village escaped destruction, but the district was the centre-point of a fight between Germans, Poles, and Ukrainians. As a result, young Bogdan learnt German and Polish in addition to his native Ukrainian tongue, and the former official State language, Russian.

The end of World War II did not restore peace in the Ukraine, or in many other parts of the U.S.S.R. Throughout the war years the efforts of Nazi propaganda to convert the Ukraine into stubborn nationalists, hating Soviet Russian domination, succeeded to such an extent that when Red Army troops occupied the area the overwhelming majority of the peasants and workers started fighting for a free and nationally independent Ukraine. Years after the Red Army had thrown out and crushed Hitler's Wehrmacht Ukrainian nationalists went into the forests and the rugged countryside, and guerrilla detachments determinedly fought their historic enemies—the Russians. (According to Moscow announcements the guerrilla warfare in the Ukraine raged until the early fifties, when "the Red Army restored law and order and stamped out all subversive attempts from Nazi-infested elements".)

The steadily growing number of Ukrainian guerrilla detachments caused Moscow great concern, especially as Red Army and police casualties mounted almost daily. Secret Police officers were sent to the trouble spots to find and arrest ringleaders and their supporters, and one of the districts suspected of encouraging the guerrilla fighters was Stashynsky's home village, Bershovitsy. But the Secret Police were unable to obtain the "confessions" they had been ordered to extort. Neither arrests and interrogations nor numerous deportations to Siberia, even executions, helped them to suppress people who had always fought against Soviet collectivization and terror.

At this time, as a result of travelling on a train without a ticket, Stashynsky fell into the hands of the Soviet Secret Police. Secret Police Captain Sytnikovsky, in charge of tracing the guerrillas in the district, heard of the arrest. He also heard that Stashynsky originated from a village of hardened Ukrainian nationalists, and that he came from a Greek Catholic Church family. The captain decided that the youth could be a useful tool to him. He began to interrogate young Bogdan, and threatened to deport him and the whole of his family to a slave-labour camp unless he agreed to infiltrate into the Ukrainian resistance groups and work among them for the Secret Police.

Stashynsky accepted Captain Sytnikovsky's proposal, believing—as he claimed later at a trial before the Federal Court in Karlsruhe—that he would be able to save his parents from exile in Siberia, and himself and his sister from imprisonment or death. And so the newly recruited informer Stashynsky was responsible for the detection and annihilation of the guerrilla group, and Captain Sytnikovsky kept his promise and left the traitor's parents and sister untouched.

Having completed his assignments in the Bershovitsy district, Stashynsky was transferred to another region. His duties again consisted of learning about nationalist guerrillas. Again he worked thoroughly.

It was decided that the young Ukrainian should receive comprehensive schooling in Marxism-Leninism because he would then be of greater use to the Soviet Secret Service and could be considered for espionage training. He was sent to the special training establishment of the Committee for State Security near Kiev, where he received political schooling, as well as instruction in Secret Service activities and German and Polish language tuition.

Bogdan Nikolayevich Stashynsky received 'genuine' documents in the name of "Josef Lehmann" and, together with his "leader officer", travelled to Warsaw. His new identity belonged to a real Josef Lehmann, who worked in a sugar factory in Poland, and Stashynsky-"Lehmann" was ordered to work in this factory and study the ways and character of the man he was to be from then on. Finally he was classed as suitable for espionage work abroad.

Accompanied again by his "leader officer", Stashynsky-"Lehmann" now proceeded to the East German city of Frankfurt-an-der-Oder, and, after a brief stay, went on to Berlin-Karlshorst. According to Stashynsky's testimony at his trial before the Federal Court in Karlsruhe, the crossing of frontiers was always smooth and without control.

The newly created "Josef Lehmann" stayed only a month at Berlin-Karlshorst branch headquarters—long enough to 'acclimatize' himself and receive additional espionage instruction. It was, however, found that he was still insufficiently equipped for his assignment, and he was consequently sent to the Soviet-controlled East German Secret Service centre in Dresden, where he worked a while and was issued with an identity-card for stateless persons and a driving licence in the names of Josef Lehmann, Siegfried Träger, Hans Joachim Budeit, and Kowalski.

On returning to branch headquarters in Berlin, Stashynsky-"Lehmann" was ordered to work as a metal-sheet-cutter in the car-park of the Soviet Delegation in East Berlin. This was to perfect his German language and characteristics. In addition he worked as a German-Polish interpreter in the East German Ministry for Internal and External Trade. Yet another of his duties was to carry out "routine orders", which consisted of noting the numbers of all Allied military vehicles in West Berlin.

Finally the day came when he was given a mission in West Germany. He was ordered to fly to Munich and hand over to a Russian resident master spy coded microfilm instructions, together with a vast amount of money, which he was to carry in a suitcase with a double bottom. He completed the assignment satisfactorily, and earned special praise, because he brought back valuable information he had obtained on his own initiative.

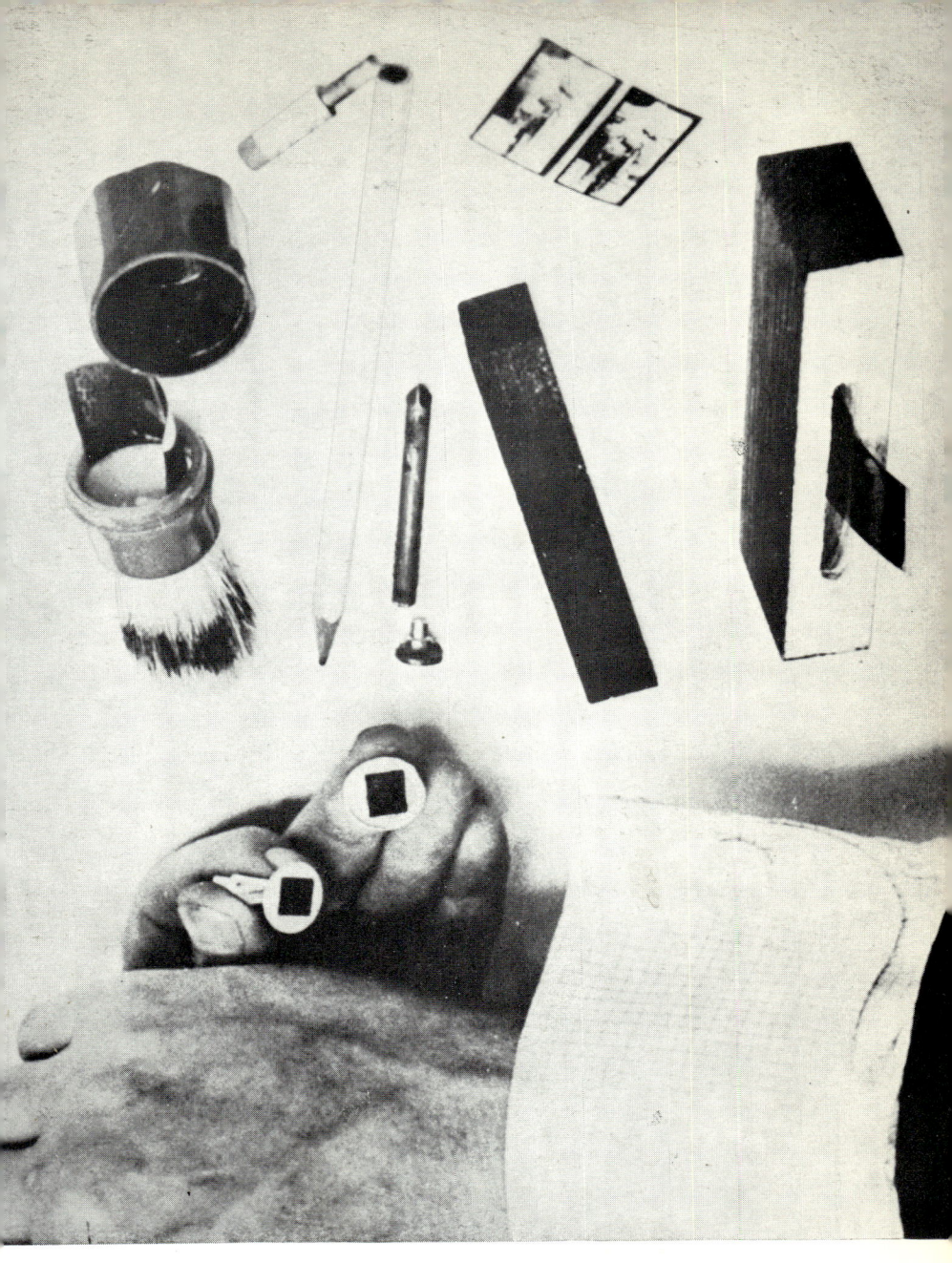

Tools of espionage. Soviet spies use hollow shaving-brushes,
nails, pencils, cuff-links, etc., to hide microfilm messages

Three miniature cameras and a cigarette-box used by Soviet spies
to hide microfilm

Photos United Press

A powerful radio transmitter used to send coded messages to
Moscow Secret Service headquarters

In an East Berlin dancing establishment the young Soviet spy met the twenty-one-year-old Inge Pohl, to whom he introduced himself as Josef Lehmann. She liked him. He quickly grew fond of the girl.

Like all other Soviet Secret Service officers, he was obliged to inform his superiors about his girl friend. Inge Pohl was immediately screened, but nothing was found against her. Nevertheless Berlin branch headquarters was not happy about the association.

Although "Josef Lehmann" was not forbidden to meet Inge Pohl again, he was cautioned to exercise the utmost vigilance and ordered to report anything suspicious.

Soon he was instructed to report to the First Directorate at Berlin-Karlshorst. There he was told to fly again to Munich—this time to recruit for the Soviet network in West Germany a Ukrainian refugee whose wife and daughter lived in the U.S.S.R. He was also told that should the recruiting attempt fail, he was to take a number of photographs for blackmail purposes.

On meeting the refugee "Lehmann" discovered that, without extreme threats, he could not accomplish his task. He photographed the man with a special camera built in a cigarette lighter. The camera was defective, and the blank film was discovered only when Stashynsky-"Lehmann" returned to Berlin branch headquarters.

For some time his duties at Berlin-Karlshorst were to direct a number of Soviet spies in West Germany. During this time he also received expert tuition in handling a "strictly secret weapon" —an aluminium cylinder weighing about seven ounces, six inches long and three-quarters of an inch in diameter. This cylinder contained a colourless, odourless liquid poison, enabling an assassin to commit 'perfect' murder.

He went again to West Germany to locate two important Ukrainian nationalist leaders—Lev Rebet and Stiepan Bandera.

The Committee for State Security in Moscow had taken the decision to assassinate these two refugees from the Ukraine, who now led the Ukrainian Liberation Movement, because, after the Hungarian revolt in 1956, and after the riots in Poland and the disturbances in other satellite countries, the Kremlin feared that even more far-reaching revolts could occur in the Soviet Union if they were skilfully organized by anti-Soviet leadership in exile.

Lev Rebet, a highly intelligent and ideologically schooled ex-Communist, was to be the first victim. Moscow considered him the "personification symbol" of the Ukrainian Liberation Movement. He was a painful thorn because he also maintained close contact with Allied counter-intelligence services.

Under the identity of "Siegfried Träger", Stashynsky went to Munich and shadowed Lev Rebet. On the day he had chosen to

E

assassinate the Ukrainian leader Stashynsky waited for his victim on the stairs leading to the editorial office of *Suchasna Ukraina* (*Contemporary Ukraine*, the publication of Ukrainian exiles in West Germany) at Karls Platz, Munich, and blew a cloud of colourless and odourless poison in his face. Seeing his victim collapse and knowing the assassination had been successful, he wrapped the murder weapon in a newspaper and threw it into the brook at Kögelmühlbach. This may appear to the layman to have been an extraordinary action for a trained agent, but the behaviour of human beings under emotional stress is not always accountable.

The official West German verdict on Lev Rebet's death was: "He died of natural heart failure."

His next assignments were "reconnaissance missions" to Rotterdam and Munich, for which he used the identity of Hans Joachim Budeit. Then he was ordered to go with his "leader officer", Sergey, from Berlin-Karlshorst to Moscow; he was to meet Colonel Gregoryi, a section chief of the Soviet Committee for State Security.

"Gregoryi told me in the presence of another man: 'It has been decided that you are to dispose of Bandera in the same manner as you did Rebet'," Stashynsky stated in evidence at his trial before the Federal Court in Karlsruhe, and continued: "It was explained to me that the weapon would be double-barrelled to exclude any possible failure. It was known that Bandera carried a weapon and was surrounded by bodyguards. . . ."

The "young hero" was allowed, as a reward for outstanding services, to stand side by side with Soviet leaders on the Lenin-Stalin mausoleum to watch the May Day celebrations in 1959.

Stashynsky flew back to Munich, using the cover name of Hans Joachim Budeit. For four days he shadowed Stiepan Bandera, who was living in exile under the name of Poppel.

Stashynsky then unaccountably began to feel his plan would fail. He abandoned the first assassination attempt, and at his second panicked.

He described the situation: "I made two steps towards Bandera, who stood beside his motor-car, and then I said to myself, 'Don't do it'. And then I turned back and went away, determined to let him live."

He threw the unused poison pistol, again wrapped in a newspaper, into the Kögelmühlbach brook.

Although he felt quite sure that his superiors in the Soviet Secret Service would order the Secret Police to keep him under observation, and anticipated that he would be accused of cowardice and not complying with orders, he nevertheless arranged an alibi in West Germany and flew back to East Berlin. When he returned he told them how Bandera had eluded him, and how he himself, under pressure, had to get rid of the weapon. To his surprise, no-one reprimanded him and he was assigned to "direction duties" at Berlin headquarters.

At the beginning of October 1959, Stashynsky's "leader officer", Sergey, conveyed to him Moscow's renewed order to dispose of Bandera, and he was issued with another weapon. On the 14th he flew from Tempelhof to Munich, and next day trailed the counter-revolutionary Ukrainian exile leader.

Again, fearing that his frequent visits to Munich must have been noticed by the West German counter-intelligence or by Bandera's own security guards, and believing that if he couldn't accomplish the assassination within hours he was sure to be arrested in Munich, he gave himself a deadline. He decided that if he did not manage to meet his victim in suitable circumstances by 1 P.M. he would once more abandon his mission, regardless of the consequences at Berlin-Karlshorst.

Stiepan Bandera arrived a little before 1 P.M. at the entrance of the block in which he had an apartment. Stashynsky went into the building ahead of him. A woman was just descending the stairs, and this made him nervous. He also had an idea that Bandera might have recognized him.

He bent down, pretending he was tying the lace on his right shoe. (He was wearing shoes without laces.) On noticing that Bandera was having difficulty with his key, he straightened up and asked whether anything was wrong. When the Ukrainian exile leader replied that nothing was wrong Stashynsky fired.

Seeing the Ukrainian refugee stumble towards the steps of the the stairs, and knowing then that Bandera would be dead within the next few seconds, he calmly left the house and closed the door.

He walked to the Kögelmühlbach and disposed of the weapon as on the two previous occasions, then went to the railway station and, twenty minutes later, travelled to Frankfurt-am-Main, from where he flew under the name of Kowalski to Berlin. When he telephoned branch headquarters he was informed that his superiors had already heard of the murder from the West German radio.

The twenty-eight-year-old Bogdan Nikolayevich Stashynsky had now reached the summit of his career in the Soviet Secret Service. At a dinner given by his superiors in his honour the chief of the Berlin-Karlshorst branch headquarters proudly announced that Stashynsky's career would continue with further schooling and training, and with many more important assignments. Soon afterwards he was called to Moscow and praised for the murders of Rebet and Bandera. The President of the Supreme Soviet invested him with the decoration of "Fighting Order of the Red Flag".

Believing he could now request personal favours, Stashynsky asked Colonel Aleksei Alekseievich, his Section Chief in the State Security Committee, for permission to marry Inge Pohl. The Section Chief refused the request, and would not discuss the matter.

Stashynsky suddenly realized that he was only a servant who had to obey orders. But he was unwilling to give up his fight to marry. He repeated his request. His Section Chief told him that if he must get married he should marry a Soviet girl who could work with him in the Secret Service.

"We have been engaged for a long time—we love each other," Stashynsky explained. His superior was adamant. Later Stashynsky was to describe the situation. "I really did love her," he said. "I couldn't jilt her.

"On the other hand, as a K.G.B., a State Security officer, I had to conceal a lot from her. I had always been determined she must not know what sort of a person I was and what I had done. But then, after I had fought with myself and had come to the decision that I must tell my future wife everything, I hoped she would understand me. . . ."

Stashynsky told Inge Pohl, on Christmas Eve 1959. Inge persuaded him to marry quickly and escape to West Berlin. He, still hoping he would be able to reach agreement with his chiefs, suggested they defer their final decision a little. But he did agree that they should create the impression that they were ready to comply with everything the Soviet officers might require of them.

Encouraged by one of his superiors at Berlin-Karlshorst branch headquarters, who considered using Inge Pohl as a "specialist agent" in West Berlin, Stashynsky appealed to the highest chief of the Committee for State Security, Shelyepin, for permission to marry. His marriage was sanctioned, but Stashynsky was pledged to return with his wife to Moscow after the wedding to undergo further schooling and training.

On March 23rd, 1960, "Josef Lehmann" married Inge Pohl in East Berlin. In May they were living in Moscow in a one-room flat in a house that belonged to the K.G.B. Stashynsky was informed he would be sent on a "special mision" to an English-speaking country, but instead he was given special tuition on West Germany. Inge Stashynsky-"Lehmann" was also sent on courses, but was not allowed to attend subjects on "advanced espionage techniques". Colonel Alekseievich did not trust her sufficiently.

The couple were unhappy in Moscow. Inge constantly begged her husband to break and defect to the West.

"When I first discovered the hidden microphones in our flat I got a terrible shock," Stashynsky explained. "We had spoken about things with each other which were far from flattering to the Soviet system and the Eastern bloc. We then realized in what danger we were. . . . But what could I do?

"My wife looked pleadingly at me. So we began to talk to each other without words and only with our eyes. . . ."

In September 1960 Stashynsky told his leader Sergey that Inge was already three months pregnant, and asked him to recommend a transfer from Moscow to Berlin so that she could be looked after by her mother. Sergey replied:

"The interests and matters of the State come first; private life is only of secondary importance. In your position children are only a handicap. It would be best to get rid of the child by abortion."

Stashynsky refused, and relations with his Section Chief rapidly deteriorated. They took to intercepting his and his wife's letters. Stashynsky's Secret Service training suddenly stopped. He was told that his instructor was ill. He was told that he should train as a barber.

At the beginning of December 1960 Stashynsky was told to report to General Yakovlyevich, head of the Committee for State Security, who informed him that he would be domiciled in Moscow for seven years and not permitted to leave, not even for a visit to East Berlin. His wife, he was told, was not restricted, and was free to go at any time. General Yakovlyevich also told him that he would not be dismissed from the Soviet Secret Service, and that, until other duties were found for him, he would be paid over two hundred roubles per month.

Stashynsky later reported: "I was suddenly aware of the fact that my life wasn't even worth a copeck."

In January 1961 Inge obtained permission to travel to East Berlin so that she could give birth to her baby due in March.

After she had left Russia Stashynsky's Section Chief, Colonel Alekseievich, and other leading officers at Moscow Secret Service headquarters suddenly changed their attitude towards him, and proposed new assignments. But he was not permitted to fly to East Berlin to be with his wife at the time of her confinement, because Colonel Alekseievich insisted that his training and work at Moscow headquarters should not be interrupted.

At the beginning of August 1961 his wife decided to return with her baby to Moscow. Colonel Alekseievich was sure that if Stashynsky was deprived of his baby son a speedy break-up of the marriage would result.

The day before Inge's departure from East Berlin to Moscow the baby died of suffocation while being looked after by neighbours as Inge was completing travel arrangements. She sent a telegram, "Peter dead please come", to her husband.

Stashynsky was grief-stricken and insisted on being allowed to fly to his wife in East Berlin. Surprisingly, they granted him permission.

Accompanied by his commanding officer, Yuryi Nikolayevich Aleksandrov, Stashynsky was flown in a military aircraft from Moscow to East Berlin, and allowed to stay with his wife each day, although under strict orders to report with her every evening to his commanding officer. They had to stay each night at closely guarded Berlin-Karlshorst.

Three days after his arrival in East Berlin, on August 12th, 1961, Stashynsky and his wife made final preparations for their escape to West Berlin. They knew that they must time their break for freedom the next day. Stashynsky's commanding officer had only that morning informed him that arrangements had been made for him to fly back to Moscow in two days, and that on his return to the Red capital travel arrangements for his wife would be set in motion. But both knew that once they were parted it was unlikely they would ever see each other again.

The Stashynskys realized the danger of what they were about to attempt. They were shadowed by Soviet detectives at almost every step they made. The house in which Inge stayed with her parents was under continuous surveillance. All they could do was to hope for luck when the moment of escape arrived.

When the couple left the Soviet district of Berlin-Karlshorst on the morning of August 13th they were, as usual, shadowed. They returned.

At four o'clock on this Sunday afternoon Stashynsky, his wife, and her fifteen-year-old brother Fritz managed to slip out of the back entrance of the house unseen as the detective's attention was diverted. Bushes and trees in the neighbouring gardens screened them, and they got away before the detective resumed his watch.

The three reached the centre of the East Berlin suburb, then walked three miles to Falkensee. No-one appeared to have trailed them.

It was already 6 P.M.

At 8 P.M. Stashynsky and his wife were due to leave the house and report to his commanding officer. If by that time they hadn't reached West Berlin, crossing-points along the frontier of divided Berlin would be notified and escape become impossible.

They reached Falkensee two hours before deadline, and Stashynsky took a taxi to East Berlin's Friedrich Strasse. *En route,* a police patrol stopped them. They feared their escape had been discovered, but when Stashynsky produced his identity-card in the name of Josef Lehmann the police officer allowed them to continue, and they knew it had only been one of the frequent routine checks the police carried out.

An hour and fifteen minutes before deadline Stashinsky paid off the taxi-driver in Friedrich Strasse. They had almost made it.

Inge's brother, Fritz, who also wanted to escape to West Berlin, implored the Stashynskys to take him with them. But he was made to appreciate that if he went his parents would be brutally persecuted for his escape.

The couple took another taxi and travelled to a railway station, where they bought tickets to West Berlin. The police control officer casually glanced at "Josef Lehmann's" identity-card, and they boarded the train to the free zone of Berlin.

Shortly before 8 P.M. they left the train at the West Berlin Gesundbrunnen station.

For Stashynsky, the Soviet spy who had murdered two Ukrainian compatriots to whom West Germany had granted political asylum, escape to the West did not necessarily mean freedom. He was aware that he might have a fair chance of remaining unconnected with his crimes, but, having broken with the Soviet Secret Service, he decided to put himself at the mercy of the West German authorities. He gave himself up, and made a full confession.

In October 1962 Bogdan Nikolayevich Stashynsky, alias "Josef Lehmann", alias "Siegfried Träger", alias "Hans Joachim Budeit", alias "Kowalski", Soviet spy and murderer, stood his trial at the West German Federal Court in Karlsruhe.

Sentencing him to eight years' hard labour, the trial judge, Senat President Dr Jagusch, said: "The court has been in a position to satisfy itself completely about the truthfulness and presentation of all facts which the accused revealed." The trial judge then pointed out that though Stashynsky had carried out the assassinations, one had to consider him more a tool than a callous murderer who had chosen and killed his victims.

Dr Jagusch went on to say: "The court hearing revealed and proved that the order to carry out the murders had come from the political leadership of the Soviet Union. Consequently, by having carried out these orders, the accused man had sunk to the level of being an exploited tool of his masters behind the scenes, and was therefore entitled to certain leniency."

He concluded:

"The accused had broken with his past in a dangerous way when, with his wife, he fled from the Eastern régime of terror to the West. And, despite the prospect of having to face prosecution for murder, which he knew was threatening him, he nevertheless gave himself up. . . ."

9

The Popular Sicilian

LUIGI SOMA'S personality was the secret of the success of his coffee bar, close to Milan's La Scala opera house. The bar was just like any other coffee bar in the city, but he had something his competitors didn't have—an ever-cheerful smile and amusing conversation that made customers enjoy their visits to Luigi's.

Then, one October morning, the door of Luigi's coffee bar stayed shut. Regulars were disappointed.

When the bar remained closed the next day, and the rest of the week, the customers asked neighbouring tradesmen what had happened to Luigi. No-one knew.

Some were convinced that Luigi had been the victim of an accident, and might be somewhere in a hospital. Others thought family problems might have taken him unexpectedly to Palermo. No-one guessed the true reason.

Luigi Soma was not his real name, nor had he been born in Palermo. In fact, he wasn't a Sicilian at all. He was a Russian resident spy operator who had been transformed into a 'Sicilian' in the Soviet Secret Service school of Stiepnaya, where he had received his training for espionage. During his eight and a half years in Italy no-one ever detected anything to indicate that Luigi Soma was in fact Antek Krakowski.

Antek Krakowski was born in the Polish town of Cracow in February 1915. The Krakowskis moved soon after Antek's birth to Warsaw, because the schoolmaster-father, Stiepan Krakowski, had been dismissed from his post owing to his Bolshevik views. Despite the shortage of manpower in almost every profession, brought about by World War I, it was impossible for the schoolmaster to find a suitable job in the capital; his political views had been reported to Warsaw, and wherever he applied he was turned down. He eventually became a professional revolutionary—employed by the illegal Bolshevik party.

Post-War Poland was difficult for Stiepan Krakowski and his family. He was several times caught actively organizing strikes or enticing workers to revolt against the Government. In 1928 the police were seeking him on a charge of high treason. If convicted, he would have received a long prison sentence, so the Polish Communist Party arranged to get him to Russia. His family followed a month later.

Being the son of a Polish 'hero' comrade, thirteen-year-old Antek almost immediately became an assistant leader in the Communist Youth League. Conscientious and intelligent, he made excellent school progress, and at the age of eighteen was recommended by the Youth League's Central Committee for a Party career. He was sent to the Marx-Engels Institute.

In October 1935 Antek Krakowski passed his finals at the Marx-Engels Institute with honours, and was appointed Third Party Secretary at the Moscow Party Committee—a very high responsibility for a twenty-year-old. Within a year he had become Second Party Secretary, and worked closely with Stalin's protégé, Nikita Sergeyevich Khrushchev. He held this post for two years, and in 1938 was transferred to duties at the Party's Central Committee.

A month before Hitler opened his *Blitzkrieg* on Russia, Antek, by then an officer of the Party's Central Committee, was classed by the Selection Board of the Soviet Secret Service as suitable for "special" training. And during his "assessment" duties at Secret Service headquarters, which during World War II was transferred to the city of Kuibyshev, on the Volga, he was chosen for the rôle of operator in Italy. He was furnished with documents of a "Luigi Soma" and, during his training, adopted the nationality and characteristics of a Sicilian.

It was not until autumn 1953 that "Luigi Soma" slipped into Italy.

Before he actually began his espionage rôle, to 'acclimatize' he stayed a fortnight in Naples, then 'returned' to his 'native' Sicily and remained in Messina a while. He then went to Palermo.

Finally he received orders from Moscow to take up residence in Rome.

As with all Russian master spies, he was equipped with substantial funds, but for appearance he took a cheap room in a lower-class part of Rome. He worked as a porter, then as a lorry-driver's mate, and later as a warehouseman. Everyone liked him.

The fact that Italy has one of the strongest Communist parties in the world, as well as a mass of fellow-travellers, greatly helped Luigi to find suitable agents and informers for the network he was steadily building.

Satisfied that neither police nor anyone else suspected him in any way, he decided to give up his warehouse job.

His next 'cover' was as a door-to-door salesman, a rôle which afforded unique opportunities to meet his contacts.

Then Luigi became involved with an Italian girl, and because of this was ordered to leave Rome.

The girl found that she was pregnant and refused her lover's suggestion of an abortion. She insisted that they marry. This was impossible as it would endanger his espionage activities.

He informed Moscow, and it was arranged that a Control Agent should deal with the girl.

Moscow ordered Luigi to transfer his network to another director, then go north. He was to remain inactive until police inquiries into the girl's disappearance were over.

A few days after the girl had apparently gone away a card arrived at her parents' home. It had been mailed in Athens and bore a message in her handwriting, stating she was well and would be writing again. Everybody now believed she had gone abroad to take a job.

As soon as it was clear that no danger threatened Luigi he restarted his activities.

Luigi chose Milan as his new centre, and opened a coffee bar.

It was, of course, almost impossible for Italy's counter-espionage to connect the coffee-bar proprietor with an espionage network, for he never personally attempted to obtain official secrets directly from anyone: he left this to his numerous agents. Microfilms of documents were dropped into an empty cup and handed to Luigi. A packet of coffee beans bought over the counter often contained considerable sums of money—reward and expense for espionage services.

Year after year this Soviet master spy operated his coffee bar and his network, undisturbed.

Luigi's activities ended through Italian counter-intelligence detecting an informer, and, through him, getting their first lead to the coffee bar. Because of insufficient evidence they could only start round-the-clock surveillance of the place.

The Soviet Control Agent learned of the counter-intelligence move, and it was the Control Agent's emergency action which saved Antek Krakowski, alias Luigi Soma.

Italian security officers discovered Luigi's technical equipment, including his short-wave radio receiver-transmitter with high-speed-transmission converter; special photographic equipment for microfilming and microdotting; code keys; plus information concerning a number of informers.

The network was broken, although the master spy escaped, and the coffee-bar regulars are still wondering what happened to Luigi.

Where is he now? Who knows? Perhaps back in Russia preparing a new alias. Or even here in Britain, undetected in our midst. Have you been to an Italian coffee bar lately? One run by a smiling Sicilian?

10

Operation Sweden

AS a result of a series of trials of Communist spies which took place in Sweden between 1951 and 1953, Admiral Helfe Strömback, Commander-in-Chief of the Swedish Navy, stated that damage done by Soviet spies was irreparable. It had been discovered that since 1941 all the secrets of Sweden's defences had been passed on to Soviet agents, and that at least five parallel Russian espionage networks had been working in the country.

Sweden succeeded in wiping out the spy networks, and those Russian agents who didn't escape in time to the U.S.S.R. were imprisoned at the 1951–53 trials, but the arrests and convictions did not end Russian and other Iron Curtain espionage in Sweden.

Since 1953, Russian, Polish, Czechoslovak, and other Iron Curtain spies and espionage networks have continued to be detected by Swedish counter-intelligence. As in all other countries of the free world, Communist Secret Service headquarters quickly filled the gaps.

An interesting example of Soviet espionage in Sweden is the case of Ernst Anderson, an officer of the Swedish Navy, who was recruited by Russian espionage and supplied Moscow with invaluable, and to his own native country disastrous, top-secret information.

The man who was actually responsible for the organization of this particular network in Sweden was the Soviet Secret Service officer Vinogradov, who posed as Second Secretary at the Soviet Embassy in Stockholm. With diplomatic immunity, he found it easy to approach Swedish Communists and fellow-travellers and recruit them as informers or espionage agents. His deputy spy operator was another Soviet citizen, Viktor Anisimov, who held the position of chief correspondent of TASS, the Soviet news agency, in Stockholm. This was, of course, shrewd strategy, because it was natural for the chief of the Soviet news agency to meet the Embassy's Second Secretary frequently.

The Swedish naval officer Ernst Anderson was recruited by a Swedish Communist who was one of Vinogradov's key agents in Stockholm. At first the agent feared it would be impossible to comply with Vinogradov's order to obtain the co-operation of Anderson. But alcohol, blackmail, and a considerable amount of cash achieved the objective.

For five years Anderson supplied the Soviet with copies of documents on armaments, dispositions, and the state of the Swedish Navy, including full details on defence installations and tactics at naval bases; potential landing-point defences on the east and west coasts of Sweden; and blueprints of Sweden's anti-invasion fortress of Boden.

But Anderson was not content with merely selling the secrets of the Swedish Navy. He also made extensive use of a camera Anisimov had bought for him to photograph airfields, including Sweden's main air base at Luleå, and he also provided the Russians with most valuable details about the Swedish Air Force.

Eventually Swedish counter-intelligence began to suspect Ernst Anderson. His career came to a sudden end.

On September 12th, 1951, Anderson obtained five days' leave from his duties in Stockholm, claiming that he had to attend to an urgent family matter. Unaware that Swedish counter-intelligence officers were shadowing him, he did not in fact go to his home town of Naşajö. He travelled to Sweden's chief naval base, Karlskrona, to obtain information on Swedish warships there.

He overstayed his five-day leave and failed to return to Stockholm until September 20th. Then, instead of reporting immediately on arrival, he went straight to an ice-cream parlour. Still unaware of the counter-intelligence officers following him, he mounted a bicycle and rode to the Southern Hospital. Before leaving the bicycle at the entrance he removed from his wallet a sheet of thin paper and placed it carefully in the cycle-pump. He then extracted further papers from his pocket and left them in the toolbag.

Swedish counter-intelligence officers acted. The papers contained the details of Karlskrona naval-base secrets—written in invisible ink. Anderson talked, and the Vinogradov-Anisimov espionage network was destroyed.

Arthur Karlsson directed a network that operated at the same time as the Vinogradov-Anisimov gang. The Karlsson case is, perhaps, even more important because his network accomplished greater successes in the industrial, military, and political fields.

Arthur Karlsson was told to become a doorman at the editorial office of the Communist newspaper *Ny Dag*, as a cover for his real work in Stockholm. Although in another Western country any connection with a Communist organization or newspaper would have been in itself grounds for suspicion, this was not so in Sweden. No-one suspected the unimportant doorman.

Karlsson's chief agent, who was his second-in-command, was a thirty-three-year-old journalist and former officer of the Swedish Army, Fritjof Enbom, who was in sole charge of "organizational matters". This meant that he was the man who recruited and directed the informers and rank-and-file spies.

Moscow's orders to the Karlsson-Enbom team were:

1. To obtain and transmit specified secret information, blue-prints, plans, etc., on Swedish inventions and production; on air-craft construction and output, as well as all other important industries; and to provide information on iron-ore fields, steel plants, and other industrial enterprises.

2. To organize in the north of Sweden activist groups of Communists and reliable sympathizers, and prepare them to be ready to give the Red Army every assistance in the event of an invasion of Sweden.

3. To provide a force of at least two hundred saboteurs who, in the event of a war between Sweden and the Soviet Union, could blow up the central arsenal and the power station at the fortress of Boden; disrupt railway transport; and spread confusion among Swedish troops and civilians by broadcasting misleading orders from underground radio stations.

Because Karlsson and Enbom were so occupied with the every-day direction of their nation-wide espionage, they were unable to carry out the orders regarding sabotage and subversion, so they put their comrade and ex-Army sergeant, Hugo Gjersföld, in charge of this aspect of their assignment.

The ex-N.C.O. of the Swedish Army trained his Red fifth-columnists so well that they would have been able, if the need arose and if armed with weapons from Russia, to seize frontier fortifications along the invasion route.

The network remained undetected for almost eleven years. When the Soviet agents were finally arrested police found a portable, powerful short-wave radio receiver-transmitter which the Soviet Embassy in Stockholm had supplied to Enbom. Police also seized general-staff maps, charts, photographs of strategic installations and detailed plans of frontier defence lines, and an arsenal of small arms and ammunition.

An official report stated:

> Railwayman Fingal Larsson had a complete plan for sabot-aging the railway system in Northern Sweden. Other Russian agents had collected highly secret information on the heavy

and medium guns sunk into granite nests. If it is remembered that these guns are the pride of Sweden's defence in the frontier and coastal regions, as they are automatically loaded, radar-controlled, and therefore most powerful and up-to-date, it will be realized that this is one of the most treacherous crimes possible.

During the sensational trial of Karlsson, Enbom, Gjersföld, and others in their network, at which altogether nine Soviet agents stood in the dock, several Russian diplomats from the Soviet Embassy and Trade Mission in Stockholm were accused of having been directly connected with the ring. But the Swedish Government was unable to proceed against them because of their diplomatic immunity.

Four members of the Soviet Embassy and twenty-two members of the consulate and trade mission were consequently allowed to leave the country, together with their families, and they embarked aboard the Russian vessel *Byeloostrov* from Stockholm to Leningrad. With them went the leader of the Swedish Communist Party, Seth Persson; the former editor of *Ny Dag*, Gustav Johansson; and a Swedish employee of TASS.

Fritjof Enbom and Hugo Gjersföld were sentenced to imprisonment for life; the other Soviet agents received prison sentences ranging from two to eight years. But the damage had been done.

The most recent and highly sensational case of Soviet espionage in Sweden centred on a fifty-six-year-old Swedish Air Force Colonel, Stig Wennerström, who worked undetected for fifteen years as a master spy for the Russians, supplying them with top-secret documents and information on military matters in Sweden and other countries, including Great Britain and the U.S.A.

When Colonel Wennerström was arrested on June 20th, 1963, the case was described in such newspaper headlines as this: "Sweden's worst case of espionage"; "The biggest Swedish espionage scandal of all time"; "Swedish Colonel sold defence secrets worth millions"; "Swedish Colonel hired by the Russians for fifteen years".

Sweden's Defence Minister, Mr Sven Andersson, said, "This case is a deeply shocking one. Colonel Wennerström has caused his country serious damage."

Colonel Wennerström described his arrest as follows:

"On the morning of June 20th, as I strode rapidly across the bridge, three men suddenly appeared. One of them stretched out his hand, introduced himself as a detective, and told me I was under arrest. I did not protest and quietly followed the detectives to their parked car."

When charged at Stockholm police headquarters with having been engaged in espionage activities for the Soviet Secret Service, the Colonel stated:

"I have not spied for them. I have been a member of the underground Soviet opposition group, working against the present régime in the U.S.S.R. This was my only contact with the Russians."

However, when confronted with irrefutable evidence of his espionage activities, he declared:

"I have spied only against the United States of America, and not against Sweden."

His interrogator did not accept this statement, and confronted Wennerström with further evidence. The Colonel then said:

"I will tell you all."

During the four months of questioning that followed, Wennerström told this story:

I was born on August 22nd, 1906, into an Army officer's family. I was a shy boy, and had few childhood friends. I did not get on too well with my father, who considered me a weakling, but my relations with my mother were affectionate. When I decided on a military career my father was surprised, and our relations improved.

During my early years I had the constant impulse to strive higher. When my young fellow-officers gathered at night for a bit of roistering I stayed in my room to study Russian. I had decided to learn the language because I thought it might come in handy at some future time, especially as few people in our country spoke and understood Russian really well.

I was trained as a naval officer, but in the 1930s I switched to the Air Force. In the winter of 1933–34 I received a military scholarship to study Russian in Riga, and it was on this visit to Riga that my interest in espionage was first awakened. Riga was the capital of the then independent Latvia, and was a famous listening-post near the Soviet Russian frontier. It was a city full of spies and informers, diplomats, and double agents.

I was first introduced to the intriguing cloak-and-dagger system of espionage when I met a British agent who talked about his activities. . . . It was the indirect start of my own involvement.

In Riga I also had my first taste of diplomatic receptions and parties. I'd always dreamed of getting into top social life, and had always tried my utmost to fulfil this ambition.

After my return from Riga to Stockholm, in 1939, I married Ulla-Greta Carlsson, daughter of the well-to-do Stockholm newspaper executive. Ulla was thirteen years younger than I. It was a very happy marriage.

In 1940 I was sent to Moscow as Swedish Air Attaché. The appointment was largely due to my command of the Russian language. At that time the German-Russian Pact was still in force, but there was growing distrust between the two countries. I established contact with my opposite numbers at other embassies in Moscow. This was one of my duties as Swedish Air Attaché, and my relations with the Germans became particularly close.

As with many Swedish military men at this stage of the War, my sympathies were with Germany, so I had no qualms about supplying my opposite number at the German Embassy with information I had collected about Russia in the course of my duty.

My appointment as Swedish Air Attaché in Moscow ended in March 1941, and I returned to Stockholm, where I continued friendly relations with the German Embassy. Two years later, in 1943, I was tipped off that our counter-intelligence had managed to break a German code, and my name had been discovered in telegrams from the German Embassy in Stockholm to Berlin as a source of information. Because of this my telephone was being tapped. I never used the telephone for any confidential conversations, so the tapping didn't worry me in the least. Although our counter-intelligence didn't discover anything else that could incriminate me, I was posted to an air base in Satanäs, on the west coast of Sweden, in October 1943.

Two years later I secured another staff post and returned to Stockholm. My main contacts were then with the Americans and Russians. I often served as an escort officer and interpreter when Soviet officers visited Swedish Air Force installations, and always got on well with them.

A year after my return to Stockholm from Satanäs, in 1946, I had my first contact with U.S. Intelligence. An American agent surprised me by revealing that my name had been found in the records of a German wartime espionage organization. The agent suggested that since I had previously worked against the Russians for the Germans, I might be willing to be similarly helpful to the Americans. I agreed. The U.S. agent then suggested a modest job: I was simply to mail a parcel (which I think contained radio tubes) as I passed through Leningrad on my way to Moscow. I had been invited to attend a Soviet military aviation show in Moscow and was to travel through Leningrad, so the job was easy. I posted the parcel.

I didn't have any other contact with U.S. Intelligence until two years later—in 1948. This time an American agent engaged me in a lengthy discussion on espionage operations, especially on the technique of a double agent. I found the subject so fascinating that, although the American agent had not suggested the venture, I decided to become a double agent myself. [American authorities

F

have emphatically denied that Colonel Stig Wennerström ever worked for U.S. Intelligence.]

Having made up my mind, my first job for the Soviet Secret Service arose late in 1948. It had come to my knowledge that Colonel Ivan Petrovich Rybachenko, the Soviet Air Attaché in Stockholm, was interested in a new Swedish airfield. I remarked to him, "If this airfield is so important I could tell you what I know about it for five thousand kroner [about £350]. He replied he would take instructions on what to do. A few weeks later, when we met at a diplomatic cocktail party and shook hands, Rybachenko said, "It's a deal."

When we next met (at another party) Rybachenko drove me home. As we parted he gave me a parcel containing money. Shortly afterwards he received from me a map showing the location of the airfield.

My decision to become a double agent was one of my reasons for having supplied Rybachenko with the map. Another reason was that I wanted that five thousand kroner; after all, the espionage business means payment for information.

There was, perhaps, also a third reason for what I did, only at the time I didn't completely realize it.

In 1948, when I was a Lieutenant-Colonel, I was informed I was being passed over for appointment as a Wing Commander. Instead I was offered the opportunity to go to Moscow again as Swedish Air Attaché. Not having been made Wing Commander meant I would never rise above the rank of Colonel. I was bitterly disillusioned.

When I handed over the map to Rybachenko I agreed to continue contact with the Soviet Secret Service on arrival in Moscow.

I took up my post as Swedish Air Attaché on January 27th, 1949, and remained there three years. The Russians treated me extremely well. Perhaps they exploited my sense of professional frustration and played up to my vanity, bolstering my ego at every turn, but before long they made me a top agent and allowed me to draw very large funds.

They invested me with the rank of Major-General—higher than I could ever have hoped to reach in the service of Sweden. I was given the code name Eagle.

My liaison in Moscow was Secret Service General Pyotr Pavlovich Lemenov. I was greatly impressed with Lemenov—a man with an almost hypnotic ability to arouse enthusiasm in his co-operators. He took special pains with me, and was my contact with Soviet Secret Service headquarters to the end of my stay in Moscow in 1952.

During my term of duty there I picked up all the information I could on Britain's air-defence system, which the Russians considered the best in the world. Through my connections in the U.S. Embassy I was able to provide a certain amount of information regarding the bomb targets in the Soviet Union being compiled by the Americans.

Towards the end of my term of duty in Moscow I learned that my next assignment would be to Washington, where I would not only serve as Swedish Air Attaché, but also be required to procure U.S. military equipment for the Swedish Air Force. General Lemenov was delighted. He had a number of specific tasks for me in the United States. The most important was to obtain technical data on the development of American aircraft, missiles, bombsights, radio and radar systems, and electronic miniaturization.

My appointment as Swedish Air Attaché in Washington started immediately after my term in Moscow ended. But, although I arrived in Washington on April 8th, 1952, it wasn't until four months later, in August 1952, that my contact, Major-General Viktor Kuvinov, Soviet Air Attaché in Washington, called on me at the Swedish Embassy. Kuvinov gave me the password "Nikolai Vasilyevich wants to be remembered" which Lemenov had arranged with me before I had left Moscow. He then handed me a slip of paper stating where our next meeting would take place.

Major-General Kuvinov gave me £1750 as starting capital, and thereafter I averaged £265 a month throughout my five years' term of duty in Washington. Kuvinov stressed that my remuneration must be kept down to sensible amounts. Spending too freely could cast suspicion. However, to reward me adequately for services rendered, they accumulated funds in my name in Moscow, to be withdrawn upon my retirement.

Major-General Kuvinov and the other Soviet contact man who succeeded him usually arranged apparently casual meetings in parks and streets. Whenever I met my contact we expressed surprise at the encounter, shook hands, and walked together for a bit. I had ready, of course, the microfilms of whatever documents were to be passed on.

I transferred the film roll to Kuvinov while shaking hands.

Another ideal setting for transfers was during a large diplomatic reception at the Soviet Embassy. I would leave the films in my overcoat in the cloakroom. Kuvinov emptied the pocket at leisure.

As Air Attaché in Washington, it was my duty to procure U.S. military equipment for the Swedish Air Force. Because of this I received information regarding the design of U.S. weapons. And, as Sweden was buying equipment under the U.S. Military Assistance Programme, and the Pentagon traditionally treats Swedish military attachés as good security risks, it wasn't too difficult for me to obtain detailed information on the U.S. weapons system. Major-General Kuvinov was delighted with the microfilms I passed.

After my term of office as Swedish Air Attaché in Washington ended and I returned to Stockholm I was appointed head of the Air Force Section in the Defence Command Office.

The years 1957–63 were the summit of my espionage career because across my desk passed, as a matter of routine, all sorts of secret documents, including operational plans, data on installations, new weapons, air-defence mechanism, and so forth. I had an additional duty—to brief the Defence Minister on guided missiles, which naturally gave me better access to classified material from the United States than I had had in Washington. I passed to the Soviet Secret Service details of Sweden's air-defence system—a semi-automatic amalgam of radar and computers which records the path and speed of attacking aircraft. I also gave them information about the Draken J-35 all-weather fighter-interceptor, bomber, or reconnaissance aircraft. This aircraft was intended ultimately to be the mainstay of our Air Force.

At the beginning of 1959 we began to acquire the following U.S. missiles—the Sidewinder, a supersonic air-to-air missile which serves as armament for the Draken; the Falcon, a larger air-to-air missile; and the Hawk, a surface-to-air missile designed for defence against low-flying intruders. It wasn't difficult for me to transfer to the Soviet Secret Service all the data they required.

Sweden also bought Britain's Bloodhound, a high-altitude ground-to-air missile. I gave Moscow all information on this weapon, too.

I provided the Soviet with information on N.A.T.O. operations and contingency plans to meet the Russian threat to West Berlin.

Towards the end of 1959 Major-General Nikolsky informed me that the Soviet Control Agent had discovered that reports that reached the Swedish security police indicated I had aroused suspicion among a few of my colleagues because of my persistent curiosity about classified documents which did not appear relevant to my work. It was also learned that Security Superintendent Otto Danielsson had obtained court permission to tap my telephone, and that he had put me under unobtrusive surveillance.

As I said previously, I never used the telephone for any important conversation. I made doubly sure to be as cautious as possible in everything I did.

I knew there was nothing the Swedish security police could get on me. I had been receiving regular cash rewards for my intelligence work from the Russians, but had kept strictly to their Secret Service rule of not throwing money about. I was, of course, spending considerably more than I earned, but I did it cautiously.

In 1960 my bank overdraft showed I had overspent some £1200, and in 1961 some £460. This was quite acceptable to anyone probing my financial affairs, as it was common knowledge that my wealthy in-laws could be helping me financially.

I knew now that the security police were greatly concerned about me, and, unable to bring any charge against me, they were anxious to prevent me from securing another post that would provide me with opportunities for espionage.

In June 1961 I was due to retire, so in March, anticipating retirement, I applied for the post of Duty Officer on the Air Force staff, as this was a post that provided access to classified documents. This application accorded with the common practice in Sweden of retiring officers taking desk work in military establishments to supplement their pension; but the security police succeeded in influencing the Minister of Defence to deny me the position.

I obtained, however, employment from the Swedish Foreign Office as a disarmament consultant, and my work consisted of helping to prepare data for the Geneva Disarmament Conference. It was thought I would not be a security risk in this job. I discovered that Foreign Minister Östen Undén had been advised of the doubts about me. The security police didn't want anyone else in the Foreign Office to be told, as they feared the possibility of a leak. The result was that they were unable to keep me under observation at work.

Once I was firmly installed in my new post in the Foreign Office, I made a practice of visiting former colleagues in the defence establishment and discreetly obtaining from them secret information. It was easy. I explained that I needed the material for the purpose of orientation for my disarmament job. Often I got what I wanted.

In July 1962 the security police tried to stop my access to secret documents by ordering that all such requests should come from the office of the Intelligence chief, Colonel Bo Westin. They tried amateurishly. I was able to continue my activities with the same efficiency as before, and earned frequent praise from the Secret Service Major-General Nikolsky.

Just before my arrest on June 20th [1963] I got the shock of my life. I had been alarmed by an incident that had occurred at a reception in the British Embassy. I had cordially approached the Commander-in-Chief of the Swedish Armed Forces, General Torsten Rapp, whom I had known for a long time. Rapp cold-shouldered me, and I suddenly feared he suspected me. As soon as I could I contacted Major-General Nikolsky and reported what had happened. He checked with the Soviet Control Agent. They told me I should flee the country. He would make arrangements for my escape. I was to leave Sweden on June 21st.

On the 20th I was arrested.

After four months of continuous interrogation Colonel Wennerström cracked and tried to commit suicide by taking an overdose of sleeping tables. The attempt failed.

Following weeks of psychiatric treatment, the second phase of the interrogation commenced. This phase consisted of producing secret military documents and checking with Wennerström whether he had submitted them to the Soviets.

When the court hearing eventually opened in Stockholm, Wennerström made no plea for mercy. He said, not without a trace of pride, in a clear voice:

"My activity has been a part of the international big-Power espionage which in turn is a factor in the cold war." Then he clicked his heels and announced: "I am prepared to stand for the judicial consequences."

Evidence was given in court by Security Superintendent Otto Danielsson, other Swedish officers and officials, Mrs Karin Rosén, and scores of witnesses. The Superintendent revealed:

"We had no hard evidence against him. We could have obtained a court order to search his home, but it was feared that if we found no evidence we might destroy the case; so, in May 1963 I and my colleagues approached Mrs Karin Rosén, Colonel Wennerström's part-time domestic servant, to enlist her as an undercover agent. She proved co-operative."

Mrs Karin Rosén, a woman in her mid-fifties, stated:

"I had long been suspicious of Wennerström. He owned an odd assortment of equipment . . . a large stand with over-arching electric lights and a camera suspended above; a safe hidden behind a curtain in the spare room; a radio, of the sort I had never seen before, built into a bookcase. The Colonel spent hours at his photography behind the locked door of the spare room.

"One morning—about a month after I had been recruited—I phoned the police to say I had found two old packages under some sawdust in the attic. Detectives discovered film rolls inside the packages. The next day Colonel Wennerström was arrested."

Wennerström was found guilty and sentenced to life imprisonment. (In Sweden life imprisonment means that the prisoner can be released, for good behaviour, after ten or twelve years.) The court calculated that he had collected some £35,000 from the Soviet Secret Service for his services.

The concluding chapter in his story was written when the man who had been able to supply Russia's espionage directors with invaluable secret information was led to the cells in the summer of 1964. The career of the ex-Swedish Air Force Colonel and diplomat and Soviet Secret Service Major-General was over.

Throughout his Swedish Government career Wennerström was considered "one of the most brilliant men" and was consequently, at one time, even aide-de-camp to the eldest son of King Gustav. In the diplomatic and social world of cocktail parties and receptions the somewhat reserved but charming Colonel and his vivacious wife, Ulla, were well known and liked. Women found the lean, athletically built man with clean-cut features that retained the image of youthfulness attractive, and sought his company.

The master spy who for fifteen years had continuously sold Swedish, American, British, and other military secrets to the Russians received his punishment, but his Soviet spy 'leaders' were saved by diplomatic immunity. All Mr Torsten Nielsson, Sweden's Foreign Minister, could do was inform the Soviet Chargé d'Affaires in Stockholm that Major-General Nikolsky, the Military Attaché, and Baranovsky, First Secretary, were *personae non gratae*, and request him to make arrangements for the two men to leave Sweden.

Sweden was shaken when the Stig Wennerström treachery was disclosed at a Press conference at the Foreign Ministry in Stockholm five days after his arrest, and when, afterwards, General Torsten Rapp, Commander-in-Chief of the Swedish Armed Forces, estimated that the damage to the country's defence would cost £20,500 million to repair.

To calm the people the Defence Minister, Mr Sven Andersson, stated that he had held discussions with the Chief of the General Staff on measures to be taken to counteract the damage caused.

The public demanded the return of the death penalty for espionage—a penalty abolished some forty years earlier.

11

The Blackmailed Yeoman

NOW let us consider the case of Nelson Cornelius Drummond, a thirty-three-year-old U.S. Navy Yeoman First Class. His arrest and subsequent trial in New York made world headlines.

His full personal details had long been filed in the Central Index at Moscow Secret Service headquarters. Each personal record in this index contains the following information:

1. *Basic Data.* (a) Present position and previous work; (b) prospects of remaining in the Service and where; (c) date joined the Service, and does he/she like it; (d) his/her relations with immediate superiors.

2. *Biographical Data.* (a) Age, parents, family conditions; (b) education, principal speciality, special technical or other knowledge; (c) attitude towards politics, party affiliation, opinions on State administration; (d) financial position; (e) attitude towards the U.S.S.R. and Soviet politics; (f) wherein he/she sees the prosperity of his/her country.

3. *Personal Positive and Negative Characteristics.* (a) Inclination to drink, women friends, family relationships; (b) whether a lover of luxury, or inclined to solitude and simple living; (c) influence of wife/husband on actions, or independence in making own decisions; (d) circle of acquaintances, and brief character sketches of same.

Although Nelson Cornelius Drummond was a coloured man, and according to Communist conception "a likely recruit because of racial handicap", no recruitment attempts for the Soviet spy ring in the United States of America were made, because the Negro sailor had no access to important classified information and was consequently of no interest. But when, in 1957, the espionage director at the Soviet Embassy in Washington, D.C., learned that Yeoman Drummond was posted to England and was likely to become of value as an informer, he contacted his counterpart in the Soviet Embassy in London, advising him to watch out for Drummond.

There was nothing in the Soviet Central Index records to indicate that Drummond was a potential espionage recruit. The file stated that he was a loyal American, content with serving in the U.S. Navy, maintaining good relations with his immediate superiors, and leading a normal life. The only way to channel him into an espionage network was to keep him under surveillance in England and find some means to secure his services.

Drummond tells how it was done, and what followed:

I was completely unaware that Soviet Secret Service agents were trailing me. I didn't suspect anything sinister when my new acquaintances invited me for a drink and discussed conditions in the United States and England, and life in the U.S. Navy. I still suspected nothing when a Russian Secret Service Colonel—a diplomat at the Soviet Embassy in London—joined us for a drink in a public house. Maybe it was because I'd already had several whiskies and wasn't as alert as I might have been.

The Russian was very friendly and talkative—and also very generous. But that evening it never occurred to me that his generosity had any sinister motive, that it was part of a plot. I thought the fellow was just being sociable. It didn't even seem strange to me that he ordered different varieties of liquors for me, whereas he and the others stuck to the same drinks, and far less of them.

I have only an uncertain recollection of what happened, but I guess that as I was intoxicated it was plain sailing for the Russians. I vaguely remember that the diplomat said something about sailors not being paid enough to live well, and that it was a pity, because one should be able to enjoy life. He then took out of the breast pocket of his coat a bundle of pound bills and handed them to me. I asked him why he wanted to give me money, and he said he wanted me to be able to enjoy myself, and he added that he was financially very comfortable. Giving some of his money to a friend made him happy, he explained. I guess that if I hadn't been as intoxicated as I was I wouldn't have accepted it.

We had more drinks, and when I was hardly able to notice what was going on the Russian diplomat gave me a piece of paper to sign. I think he said something about wanting to have a note from me that he'd given me two hundred and fifty pounds as a present, so that later he'd know what he'd done with his money. I thought this fair, and signed the piece of paper. Afterwards another drink or two, but what happened later is a complete blank to me. I found out next morning that the diplomat and the others had taken me to my London address to sleep off my drunkenness.

My next meeting with the diplomat was not as pleasant as the first. The meeting took place at my London address. It was the day after the drinking session.

The diplomat now demanded that I provide him with all the classified material I could lay my hands on. When I said I wouldn't betray my country, and threatened to report him to our security service, he produced a photostat of the receipt I had signed in my intoxicated state in the public house, and warned me that the document would be handed to the U.S. authorities if I refused to co-operate. I honestly didn't know what I'd signed. When I saw the photostat I got the shock of my life—I was terrified—I had signed a receipt for £250 which confirmed that money had been paid to me for having supplied the Soviet Secret Service with classified U.S. Navy documents. I was flabbergasted.

I told the Russian I would make a full statement to my superiors on what had happened. I was convinced they would believe me, as they could check the truthfulness of my statement by ascertaining that I had not passed any classified or other document to the Russians, or anyone else.

The Russian was prepared for such an event. He presented me with photostats of classified documents which, he stated, would be attached to the receipt to prove that the £250 had been paid to me as remuneration for supplying these naval secrets. He added, however, that if I was "sensible" and co-operated fully I would be paid much larger sums of money in cash for my services. To "break my stubbornness", as he called it, he played his trump card: "If I am forced to hand over these highly compromising documents to the U.S. authorities the facts will not be given by Soviet sources, but by an American double agent." And, the diplomat added, he left it to my imagination to work out if the U.S. authorities would believe my story when they were presented with "conclusive" proof about my "activities".

For a long time I studied the photostats of the documents (which I had never seen before), and found, to my horror, that they bore the markings and reference of the archive to which I had access. I realized that the Russian hadn't exaggerated when he implied that my superiors would hardly believe my story. I felt sure I was completely trapped. I panicked and undertook to supply their espionage network with U.S. naval secrets.

But I still did not betray my country—I mean, I only gave them classified documents which I judged would do no harm to the United States. The Russian diplomat didn't fall for it. He told me he was dissatisfied with my co-operation and demanded I supply the "real" stuff. He threatened again that he would expose me to the U.S. authorities if I refused to comply. I knew then that, having passed even unimportant classified documents, I was in deep waters. I had no alternative but to give the Russians what they wanted. I did.

I've never felt as rotten in my whole life as I did when I became a Russian spy. I played with the idea of suicide, but guess I didn't have the guts to blow my brains out. I didn't even have the courage to confess to the U.S. what had happened and what I'd done. I lived in continuous fear that I'd be found out and arrested. I couldn't sleep properly, and when I did I was haunted by nightmares. I was living in hell.

I've never been a great drinker—I liked a drink or two, but no more—and the first time I yielded to temptation and drank and drank till I could think no more was the time the Russian diplomat, the Soviet Secret Service Colonel, got me drunk in London. When I became a spy I took to excessive drinking. The alcohol let me forget my miserable existence.

I'd never been a skirt-hunter. Sure, I had a girl now and then, but I was no different from any other guy who lives a normal life. But when I started drinking all that changed. There were plenty pretty dolls in the drinking clubs I went to, and I had affairs with lots of them. Again, it sort of helped me to forget the hell I was in. I had plenty of dough and could entertain girl friends lavishly at expensive restaurants, buy them nice presents. All this time I was borrowing from the files classified documents which I let the Russians photograph.

My association with the espionage network in London was short-lived: it lasted only a few months. But during these months I was always paid on the spot for my "appreciated co-operation", as the Colonel put it. The cash payments varied according to the importance of the documents, but I never got less than a hundred pounds a document. My funds never ran dry.

The ending of my association with the network was due to my alleged misconduct with a British female national. The Office of U.S. Intelligence in London began a security investigation on me, but my link with the network wasn't discovered. However, having been involved in a scandal, I was posted back to the U.S.A. and given the job of Administrative Assistant in a Mobile Electronic Technical Unit at the U.S. Naval Base, Newport, R.I.

Before I was shipped back I saw Ralph, the contact to the Colonel: I had to tell him about my home posting, as otherwise I'd have been in big trouble. When I told him he adopted a funny attitude and said I'd have to explain to the Colonel. I was rather surprised because up till then Ralph had always behaved like a pal. Anyway, he said I'd have to wait till he (Ralph) had spoken to the Colonel first. He'd meet me later.

I met Ralph, as arranged, at seven-thirty the same evening outside the Dominion Cinema in Tottenham Court Road. As we walked along Oxford Street towards a pub he told me the Colonel would meet me at eight o'clock sharp at the ticket machines in Piccadilly Circus underground station.

The Colonel arrived bang on time and seemed to be in a hurry. "I have my car round the corner," he said, and asked me to follow him out of the station. As we drove along he told me he was disappointed with me because I'd been involved in a scandal with a woman. He wouldn't listen to the explanation that I hadn't been at fault at all. He went on lecturing me that agents must not get involved in matters which can interfere with their work, and said in a sort of threatening way that his and my superior wouldn't like my assignment in London being cut short because of such an idiotic love affair. When I told him my home posting to the U.S.A. brought with it my appointment as an Administrative Assistant in a Mobile Electronic Technical Unit at the U.S. Naval Base near Newport, R.I., his mood improved, and he remarked that the change of duty might not be bad after all. We pulled up at a pub and had a few drinks, and as we parted he said he would be in touch with me. He didn't make contact again, but that may have been due to the fact that I left London almost immediately.

Back home in the States, I immediately began my job as an Administrative Assistant. I wasn't approached by the Russians. I thought my association with the Soviet Secret Service was terminated once and for all, but my new-found freedom didn't last.

Soon after my return I was contacted by a man, a Russian, who introduced himself as Mikhail Stiepanovich Savelyev, First Secretary of the Soviet Mission to the United Nations Organization in New York. As he wanted to talk in private, we decided on a car drive in the country. He told me the Secret Service Colonel in London had notified his counterpart at the Soviet Embassy in Washington, D.C., of my home posting.

I wanted to stay out of the spy racket and told the U.N.O. man so. He made the same threats as the Colonel in London, and I knew I was caught. I had no other choice but to continue spying.

The Russian promised he would make my task as easy as possible and would take every precaution to see that U.S. counter-intelligence couldn't track me down. He said that he didn't approve of "primitive" methods being used in the spy business, and made it clear that, in his opinion, "borrowing" secret documents for photographing was much too risky because this method afforded counter-intelligence too many opportunities to pounce. He said he would teach me to use modern equipment so that I could work independently and safely.

We met again at the weekend, and he showed me how to take photographs with a microfilm camera, how to use 'flash paper' that burns instantly, and pencils that write invisibly. He showed me how to conceal microfilms in specially constructed inconspicuous containers.

From the beginning of 1958 until the summer of 1961 I complied with his orders and was paid in cash for every document I microfilmed. Apart from microfilming, I also 'borrowed' top-secret documents from my office at the Naval Base, after it closed down on Friday nights, and returned them to the files by Monday.

The effect on me was the same as in London. I took to drink and women again. I prayed for a miracle that would enable me to get out of the U.N.O. man's control.

My spy leader suggested one day that I purchase the Havana Bar and Grill, near the Newport Naval Base. He felt this would provide an ideal place for meeting contacts. He gave me the money to make the purchase, and I bought it in my name. He was right—it was very suitable for meeting contacts because it's natural for people to visit a bar and grill, and for strangers to talk to each other over a drink or steak. It was easy to pass on to contacts containers of microfilms, and equally easy for them to pay me on the spot. Journeys to New York were eliminated, so there was no longer much danger of an alert snooper picking up the fact that I used to travel there quite a lot.

In the summer of 1961 my spy leader instructed me to meet him in New York. I was to use a ticket for a Broadway show and pretend not to know the occupant of the adjoining seat. We met as arranged, and during the show he handed me his message, which was written on flash paper. During the interval I went to the toilet to read the message. It told me that the U.N.O. diplomat had learned that U.S. counter-intelligence suspected him, and that consequently he was leaving for Moscow. Before he left he would hand over to a colleague, Vadim Vladimirovich Sorokyn, a Third Secretary of the Soviet Mission to the United Nations Organization in New York, and he told me to meet my new leader that Saturday evening in Forty-first Street. He said his successor would approach me and identify himself by asking the way to Lexington Avenue. I was to answer that I'd show him the way, and we would walk along together.

I burned the flash paper and flushed the remains down the toilet. When I returned to my seat Savelyev never once looked at me. After the show we left the theatre without speaking a word to each other, and went in different directions.

My meeting with my new leader, Sorokyn, went according to plan. He ordered me to continue as during my association with Savelyev. But, although Sorokyn was even more careful than Savelyev, U.S. counter-intelligence caught up with him only a few months after he had taken over from Savelyev, and he had to leave New York in May 1962. Before he went he informed me my new leader would be Yevgeniy Mikhailovich Prokhorov, a Second Secretary of the Soviet Mission to the United Nations Organization in New York.

Prokhorov was an impatient man. He repeatedly said he wanted to prove to Moscow that he was particularly efficient and could obtain better results than anyone else. He asked me to supply a greater number of secret documents than ever before, and promised to pay a hundred dollars over the usual rate for any documents in excess of the average number I had usually passed on.

Everything went smoothly, and he was satisfied, but in mid-September 1962 he suddenly warned me to take it easy and to be extra careful. He devised improved safety precautions, but he assured me there was no reason to assume *I* was suspected by U.S. counter-intelligence.

I didn't know it at the time but those new safety measures had come too late: F.B.I. agents had already begun to suspect me and were keeping me under secret surveillance. The use of code names for Prokhorov and his colleague Vydrov, a Third Secretary of the Soviet Mission to U.N.O. in New York, the use of cuff-links with the head of a horse for identification and recognition, and the hiding of spy material in ingeniously constructed containers which were left in prearranged 'dead drops' were no longer safe from detection. . . .

Unaware that I was being trailed by F.B.I. agents, I drove my car direct to the parking-lot of the Larchmont Diner, Larchmont, N.Y. F.B.I. agents were waiting there and watched everything that went on.

As Prokhorov sat in my car, leaning against the window and talking with me, F.B.I. agents closed in and seized the eight confidential Navy documents I had brought along, and which were on the seat between Prokhorov and myself. They arrested me, Prokhorov, and Vydrov in the parking-lot. After the two U.N.O. secretaries identified themselves and claimed diplomatic immunity they were released and allowed to return to Moscow.

I was left holding the baby.

U.S. Navy Yeoman First Class Nelson Cornelius Drummond was indicted by a Federal Grand Jury in New York on October 5th, 1962, on espionage charges. The first count of the indictment charged that:

"Yeoman First Class Nelson Cornelius Drummond has conspired to turn over to the Soviet Union or its agents documents, writings, code books, signal books, sketches, photographs, photographic negatives, blueprints, plans, maps, models, notes, instruments, appliances, and information relating to the national defense of the United States with intent and reason to believe that they were to be used to the injury of the United States and to the advantage of the Union of Soviet Socialist Republics."

The second count accused Drummond of attempting to obtain information relating to naval weapons systems, maintainance data relating to submarines, and electronic data.

On May 13th, 1963, Yeoman Drummond's trial for his life opened at the Federal Court in New York. He testified that since 1957 he had received between $20,000 and $24,000 from the Russians for "worthless" documents, but denied that he had acknowledged in his statement to the F.B.I. having given "one or two secret documents" to the Russians, and contended that he was "not allowed to read the statement" by F.B.I. agents before he signed it. However, when shown a number of corrections on the typewritten and signed statement, he admitted that these corrections were in his own handwriting.

Drummond's trial ended on May 23rd, 1963, in a deadlocked jury. The foreman of the jury told the court that the vote had been eleven to one for conviction five minutes after the jurymen entered the jury room; that it was still eleven to one on both counts of the indictment twenty-four hours later; and that there was no hope of reaching a unanimous verdict because of the hopeless deadlock. Federal District Judge Edward Weinfield then dismissed the jury and set a second trial on the same indictments for June 3rd, 1963.

Nelson Cornelius Drummond was eventually found guilty and sentenced to life imprisonment.

12

A Ski-ing Instructor with a Difference

ALTHOUGH neutral, Switzerland is nevertheless an important target for Communist espionage. The numerous occasions when Iron Curtain diplomats have been requested to leave the country prove that Russian, Czechoslovak, Hungarian, Polish, and other Communist embassies, consulates, trade missions, and diplomatic or semi-diplomatic institutions in Switzerland cover espionage direction centres.

As in other countries, a considerable number of espionage rings work independently of those cloaked by diplomatic privilege.

The espionage network of Xavier Schmeisser was for a long time able to pass to Moscow information on Swiss defence installations and plans, on weapons on the secret list, and other strategic information.

Swiss counter-intelligence detected the network, which operated under the cover of the Lucerne publishing house Nova Vita, which was owned by Xavier Schmeisser, specializing in Christian literature, and which even published anti-Communist pamphlets!

After years of success Schmeisser and another agent aroused suspicion, and a police raid on the Nova Vita offices unearthed 160 microfilmed espionage reports.

Swiss security proved that Xavier Schmeisser's organization was an offspring of the Soviet espionage centre at 192 Route de Florissant in Geneva, which was established at the end of the thirties, and from where, during World War II, the short-wave radio stations operated with remarkable success in keeping Moscow headquarters informed on the Wehrmacht's moves, and passing on plans of German military preparations obtained from a source in the Nazi High Command.

In 1946 Alexander Rado was instructed by Moscow to found another espionage network in Switzerland and, with an initial

East German Secret Service headquarters in East Berlin

East German Secret Service headquarters in Berlin–Lichtenberg

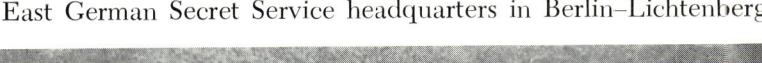

Various electronic snooping devices, ranging from a microphone concealed in the olive of a Martini to a bugged tie-clasp

expenditure of some 300,000 Swiss francs, Xavier Schmeisser established his unit.

Another case involved spies who were able to work with diplomatic immunity. Two senior officials of the Soviet Embassy in Berne, Boris Frolov and Nikolai Modin, were arrested by Swiss counter-intelligence officers while making contact with an agent in Zurich. Although it was established that they were negotiating the purchase of Swiss military secrets as well as information on missile-launching sites in West Germany, all the authorities could do was summon the Soviet Ambassador, Nikolai I. Koyukin, to the Swiss Ministry in Berne and inform him that Frolov and Modin were being deported for having engaged in espionage.

Almost every year Soviet spies are detected and arrested by the Swiss counter-intelligence and security forces.

One of the most interesting examples of Communist espionage in Switzerland is the case of "Anton Huber".

Huber was an officer of the Hungarian Secret Service who for years successfully directed in Switzerland a spy web that covered the country and stretched into Austria.

Anton Huber was, in fact, Miklos Bondi, who came from a Hungarian workman's family in Pest on the Danube. He was born in 1927. During World War II, Miklos worked as an apprentice in a German-Hungarian firm in Budapest and acquired a good knowledge of the German language. This was one of the main reasons why the Hungarian Secret Service later found him suitable for espionage in a German-speaking country.

Although Miklos's father belonged to the Communist-led anti-Fascist movement in Nazi-occupied Hungary, he was not discovered by the Gestapo.

Then, when the Nazi Wehrmacht was crushed and Russia liberated Hungary, Miklos joined the Communist Party, and soon became Party District Secretary. In 1948, a year after Communist rule had been established in the country, he was sent to the Matyas Rakosi Institute for spy training. After a nine-month course he passed his final examination and went on for three years to the Hungarian Secret Service school, Bela Kun College, for advanced espionage schooling and training, and for additional German-language tuition.

In the late summer of 1952 Miklos Bondi was ready. Budapest Secret Service headquarters supplied him with documents in the name of "Anton Huber", and, assuming this identity, he went to Austria to 'acclimatize' himself and become a mountain guide and ski-ing instructor. Assisted by Austrian Communist fifth-columnists, "Huber" settled among the genuine guides and ski-ing instructors. This good-looking young man became a popular mountain guide in the summer and a ski-ing instructor in winter.

In July 1953 he was at last ordered to Switzerland.

During the ten months he stayed in Austria he wasn't required to run any espionage network: his only duties consisted of passing on from informers to couriers inconspicuous containers of microfilmed secret documents. In Switzerland, however, he was to be a resident espionage network operator.

Within two months he had twenty agents and informers working for him.

In 1956 "Anton Huber" ran into trouble from, of all people, the Soviet resident spy director in Switzerland!

For some time the Russian espionage chief had received reports of Huber's successes. He decided to utilize Huber's informers to improve his own network. Huber was unwilling to 'share'. He suspected that the Soviet approach could be a test to learn whether he was completely loyal to his superiors, or whether he could be bribed.

Huber reported the approach to his own headquarters, but instead of sending his report as a microdot message affixed under a postage-stamp to Budapest headquarters, he dispatched it through one of his contacts who was ordered to hand it to a courier travelling to Hungary. The contact secretly worked for the Russian resident director in Switzerland, who consequently intercepted the message.

The same evening Huber was stopped by two men as he was walking home, and hustled into a car. He was told of the interception of his report.

Huber became a Hungarian-Russian master spy in Switzerland and, unknown to his Budapest headquarters, enabled Moscow headquarters to obtain information which, until then, had not *automatically* been forwarded to Soviet intelligence.

Huber worked unsuspected in Switzerland for almost ten years. Attention finally centred on him, but, unfortunately for Swiss counter-intelligence, he was warned of the security probe and left for Austria. Acting on the advice of the Swiss authorities, Austrian counter-intelligence traced him, but Huber was not brought to trial. Before the security officers could take him into custody he was found dead. The pathologist stated that Huber's skull had been battered either by a blunt instrument or by his fall down a mountain slope. Police considered Huber had been struck on the head, and been thrown down the mountain.

The Swiss found his equipment as well as information on other members of his network.

Switzerland is a natural meeting-place of spies of all nations, and Switzerland is well aware of the fact that she is one of the targets of concentrated Communist espionage. The Swiss Federal President has openly charged the Swiss Communists with being in the pay of Moscow. And the I.P.I. (International Press Institute) in Zurich summarized an investigation into Soviet espionage being carried out under the cloak of the Russian news agency TASS, by noting that:

"Only a fraction of the information TASS correspondents abroad send to their head office in Moscow is ever printed. The greater part of their work consists of the gathering of military, political, and economic intelligence. . . ."

Sir Percy Sillitoe, K.B.E., former head of Britain's M.I.5, said: "Being familiar with what a spy is up to, and being able to anticipate the methods he may use and which targets he is likely to choose, are important steps towards the detection of master spies and their spy webs." The same principles obviously apply to the Swiss counter-intelligence and security forces. Their repeated detections of Soviet and other Communist master spies and their networks are evidence of their efficiency and their constant fight to preserve freedom and independence.

13

The Fake Frenchman

IT is well known that Soviet spies operate throughout the whole free world, and that Communist master spies nearly always slip into a country so ingeniously that it is usually impossible for the authorities to detect them before they can cause damage. But there are occasions when spies could have been detected—had the authorities applied sufficient vigilance.

The case of Jaroslav Sterba is an example. He was an officer of both the Czechoslovak and the Soviet Russian Secret Service. After Sterba succeeded in obtaining from the French Consulate in Prague the required official documents he found little difficulty in worming his way eventually right into French counter-intelligence.

But for a run of bad luck, he might have succeeded in spying for Prague and Moscow to this day, instead of ending his successful espionage career within four years.

Jaroslav Sterba was born in 1938 in Northern Bohemia, in the town of Liberec, shortly before Hitler occupied the Sudetenland. His father, Vasek Sterba, an embittered anti-Nazi, escaped by taking his family by car to Prague. But later Hitler's Wehrmacht occupied the rest of the Czech lands, and the Gestapo began to arrest anyone with an anti-Nazi background.

One of the first grabbed was Jaroslav's father. During the months he had been in Prague he had become a friend of the prominent Communist journalist and writer, Julius Fucik, as well as of a number of other Communist leaders. This was sufficient for the Gestapo to arrest the refugee, and for the S.A. and S.S. sadists to torture Sterba in the soundproof cellars of Petschek Palace, Prague Gestapo headquarters. On discovering that he had also played a leading part in the newly born Czech underground resistance movement against the Nazis, they beat him to death.

Julius Fucik, as well as other Communist leaders, had gone into hiding, but when news of the death of his friend Sterba reached him he realized that the rest of the Sterba family was in danger, and he did his utmost to save them. His comrades got the family to Moravska Ostrava, and from there Moravian miners led them safely through underground coalmines into Poland. After being handed over to Polish Communists the Sterbas soon found themselves in Russia.

They first stayed in Moscow; the mother mastered a number of languages and was therefore useful to the Soviet Publishing House for Foreign Languages. Then, when Radio Moscow increased its anti-Nazi German-language propaganda broadcasts, Mrs Sterba was transferred to the Radio Centre, where she broadcast daily to the Germans. As her duties left her insufficient time to look after her children, Moscow Radio arranged for them to be taken care of by a Soviet children's home.

Hitler's troops advanced, and the Soviet Government was evacuated from Moscow to the safety of Kuibyshev. Mrs Sterba and her children also went, because she had been ordered to continue broadcasting from the safe area. Mrs Sterba became a convinced, trusted Communist; so did her children, who grew up in Soviet children's homes and schools.

When Czechoslovakia was liberated at the end of the War the Sterba family returned to Prague with many other Czechs and Slovaks who had survived in Russia. During the short-lived Coalition Government Mrs Sterba worked in the Central Committee of the Czech Communist Party, preparing the ground for her country to join the Soviet bloc. Her children were active young Communists.

The most intelligent and completely Sovietized child was Jaroslav. During the three years in which post-War Czechoslovakia enjoyed a democratic and free life the little boy became a Pioneer leader. And in February 1948, when the Communist *coup d'état* converted the country into a Russian satellite, ten-year-old Jaroslav was sent to the Soviet-controlled school in Prague-Dejvice, where bilingual tuition was in Czech and Russian, and where emphasis was laid on Marxist-Leninist schooling. Children selected for the school also received extensive French and German tuition. Created for the Czech Communist élite, it was the cradle for future Communist Party executives, diplomats, and— spies.

Having attended the school for four years Jaroslav passed the "examination of the first cycle"—schooling of the Czech, Russian, French, and German languages and in all fields of Marxist-Leninist theory, *i.e.*, in comprehensive Communist ideology, and in "Revolutionary Strategy", which entailed preparing the pupils for intelligence activities, sabotage, and other subversive actions. It was now the summer of 1952. He was recommended for "specialized" schooling. For the next three years he attended the closely guarded Czechoslovak Secret Service school near the popular mountain spa of Joachimsthal. This school was named *Technicka Akademie*—Technical Academy.

Students had to rise at 6 A.M.; from 6.30 to 7.15 A.M. they engaged in outdoor physical exercises, regardless of the weather. After cold showers and breakfast they started classes, which went on until 6 P.M. There was an hour break for lunch, and half-hour breaks in the morning and afternoon. After dinner they assembled at 7.15 P.M. in the communal room to listen to lectures or engage in discussions on Communist tactics and allied subjects. At 9 P.M. came "Lights Out".

At the Technical Academy instructors were Russians sent to Czechoslovakia from Soviet Secret Service schools where they had been senior officers and tutors.

Jaroslav was among the ten best pupils at his time in the Academy, and he frequently received awards.

On January 1st, 1956, the final examinations commenced. A week later Jaroslav passed with honours, and was assigned to work in the Prague headquarters of the Czechoslovak Secret Service, after a holiday in the Tatra Mountains.

His career as a Czech and a Soviet spy had begun.

At first Jaroslav Sterba was entrusted with general duties at Prague headquarters. He worked in the Central Index, then in the Communication Department, the Transport Division, the Coding Section, and in almost every other department, to gain varied practical experience in the work at headquarters. His above-average knowledge of French enabled him to be transferred to the Foreign Directorate to work in "Section France".

Czechoslovak State Security's Lieutenant-Colonel Antonin Vaverka thought so much of him that he promoted him to Assistant Directing Officer and let him take an active part in the direction of Czechoslovak master spies and their espionage networks in France.

In the summer of 1956 Lieutenant-Colonel Vaverka decided that Jaroslav should be prepared for work in France. He was provided with a Frenchman as special tutor to perfect his knowledge of the French language.

In 1957 Jaroslav was ready, but instead of following the usual Soviet Secret Service pattern of providing the agent with documents of a genuine French national who could no longer be traced, Lieutenant-Colonel Vaverka considered it sufficient to provide him with false documents.

Jaroslav Sterba went to the French Consulate in Prague, and presented a forged birth certificate with a French name. He said his parents and grandparents were French citizens, and that he wished to claim his rightful French citizenship and go to France.

Consular officials were ready to help, especially when Jaroslav emphasized that he was anxious to serve his term as a conscript in the French Army.

The Consulate made routine inquiries, but Prague Secret Service headquarters had taken all the necessary precautions for such an eventuality; the French inquiries only brought corroboration of Jaroslav's statements. In 1958 the fake Frenchman entered France to serve his military term.

From then on it was easy for Jaroslav, who, unknown to Prague headquarters, had also been recruited by the Soviet Secret Service as their special agent in France. He was liked by his fellow-conscripts in the Army, and his officers rated him highly.

During his French Army service he was transferred to French Occupation Forces in West Germany because his officers wanted to utilize his knowledge of the Czech, Russian, and German languages. To cap it all, he was attached to the Radio Monitoring Section of the French Army, in West Germany—a position that enabled him to mix freely with all grades of military personnel and learn important secrets. These he duly passed on to Prague and Moscow.

When his conscription term ended he left the Army with an excellent record. This, together with his having been able to make friends with influential officers and civilians, helped him obtain employment *in the French counter-intelligence.*

Until the end of November 1962 the Czech-Russian double spy in France, who had managed to move so deep into confidential departments, regularly transmitted military secrets to his espionage directors. Working in French counter-intelligence, and having first-hand knowledge of what was being done against Russian and other Communist spies in France, and knowing so much concerning French intelligence activities in Russia and other Iron Curtain countries, he was able to give authentic information that helped to hit hard against France's intelligence and counter-intelligence.

Despite his extraordinary success as a master spy in France, and despite his reputation as a devoted, efficient, and patriotic officer of the French counter-intelligence, his unique career came to an unexpected and sudden end.

All the evidence required was found in his apartment—short-wave radio receiver-transmitter with high-speed broadcast converters; Czech and Russian codes; all the utensils for using invisible ink; and other espionage technical equipment. They had been cleverly concealed in ingenious hiding-places in the apartment. And it had taken the French four long years to catch up with their owner.

Jaroslav's career in France shows that the recommendations of British committees on security are essential to the effective fight against and detection of spies.

It would, however, be unfair to select the case of Sterba as wholly typical, as it could lead to the unjustified conclusion that the French authorities and counter-intelligence are always at fault. The French Deuxième Bureau rightly enjoys the international reputation of being one of the most efficient organizations of its kind, and numerous arrests of spies support this reputation.

An illustration of the French counter-intelligence is the case of Demyan Mironovich Sheykov, whose cover was almost perfect, yet French spy-catchers discovered the dangerous master spy and smashed his widespread network.

Demyan was born in the Caspian Sea oil town of Baku a year after World War I had started. His father was one of Stalin's devoted lieutenants. In the early twenties the family moved to Moscow, where Demyan ultimately went to the Technical College. The Party Organizer selected him for "special" schooling and training.

Demyan's espionage career started when he was nearly twenty years old. The pattern for him was Marx-Engels School, Gorky; Lenin Technical School, Verkhovnoye; "assessment duties" at Moscow Secret Service headquarters. He was sent to the key spy school at Stiepnaya, near the northern border of the Kazakh Soviet Republic. He was from then on known as Pierre Durant.

In 1948, when the Berlin crisis was in full swing and it seemed as if the world might be thrust into another war, Durant, then thirty-three, was sent to Morocco, to acclimatize. For three years he worked as the head of Soviet espionage in Marrakesh and Casablanca, and then transferred to Algiers, where he worked for another four years.

After some seven years' successful work in French Africa he was instructed to leave Tunis and travel to France itself.

He decided to become, of all things, a Paris bus conductor! This occupation enabled him to meet agents and informers with the greatest ease, and a bus conductor was unlikely to be suspected of being a Russian spy.

Within six months Pierre headed several spy networks, and dozens of agents and informers regularly supplied him with secrets from the French Army, Air Force, Navy, industry, research institutes, and laboratories. He continued successfully for almost six years. This is no reflection on French counter-intelligence. Any security force would have found it almost impossible to uncover such a superbly efficient and cautious ring.

France's counter-intelligence nevertheless eventually did. A security officer accidentally noted a bus conductor who too frequently bought a brand of chocolates too expensive for his moderate means. He trailed Pierre, and discovered that he always bought the chocolates in the centre of Paris, then travelled to a suburban flat and, an hour or so later, journeyed across the city to take the chocolates to his girl friend. Yet he seldom stayed long at the girl's apartment.

A visit was paid to the girl's apartment while she was out. There were several boxes of chocolates around, and it was found that two chocolates were missing from each box. Always the same type of chocolate.

Pierre and his girl friend were followed. Then on the third day French counter-intelligence acted. Pierre and the girl were arrested. The chocolates were examined. The two particular types missing from the boxes in the girl's apartment contained—microfilms.

Georges Paques was a barber's son, and he was clever. He did not find it difficult to get into the French Civil Service.

The ambitious young man worked as hard as he had done during his school life, and his pleasant manners, his initiative and reliability, brought him rapid promotion. Paques was able to boast that he held major Civil Service positions in seven French Governments, and that his services were always fully appreciated.

At the end of World War II he got mixed up with Communists. He had a certain admiration and sympathy for Russia because the Red Army had played such an important part in crushing Hitler. Georges expressed his views. When he was in due course approached to supply the Russians with secret information from his Government office, and was at the same time offered substantial rewards for collaborating, he refused.

Georges Paques would be of considerable value as an informer to the Soviet Secret Service, and it was decided to win him over. The Russian recruitment attempts started with involving Paques, over a drink, in political discussions. They spoke to him of ideological motives and duty to the Communist Party. When these attempts came to nothing the known pattern was followed. The "stubborn" Frenchman was filled up with cognac, and when he no longer knew what he was doing was given a sum of money for which he unknowingly signed a "receipt". What he also didn't know was that the receipt said he had been paid for supplying top-secret documents.

The scene was now set for blackmail, and, like so many other men and women before and after him, Paques panicked. Instead of seeking the help of the French security authorities or his

superiors in the Ministry, he yielded to his blackmailers' pressure
and agreed to become a Soviet spy.

Once recruited, Georges Paques worked obediently for the
Russian espionage network in France. He continuously supplied
his contacts with top-secret documents and other classified information to which he had access in the Ministry. But, though his
masters were satisfied with his activities, praised him, and paid
him additional bonuses, they wanted more from him—closely
guarded military secrets. Paques had such a brilliant career
record in the French Civil Service—which earned him a large
entry in the French *Who's Who?*—that they believed he could
climb to still higher positions.

Paques' Russian "leader" in Paris informed him that he was
to make every effort to get himself promoted to the French
Defence Staff H.Q., so that he would be able to have free
access to military top secrets. Prompted by the prospect of being
paid still larger amounts of money for information of prime importance, and also by his own ego, Paques agreed to his "leader's"
proposition. His efforts were successful, and in 1958—he was then
forty-nine years of age—he was given a senior appointment at
the French Defence Staff H.Q., where experts thrashed out military policies, often in the presence of General de Gaulle himself.

From then onwards Moscow Secret Service headquarters were
fully informed on what was transpiring behind closed doors at
the French Defence Staff Headquarters. And, ironic as it may
seem, Russia's military leaders often knew all about French top-
secret armament developments and stategic plans and moves long
before France's closest allies were given the information.

In 1962 Georges Paques was named Deputy Head of N.A.T.O.'s
Press Service, and transferred his office to the A-shaped N.A.T.O.
building quarter of a mile from the Arc de Triomphe. He had
now full access to the meetings of the N.A.T.O. Permanent Council, in which delegates from fifteen nations discuss secret defence
planning.

From now on Georges Paques leaked vital secrets to his Russian
spy associates. He supplied them with classified documents from
the N.A.T.O. Council meetings, and full documentation of the
West's retaliation plans in the event of a nuclear attack on
Europe.

The jovial and brilliant Paques worked so carefully and skilfully that no-one ever dreamt he could be a spy. Nor did anyone
query how he could afford to live with his Italian-born wife
in a £20,000 luxury second-floor apartment in the Place des
Ecrivains Combattarts, in the Bois de Boulogne area.

Fortunately for the free world, a high-ranking Soviet Secret
Service officer defected to the West—Mikhail Goleniewski, who

insists that he is, in fact, the Grand Duke Aleksei Nikolayevich Romanov, son of Nicholas II. He helped to trap Vassall and Philby, Lonsdale, Blake, and Wennerström, and he also pointed the finger at Paques, and only then did N.A.T.O.'s counter-espionage service, together with the French D.S.T., move in on the traitor.

Conclusive proof was needed to enable the spy-catchers to arrest their man and hand him over to the French Security Court for conviction.

Georges Paques was kept under surveillance; and this difficult job was carried out with such great skill that neither Paques nor the Soviet Control Agent noticed anything.

Then, in August 1963, the work of the French security agents met with success. They were able to pounce on Paques in his luxury apartment. He was handling two copies of classified documents from N.A.T.O. Council meetings when they caught him.

14

The U.S. Diplomat Spy

IRVIN C. SCARBECK, twice married and with four children, had a promising career ahead of him in the State Department, Washington, where he was a senior official. But promotion came his way, and he was posted to the U.S. Embassy in Warsaw, as Second Secretary, and Irvin Scarbeck met disaster.

He was happily married to his German-born wife (she was his second wife, and a mother of three). He knew that the Communist Secret Service employed beautiful women to blackmail and recruit agents. Nevertheless he fell for the old trick, and was ensnared. Finally he was detected, arrested, and sentenced to thirty years' imprisonment.

Scarbeck tells how it all happened. . . .

When I was told I was to be posted to the U.S. Embassy in Warsaw to be acting Second Secretary I was briefed in great detail on the known methods Communist agents use to recruit informers. The briefing was a short, thorough course on what to do and not to do. I was to be on guard always, careful not to get involved with women, permanently aware of the common practice behind the Iron Curtain of using listening devices.

When I arrived in Warsaw this was all repeated, and it was impressed on me that I was in a country where *no-one* could be trusted.

I complied, of course, but the longer I stayed in Warsaw and the more local people I met, the more I became convinced that there was spy mania in Washington, and that the cunning of the Communist Secret Service agents was greatly exaggerated by our Government circles. No-one made the slightest move to involve me or seek any information. No-one asked a single question that could have been considered an attempt to get confidential information. There was ordinary small talk about life in the U.S.A. in general, about cars, theatres, cinemas, entertainment, restaurants, television, radio programmes, and things like that.

Then I met Urszula Discher.

Until then I had met only Polish men. Urszula was the first Polish girl. She was lovely. But when we first became acquainted the thought crossed my mind that this could be the "beautiful woman trick approach" about which I had been lectured in Washington, and at the Embassy in Warsaw.

I first met Urszula in a Warsaw café, and she didn't seem to even notice me. I couldn't keep my eyes off her. She was reading, and she never looked up once. I wondered how to approach her. I felt I had to make her acquaintance, to talk with her, to find out who she was.

I saw her take a cigarette and search her handbag for matches. I crossed to her table, and offered a light. She thanked me with a smile, then immediately turned her eyes back to what she had been reading. I asked if she minded if I sat at her table. She said she didn't, but there was no encouragement of any sort. I felt she couldn't be a Polish Secret Service agent; if she was she would not behave this way. She would show at least some sort of interest.

We eventually talked, and I became still more convinced about her, because she showed no interest in anything of possible use to an espionage organization.

We met frequently, and I fell in love with her. But although we knew each other well and were on intimate terms, she never once asked me about my work at the Embassy. It was simply a love affair.

Then, a day before Christmas Eve (December 23rd, 1960), I was with Urszula in her apartment. In the middle of the night Polish Secret Police officers burst in and found us in bed. They took scores of flashlight photographs. Urszula started crying uncontrollably.

One of the officers, who introduced himself as a police captain, informed me that my intimate association with a Polish female was illegal in Poland: I was in breach of Polish law, and was told I would have to face the consequences. My Embassy would be informed; Urszula would be arrested and brought before the court on a charge punishable with a prison sentence. The police captain kept telling me that once the U.S. Embassy was informed of my crime my diplomatic career would be finished, I would face court proceedings, and was liable to a considerable prison term in Poland. This apart, he continued, my marriage was certain to break up, because of my mistress.

"You laid your trap extremely well," I replied.

"You have it all wrong, Mr Scarbeck," the Secret Police captain replied. "Urszula Discher is no agent of ours. I'll tell you how we were able to catch you. We watched you, as we do all foreign diplomats. As we saw your romance with Miss Discher progress, we kept you and her under continuous secret surveillance. Simple! The fact that we are arresting your mistress and bringing her before the court should be sufficient proof for you that she is not our agent."

He spoke English well, and he convinced me that Urszula was no Secret Police agent. I could, he said, save myself and Miss Discher from disgrace, arrest, and ruin if I wished. He told me that in certain circumstances crimes need not be brought to the attention of the courts, that if I co-operated with the Polish authorities he would not report the incident.

"What do you mean by 'co-operate with the Polish authorities'?" I asked.

"We'll discuss that at headquarters," he answered. We dressed and were led to cars.

During the journey from the apartment to police headquarters Urszula travelled in one car and I in the other. When we arrived we were taken to different rooms without being allowed to speak a single word to each other.

I was kept waiting a long time in the room—a typical office with filing cabinets, a large desk with several telephones, two chairs. A guard was standing by the door. We didn't talk.

A Secret Police Colonel came in, took a folder from the filing cabinet, and sat down at the desk. He then repeated the story the captain had told me at Urszula's apartment—about my diplomatic career being finished and so on. At the end of his lecture he offered me a cigarette and said:

"We are not unreasonable people. All you need to do to have the crime erased from the files is to provide the Polish authorities with some information."

"You are trying to blackmail me into working for you as a spy," I protested.

"I am not doing anything of the sort," he replied. He said it in a quiet voice that sounded as if he were amused. "I am just telling you what you can do to save yourself and your mistress. The choice is entirely yours. If you decide you want to face it, then it's all the same with me. You will be charged in accordance with our law and brought before the court for sentence, the U.S. Embassy will be notified, and that is that. Your trial will be a public trial and will be reported in full in the Press."

He seemed to enjoy this because he dwelt at length on what an international scandal the trial would be, and how it would damage the reputation of the U.S.A. and American diplomats. When he had exhausted the theme he repeated that the decision was entirely mine and no pressure would be used to influence me either way.

"If, however, you decide you don't want to end in disgrace, just say," he went on. "If you agree to co-operate with the Polish State—that is, if you agree to provide us with confidential information—all records about you and your mistress will be destroyed." He looked at me triumphantly and said, "We are generous people, Mr Scarbeck, and we understand love affairs even if they are not within the law. If you co-operate we won't officially know of your association with Urszula Discher, and you can, of course, continue your love life as before. We don't mind our agents enjoying themselves. Apart from this, we also pay generously for valuable service rendered. We are proud people, Mr Scarbeck, we don't solicit presents, we pay for co-operation."

As he said this he rose from his chair and said he would leave me alone awhile to think matters over. As he left the room the guard re-entered.

The Colonel reappeared with a file in his hand. Standing next to me, he opened the file and showed me large prints of photographs taken by Secret Police officers when they entered Urszula's apartment. He said that, depending on my decision, the prints would be given to the U.S. Embassy, the court, and the Press.

"Have you come to a conclusion, Mr Scarbeck?" he asked as I looked at the photographs.

I told him I had.

"Splendid," he said. "I thought you would be governed by common sense and would not refuse our generous offer." He produced from the file a typewritten sheet of paper and, handing it to me, said, "If you sign this your criminal offence record will be destroyed at once, and I will see that the same is done with the photographs and the negatives. You can be present when they are destroyed, so that you will know we have kept our word."

The typewritten sheet of paper was an agreement confirming that I had joined the Polish Secret Service, and undertook to supply confidential information, data, and documents whenever required to do so. I noticed that it bore a date shortly after my arrival in Warsaw. I pointed this out to the Colonel, and he said this had been done to safeguard me, and not to connect my agreement to work for the Polish Government with that night's happenings. There was nothing left for me to do but to sign the document, which the Colonel witnessed.

He returned the document to the file, then led me to another room. He summoned another officer, who handed him a file containing all the data about myself and Urszula, and also a bundle of compromising photographs taken earlier that night at Urszula's apartment, and the negatives of the photographs. He invited me to satisfy myself that it was the dossier on me. After I had done so he pushed all of it into the stove and burned the lot.

As he led me to another room the Colonel told me that one of his men would approach me in due course, and that from then on this man would be my only link with the Polish Secret Service. He told me his contact man would identify himself by the pass-code "Antek wishes to be remembered", and that he (the Colonel) was certain our co-operation would be satisfactory and beneficial to all concerned.

I was reunited with Urszula, and we were allowed to leave. She was very upset about what had happened, and sobbed a lot. She was frightened we might be rearrested at any time. It was obvious she had not been told about my recruitment to the Polish Secret Service. I did my best to convince her that I had been able to straighten out the matter and that no danger threatened either of us. She wasn't easily convinced. "As long as one lives in Poland there's no guarantee one won't end up in the hands of the Secret Police," she said.

When I eventually left Urszula I wanted to be on my own, to sort things out in my mind. I walked the streets of Warsaw for hours, reliving in my mind all that had happened that night, considering whether I should make a full statement to my people at the Embassy about what had happened. After all, I had not given the Poles any information of any sort. I was not a spy—yet. But would they believe me? There was the agreement I had signed, and the back date it bore. If I confessed and presented my Embassy with the facts the Poles were sure to present them with the agreement, and it was more than doubtful that my story would be accepted. And how could I be sure that *all* the negatives of the compromising photographs had been destroyed? Perhaps they had kept one or more negatives and, if I double-crossed them, would publish the pictures. My career as a diplomat and senior Government official would be finished, so would my marriage, and I was certain to be arrested, prosecuted, and sent to prison.

I decided to stick to my agreement with the Poles to supply them information. But I made up my mind never to let them have anything of real importance. I was determined not to betray my own country.

Days passed, and there was no approach from the Colonel's contact man. I hoped against hope that the Poles were not going to hold me to the agreement. But then a man came to me and said, "Antek wishes to be remembered." There it was.

The contact gave me the following orders:

I was to meet him next evening at six-thirty sharp, and bring classified documents to be photographed at once and then returned. I had no alternative.

The following evening I met him and handed over some documents giving relatively valueless information. They bore the

A carved replica of the Great Seal of the United States which, presented by Russia, contained hidden microphones. The Russians were able to overhear every word spoken in the American Ambassador's study

112

Side view of a microphone (*below*) and probe tube (*right*) which were buried in the wall of the United States Embassy in Moscow and had, for years, been betraying confidential conversations of American diplomats to Soviet Secret Service headquarters

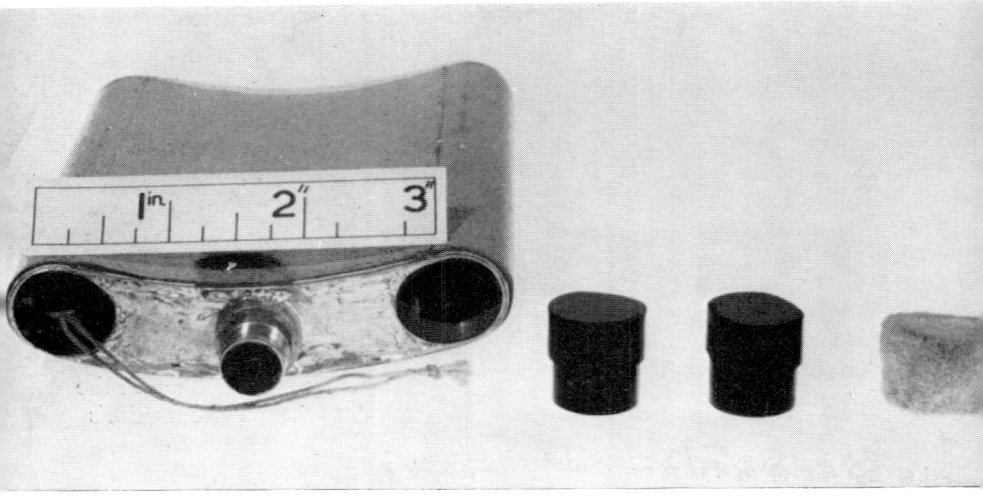

Container used by Soviet spies for hiding microfilm

The torch and the Yardley container were provided with false compartments for hiding microfilms

Photo United Press

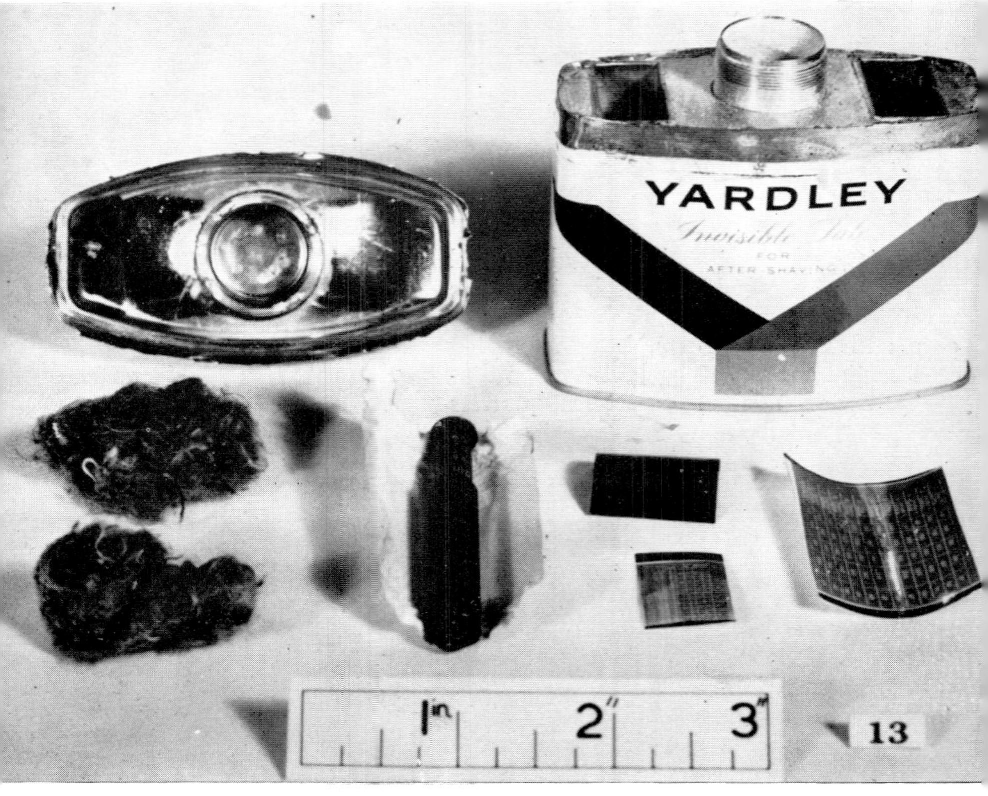

13

classified marking, and the Poles seemed happy. The documents were photographed, then handed back to me so that I could return them to the Embassy files.

Although I had given the Poles unimportant information, I felt bad. The fact remained that I had passed on documents from our files, and this was a betrayal of the trust invested in me as Second Secretary at the Embassy.

My meetings with the contact man were regular. It was always the same procedure: they photographed the documents, handed them back to me, and I returned them to the Embassy files.

In March (1961) Urszula told me she had been visited by Secret Police officers who told her that they weren't satisfied with my behaviour, and that if I didn't come up to expectation she would be arrested and sent to prison for a long time. I at once got in touch with my contact and told him I wanted to meet the Colonel to find out from him what it was all about. The outcome was that the Poles accused me of not keeping my part of the agreement. They wanted the real stuff.

I made it clear that I resented very much Urszula being threatened. At last they agreed to give her an exit permit from Poland so that she could live abroad. The promise was conditional on my supplying them with more important documents. I gave them some almost immediately, and Urszula received her exit permit to leave Poland. She went to live in West Germany. When she was safely there the Poles told me, "You're a fool," but didn't elaborate on what they meant.

My contact became increasingly insistent that I provide more secret material. To pass them something big with classified marking I gave them an English translation of a six-hundred-page Soviet economic report, which they photographed. They were very angry later when they learned what they had copied.

Shortly afterwards my contact told me something that shook me. He said there was a new security officer coming to the U.S. Embassy in Warsaw. I didn't even know we had one coming. The new security officer, Mr Victor Dikeos, arrived, and discovered my love affair with Urszula. He also discovered that I had been passing American secrets to the Polish Secret Police.

Irvin C. Scarbeck was taken to Frankfurt, West Germany, for questioning by Mr Kenneth Knauf, a State Department security officer, on June 5th, 1961. Early in the interrogation Scarbeck tried to convince the security officer that he was innocent. "If someone says he knows I have passed secret documents . . . he's trying to frame me," he insisted.

Mr Knauf reminded Scarbeck that he had already admitted that the Poles had helped arrange to get his Polish mistress to

H

Germany from Warsaw. Insisting that Scarbeck was "holding out", Knauf persisted: "You must have given them a present. Nobody's been this lucky in the history of intelligence. You took documents out . . . they photographed them . . . you brought them back." In the end Scarbeck confessed.

He related how he had read a secret report prepared by the U.S. Ambassador to Poland, Mr Jacob Beam, dealing with American-Polish relations during the past four years. He maintained that he did not turn over the document to the Poles until he had decided that there was "nothing in it that affected the security of the United States". He insisted: "It helps cement relations."

Scarbeck was arrested on June 13th by F.B.I. agents and charged that between January 1st and May 30th, 1961, he had passed information to Polish agents.

According to the indictment handed down by a District Grand Jury on July 21st, the ex-diplomat gave the Poles information from three documents.

The first of these was an examination of United States policy towards Poland during the last four years, prepared by the American Ambassador to Poland, Mr Jacob Beam.

The second document was an estimate of the effectiveness of the Polish armed forces, prepared by United States Military Attachés at the American Embassy in Warsaw.

The third document was an Embassy weekly summary report to the State Department that included an item about the discovery of a new Polish airfield near the border of Czechoslovakia.

The indictment also charged Scarbeck with wilfully and unlawfully removing a copy of the Ambassador's report from the American Embassy in Warsaw.

Scarbeck stood trial in October 1961 before the District Court in Washington, D.C.

He did not take the stand to testify. The defence presented only three witnesses. One of them was Urszula Discher, who merely responded with a negative answer to the one question asked of her: had she ever worked for the Polish Secret Police? The other defence witnesses were psychiatrists. Both said they were unable to determine—because of inadequate time for examination—whether Scarbeck might have been mentally ill when the crimes were committed, and therefore not responsible for his actions.

The trial lasted nearly three weeks. At the end the weary jury, which had been locked in the United States courthouse for more than two weeks during the trial, brought in its verdict at 10 A.M. on October 17th, 1961. The jury spent fifteen and a half hours in deliberation, stretching over a three-day period. They decided that Scarbeck was guilty of turning over information from the three documents named in the indictment, but found him not guilty of the fourth indictment count. Justice Department Attorney Mr Paul C. Vincent said that in his view "it was a very fair verdict and the Government is satisfied".

It was announced that Scarbeck would be sentenced later, following preparation of a pre-sentence report by the court's probation officer.

On November 9th, 1961, Scarbeck was sentenced to thirty years' imprisonment for passing classified material to Polish Communists. The sentence, the maximum permissible under the law, was imposed by Federal District Judge Leonard P. Walsh. The Justice Department said that Scarbeck would be eligible for parole after ten years. He would then be fifty-one.

Mrs Scarbeck returned to West Germany about two weeks before the verdict.

15

A Flexible 'Shipper'

THE chief Soviet Secret Service resident operator in the
Netherlands successfully worked for over seven years in the
country, and was listed in Moscow headquarters' files under the
cover names of "Van der Bergh" and "Robijns", also as "Anton",
"Hein", and "Karl". He came from a family of spies; his real
name was Pyotr Davidovich Zlotniysky, but no Dutchman who
met him was ever able to detect the slightest trace of Russian
origin.

One of the main reasons Zlotniysky was chosen as a Soviet
Secret Service resident operator in the Netherlands was his unusual background.

His grandfather, Igor Aleksandrovich Zlotniysky, had been an
officer of the Tsarist Secret Police, Okhrana, in Kiev, and was
classified by St Petersburg headquarters as "a specialist in tracking down subversive elements". Unknown to his Okhrana superiors, who frequently praised him for his successful arrests of
terrorists, he was a double agent who passed on important information to Lenin's organization and was responsible for many a
Leninist escaping arrest and punishment. Until his retirement in
1905 he managed to continue double activities so well that, on
leaving the Okhrana service, he was presented with a special
diploma and an inscribed gold pocket-watch.

His only son, David Igorovich Zlotniysky, born in Kiev in 1872,
emulated his father. At the age of seventeen he joined the Russian
revolutionary movement. Eventually he enlisted in the Rostov
police force. He carried out his double rôle so efficiently that in
1896 he was promoted to Okhrana plain-clothes detective.

Eight months after the retirement of his father matters became
more difficult for the double agent—then an Okhrana lieutenant.
For Okhrana Captain Kapronov received word from an informer
that Lieutenant Zlotniysky was a member of the Bolshevik movement, and sent a roptr to St Petersburg which stated:
". . . Lieutenant D. I. Zlotniysky harbours revolutionary sympa-

thies." The informer's accusation could not be proved, and the suspect therefore could not be arrested and charged. As a precautionary measure it was decided to transfer him from Okhrana service to a clerical post in the Ministry of the Interior, where he would be under strict supervision.

His transfer to St Petersburg—then the centre of the revolutionary movement—soon enabled Zlotniysky to become a leading member of the illegal Bolshevik Action Committee. Because he was suspect the Okhrana kept him under secret observation, and eventually managed to arrest him as he was distributing leaflets. He was sentenced to two years' exile in Siberia.

Although his wife had just given birth to their son Pyotr, Zlotniysky was not downhearted at being sent to enforced residence in Irkutsk. He was a fanatical Bolshevik, and exile in Siberia was in fact an important stepping-stone to a future Party executive post; it brought him in direct contact with the prominent Leninist leaders.

When, in 1917, the Bolshevik revolution succeeded and the Soviet Secret Service was established, Zlotniysky became Dzerzhinskiy's espionage executive officer. But he did not live to see the Soviet Secret Service grow into a dangerous worldwide espionage network, for in 1919 he died of pneumonia.

Like so many other children of Old Bolsheviks who had died, the thirteen-year-old Pyotr Davidovich Zlotniysky was 'adopted' by the Party. He was a bright boy. His school records showed him to be "an exemplary student", also "an exceptionally active young Communist". In 1927 he finished his college education and practical training, and became an official of the Central Committee of the Russian Communist Party—responsible for compiling economic reports for Stalin's Politburo.

This is the background of the man who, from 1953 to 1960, was the Soviet Secret Service resident operator in the Netherlands and considered to be one of the best spies Russia has ever had.

When, in the middle thirties, Stalin's Politburo ruled that "the Soviet Secret Service must be developed into a powerful worldwide striking force", and it was decided to train even greater numbers of future spies for service abroad, one of the persons the Central Committee of the Russian Communist Party recommended as "suitable for special intelligence training" was Pyotr Davidovich Zlotniysky. But although his recommendation came from no less an authority than the Central Committee, it nevertheless took the Selection Board of Moscow Secret Service headquarters eleven months to accept him for spy training. Not before 1937 was he ordered to attend the elementary courses at the Marx-Engels School, Gorky.

In 1938, after having undergone all the preliminary training at the Marx-Engels School and the Lenin Technical School, and having been found suitable for future Secret Service work by the Selection Board in Moscow, Zlotniysky was sent to the First Directorate for "assessment duties" and, after three months, was assigned to the Division for the Netherlands.

Because of the outbreak of World War II in Europe, and the need for increased espionage activities in the West, Zlotniysky stayed longer than usual at Moscow Secret Service headquarters. He was found to be "a most promising officer with exceptional understanding of Dutch affairs and mentality", and was eventually promoted to Assistant to the Director of the Division for the Netherlands.

In 1942 he was sent to Prakhovka, the super-spy school for agents to be assigned to Holland. From the day of his arrival at this institution he became "Hein".

The original Prakhovka school had been evacuated after Stalin's scorched-earth policy had been carried out. The newly created "Hein" was one of the first arrivals at the emergency school which was established near Ufa, in the Bashkir Soviet Republic.

During his stay at Prakhovka, where he was converted into a 'Dutchman', Zlotniysky-"Hein" was among the institution's best students. Entries in the school's records stated that he was "a very promising" future resident operator.

In 1947 the Prakhovka school was rebuilt and re-opened on its original site, some seventy miles north-east of Minsk, the capital of the Byelorussian Soviet Republic. The two hundred or so square miles of the school training area stretched towards the border of the Latvian Soviet Republic. "Hein" returned to the new school. In October 1952 he was classed as ready for work as a resident operator in the Netherlands.

In mid-February 1953 "Hein" walked off a ship in Rotterdam and headed for Amsterdam. Possessing genuine documents, he had no difficulty in finding accommodation in the city.

He decided to establish his headquarters in Antwerp. His reasons were:

"One can go from Antwerp to Rotterdam and back as easily as from one Soviet town to another. I ask therefore for permission to be allowed to direct operations from Antwerp instead of from Dutch territory. My organization would be completely undetectable. By not engaging in any activities in Belgium itself the Belgian authorities can never have grounds to even suspect me; and having no equipment in Holland, the Dutch authorities cannot become dangerous. . . ."

The suggestion was a deviation from the strict Soviet Secret Service rules which insist that a resident operator must work independently in the country of his assignment.

Some of the Russian intelligence chiefs were in favour of the suggestion, pointing out that "flexible arrangements must always be considered if they can help the security of the organization and guarantee the flow of information".

"Hein" was allowed to set up headquarters in Antwerp.

He decided to use the 'cover' of a reputable shipper—a status which would enable him to go anywhere without creating suspicion. In Antwerp he found accommodation and considered setting up his own firm and developing a genuine business. Like all resident operators, he had large financial resources at his disposal, and it was not difficult to open offices and employ specialized people in Antwerp.

As he was about to put his plans into action an unforeseen occurrence caused him to pause awhile. A genuine Antwerp shipper, with whom he had become friendly during frequent visits to the bar of his favourite hotel, told him one evening that he was looking for a partner. This was the perfect solution for "Hein".

The Antwerp shipper often came to the hotel bar, and each time he talked of plans for expanding his business. He did his best to persuade the "rich Dutchman" Hein to come in with him. The spy said he was "interested", but had not yet had time to make up his mind.

Then, at the end of April, he decided to create the impression that the shipper had succeeded in convincing him that the proposition was sound and profitable. "Hein" became a partner in the firm. The shipper accepted his explanation that he could not be continuously at the offices as other business interests made it essential for him to travel frequently.

Having established his 'cover', he began to organize his network. It was plausible for him to have to travel extensively and meet a great variety of people, and he soon had reliable sub-agents in Amsterdam, The Hague, Rotterdam, and other centres.

Perhaps one of the cleverest moves he made was to use a travel bureau for his activities. He was able to get a footing in several innocent businesses, and managed to arrange for agents to become employees in travel bureaux, working as counter clerks, travel couriers, translators, etc. These people were able without risk to get in regular personal touch with scores of informers.

The nature of the travel businesses made it easy for secret reports to be passed on from informers to sub-agents, and for the sub-agent to pass payment and special instructions for future work. Travel couriers, accompanying parties of tourists to foreign countries, had excellent opportunities to carry microfilms in both directions.

During his seven years' activities in the Netherlands "Hein" was an efficient operator who also specialized in collecting 'facts' that could be used to recruit informers, and in the manufacture of compromising 'evidence'. He found blackmail to be one of the most effective weapons for forcing victims to work for him.

One of his favourite methods was to get victims into the apartments of women agents and have them photographed by hidden cameras. Another of his methods was to lend would-be informers money and ask for a receipt. This was then doctored, and the unsuspecting individual shown a photograph of the receipt which had been forged to state that the money had been paid for intelligence information. Threats to hand over the 'proof' to the police, and offers to pay handsomely for the supply of secret information, were usually enough to 'persuade' any hesitant party.

In 1960, however, one of his key operators was suspected, and "Hein's" spy web was put out of business.

The case of Mademoiselle Germaine, were it not recorded in official files, might be queried by many as the product of a vivid imagination.

Mademoiselle Germaine, a typical French miss, was in real life not French at all, but the daughter of a Rumanian father and a Georgian mother. The father, Soltan Cornescou, had come as a young man to Odessa in 1913 because he hoped that the busy Black Sea port might provide him with better opportunities than his own country. He found employment in a shipping firm, and a year later married Marfa Kalidze, daughter of the firm's Georgian manager.

In the middle of World War I, in October 1916, a daughter—Irina Soltanovna—was born to the Cornescous. Irina, thirty-one years later, entered the Soviet Secret Service spy school of Stiepnaya as—Mademoiselle Germaine.

Irina's favourite subject at school had been French, and it was arranged for her to enlist as a student at the University of Moscow, where she graduated in 1937, with a diploma in French.

Her first job was as French translator with the Publishing House for Foreign Languages in Moscow, and soon afterwards she was called to do editorial work for the Radio Centre. She was transferred to the French Section of the Comintern.

After the German-Russian war began in June 1941, Irina was posted to the Soviet Ministry for Foreign Affairs, where she became assistant to the head of the French Section. Her diplomatic career ended in 1945. With World War II over, Stalin decided to build up subversive forces overseas. Irina Soltanovna was one of those earmarked for work in France.

Irina was put through Secret Service training at the Marx-Engels School, and the Lenin Technical School, followed by a period of "assessment duties" at Moscow Secret Service head-quarters, and then training at the French-speaking division of the spy school at Stiepnaya. When passed as ready for espionage abroad the forty-one-year-old (but much younger-looking) master spy was sent to France as Mademoiselle Germaine.

After an 'acclimatization' period in Paris she decided on the cover of a French governess in the family of an influential man.

The only posts a Paris agency could offer were with a banker, a household where she might never come across any useful infor-mation; with a textile merchant in Lille, an offer she discarded for the same reason, and also because it was in a provincial town; with a businessman in Toulouse, again 'out of the way' and there-fore uninteresting; and with a director of a Belgian steel concern who was resident in Paris as their representative—also an un-attractive post for her. Realizing that she needed to establish her 'cover' as fast as possible, she chose employment with the Belgian family, determined to change the job as soon as she could find something better.

Living with the family had drawbacks: it was impossible for her to keep technical espionage equipment in her room because of the danger of its being discovered. But having a substantial sum of money, and a list of names and addresses of people suitable for recruitment as agents and informers, she was soon able to find a hide-out for her technical equipment. She recruited a team and set up her first network.

To her surprise the Belgians with whom she stayed proved to be an excellent choice. Not only did they treat her as one of the family, but they were keen on entertaining, and their guests in-cluded French and other West European industrialists, scientists, technologists, officers, and even members of the Corps Diplo-matique. So, almost from the beginning, Germaine was able to pick up important secret information on vital industrial, political, and even strategic subjects.

After less than four months her employers said the family would be returning to Brussels, and suggested that she accompany them. As headquarters had assigned her to France, and she could not change her place of assignment without con-sent, she had to postpone her reply until Moscow informed her what to do.

Because of the urgent need for a decision, she transmitted a coded high-speed short-wave radio message to headquarters. Her superiors had been pleased with the information she had regularly passed, and permitted her to change the country of her assignment. She was ordered to go with her employers to Brussels, and continue from there her activities as a resident operator.

In Brussels her employers entertained even more important personalities than they had done in Paris, and, equipped with special miniature but highly selective 'limpet' microphones and wire recorders, Germaine was often able to obtain and transmit to headquarters information of great importance.

She wasn't, however, content with the information she obtained at home. She considered it her duty to set up an espionage network to penetrate into the most important Belgian military, research, and other closely guarded establishments. Within six weeks of arriving in Brussels she had two webs operational, and numerous agents and informers supplied her with calculations, blueprints, plans, reports, and many other documents from all over Belgium.

Her second-in-command, a Paul Veken, was a Belgian who concealed his Communist fanaticism and was considered to be a very religious office clerk. He was therefore excellently suited for his rôle in her network. It was safe for her to meet him whenever necessary.

Despite her excellent 'cover' and the caution that made it possible for her to remain undetected for almost four years, she eventually made mistakes that led to her detection.

The greatest was being convinced that the park to which she daily took her employers' children was ideal for her frequent rendezvous with her second-in-command, Veken. She didn't seem to realize that it might arouse suspicion if he came almost every day to the park, played with the children, chatted with her, but never dated her during her off-duty times.

It was clever of her to bring tempting-looking sandwiches which she offered to Veken; not so clever that he always ate only one or two, pocketing the remaining ones. These contained microfilms. It was also odd that she and the children ate only some of the pastries which Veken brought, and that Mademoiselle took the others home with her—the ones that contained information for her.

Belgian counter-intelligence spotted the mistakes, and, after almost four years of successful work as a Resident Network Operator in Brussels she and her lieutenant were arrested. Microfilms containing important military and scientific-technological secrets were recovered, her network centres found, and most of the spy ring's agents and informers caught.

16

Treachery was their Business

FOR ten years Heinz Felfe, a top-ranking officer of the West German Secret Service, worked undetected for his Russian masters, photographing documents after office hours at the Munich-Pullach headquarters of General Gehlen's Federal Intelligence Service. There, too, he made tape recordings with which he supplemented the information obtained from the microfilmed photographs. He sent it all to Moscow Secret Service headquarters. Soviet intelligence directors were consequently fully informed on every move in the Counter-Intelligence Department against Russia in General Gehlen's Federal Intelligence Service; of all activities in the West German Federal Office for Protection of the Constitution; and exactly what U.S. intelligence service was doing.

To top it all, apart from supplying the Russians with fully comprehensive intelligence and counter-intelligence data, Felfe and his associates, Clemens and Tiebel, also passed on N.A.T.O. secrets of utmost importance to Soviet strategy. And if Soviet Secret Service officer Klimov hadn't defected to the U.S. intelligence service in Helsinki, Felfe, Clemens, and Tiebel might have still been acting for the Soviet Secret Service inside the Federal Intelligence Service.

Klimov had been a senior staff officer at Moscow Secret Service headquarters for a considerable time, and knew every angle of the espionage business. When he was transferred to "foreign duties" he started toying with the idea of defecting to the Americans. He was, however, aware that if he didn't want to risk being turned away he could not come empty-handed, but would have to present the U.S. authorities with important documents and information. With all the care and skill he had acquired during his work with the Soviet Secret Service, he prepared his escape.

When he finally defected to the U.S. intelligence service in Helsinki he was able to bring them material of great value. Among this was precise information about Heinz Felfe, West German counter-intelligence top brass, Felfe's confederates Clemens and Tiebel, data on their cover names, their contacts, Soviet superiors, their activities, and methods.

After Klimov was interrogated and cleared, his information checked, counter-checked, and found correct, U.S. authorities passed the facts on the Felfe-Clemens-Tiebel trio to their counterparts in West Germany. Provided by the U.S. intelligence with conclusive evidence of the espionage activities of Felfe and Co., West Germany's Security Police acted.

When Felfe was arrested by officers of the West German police on November 6th, 1961, he was convinced that no-one could prove he had been working for the Soviet Secret Service. He was certain that when confronted with the Investigation Judge he would not only be released, but also receive an apology, for, after all, he was one of the top officers in the Federal Intelligence Service and, as such, held enormous power. So when West German plain-clothes officers requested him to accompany them to headquarters and he obtained from them the information that he was to be charged with espionage for Soviet Russia, he threatened them and their superiors that he would see they were all punished for their "idiotic mistake". And when he eventually faced the Investigation Judge he demanded immediate release, claiming the charge was "too ridiculous for words". He said he had "no desire to waste time with answering silly questions".

Felfe was not released. Instead the Investigation Judge challenged him with details of his espionage for the Soviet Secret Service. Realizing it was impossible to refute the conclusive evidence, Felfe decided to make a voluntary confession to create the impression that he wanted to co-operate with the West German authorities. But to make his treachery appear less serious he insisted in his voluntary confession that he had passed on to the Russians only "information which did not harm the interests of the West German Federal Republic". He vehemently denied having passed military or other vital data.

The case of Felfe, Clemens, and Tiebel is of interest because it establishes, among other things, that Moscow Secret Service headquarters will readily disregard Communist anti-Fascist principles if notorious ex-Nazis, holding sufficiently important positions, are willing to work for them.

Here, then, is Heinz Felfe's own confession. . . .

I was the son of a minor officer of the Criminal Investigation Department. I was born in 1918 in Dresden. Like so many youths of the post-World War I period, I was discontented with life in the democratic Weimar Republic and believed Hitler's Nazi propaganda that the Third Reich would hold ample opportunities for *every true* German. I saw my opportunities in the N.S.D.A.P. (Hitler's Nazi Party).

My initiative and conscientious activities in the S.S. were noticed and appreciated, and in time I was promoted to the high rank of S.S. *Obersturmführer*. My duties in the S.S., which entailed, among other things, special investigation work, were the stepping-stones for my gaining considerable experience in all branches of intelligence. My abilities in this field were eventually noted by my superiors in the S.S., and I became an officer of the *Geheimdienst* (the Nazi secret security service).

I worked under S.S. *Obergruppenführer* Schallenberg in the Department of Foreign Eastern Countries, where I learned every trick of practical espionage. I liked espionage work, and was certain this was the profession I was born for.

[Felfe often boasted to colleagues in the Nazi Secret Service that he was "a born spy" and that, throughout World War II, he was considered by the heads of the *Geheimdienst* to be "one of the most capable and reliable intelligence officers in the Third Reich".]

My career as one of the top men in the Secret Service continued throughout World War II. In the spring of 1945, at the end of the War, I found myself in Holland. I marched in full S.S. uniform into British prisoner-of-war custody.

When I was freed in November 1946 my first step was to contact my friend and comrade in the S.S. and the intelligence service, Erwin Tiebel. I wanted to find out whether I was more or less safe in West Germany, or whether there was any likelihood of my being arrested and prosecuted on war-crime charges.

Tiebel was a solicitor, and therefore was able to make inconspicuous inquiries on how the hare was running. He ascertained that neither the Allied nor the West German authorities were interested in my past. He said it was safe for me to angle for a post as a police commissar. He behaved like the good old friend he had always been, and, in fact, did his utmost to find me employment as a police commissar. These efforts failed, however, and so did my own. I had to be content with becoming an official in the Federal Ministry for All-German Affairs. My job was interviewing refugees.

In mid-1951, after almost five years of this, my employment was terminated. I was a respected official, but this didn't automatically open the door to another well-paid top position.

I contacted my former comrade at the *Geheimdienst*, ex-S.S. *Hauptsturmführer* Hans Clemens. I had been his superior during his service in the *Geheimdienst,* and thought he was the man to help me, as he held a senior post in the Federal Intelligence Service of General Gehlen.

Hans also came from Dresden, and intended to become a professional musician, but as he was only a moderate player he was more often unemployed. He also joined the N.S.D.A.P. in 1931, and when the Führer established the Third Reich gave up his career as a musician to become a Gestapo investigator. His efficient, cold-blooded, and ruthless interrogation of political and racial prisoners earned him promotion, and he became officer-in-charge of Dresden Security Service headquarters. Determined to prove to his superiors that "only terror induces suspects to talk and sign confessions", he increased his brutalities towards political and racial prisoners. He earned himself the nickname "The Tiger of Pieschen". (Pieschen is a Dresden district.)

Clemens's 'successes' were eventually noted by Reich Security headquarters in Berlin. They were in urgent need of experienced officers for their Department VI—Foreign Espionage. Clemens appeared to be right for the job. He was put in charge of "securing contact with Switzerland". It was his task to send spies to that small but important neutral country to set up intelligence networks for the Third Reich. As I have previously said, I was Clemens's superior.

As for Clemens's past—during the War he was posted to Italy. He became known to the Italians as "The Tiger of Como" because of his unprecedented brutalities towards the population, and especially because of his part in the shooting of 330 Italian hostages.

At the end of the War he was brought before the War Crimes Court in Rome and, in the so-called Keppler Trial, was charged with having been an accessory to the shooting of these 330 Italian hostages. He admitted that he had been in charge of the execution squad for several hours, but, despite his admission, was—to his surprise—released in 1948.

He was allowed to return to West Germany, and was still an ardent hater of what he termed "wishy-washy democracy" and "aggressive Communism". He couldn't find a job that would have enabled him to live well, so, as you might say, "he sold himself body and soul" to the Federal Intelligence Service of General Gehlen and to the Soviet Secret Service.

When I approached Hans in mid-1951 he was only too pleased to be able to repay me for the many favours I had afforded him when I was his superior in the *Geheimdienst.* Hans said he would be able to get me into the Gehlen organization because the General was very interested in unemployed Nazi intelligence-service people.

He suggested I should meanwhile travel to the Soviets, as our ex-S.S. and *Geheimdienst* comrade, Erwin Tiebel, had already done. I wasn't very happy with the suggestion because I feared I might be arrested and tried on war-crimes charges. Hans explained that the Russians conveniently had forgotten Tiebel's anti-Soviet wartime activities, treated him royally, and offered him a collaboration job with their Secret Service. He added that the same would also be the case with me.

I accepted his proposition. After all, he had also been welcomed by the Russians and was in their service.

Hans's wife, who lived in the East German town of Dresden, arranged a meeting between myself and a top-ranking Soviet intelligence representative—a Russian Secret Service colonel who went under the cover name of Max.

We met in the Soviet Sector of Berlin in September 1951.

We drove to a villa in Karlshorst, where we had a magnificent dinner. The champagne really flowed, and Max and I discussed the possibilities of East-West business, and whether the Russians would help me to establish a concern that could be developed for intelligence purposes.

Max didn't think much of my proposition, but told me the Russians would be interested in me as an espionage agent—if I could find a position in West Germany that would enable me to obtain important documents and the kind of worthwhile information Moscow required.

Although during this first meeting with Max I wasn't, as yet, given direct orders regarding my future work as a Soviet agent in West Germany, I was nevertheless requested to sign an undertaking that I had joined the Soviet Secret Service; I was handed five thousand D-Marks as advance payment for services to be rendered, and ordered to report to Max any development in my envisaged employment with the Gehlen organization.

On my return to the Federal Republic former S.S. *Standartenführer* Kriechbaum, who held a senior post in General Gehlen's Federal Intelligence Service headquarters at Munich-Pullach, came to see me. He said that our mutual friend Hans Clemens had asked him to call on me and find out whether I still wished to resume my "old trade"—meaning intelligence work—or whether I had changed my mind. When I assured Kriechbaum that I was more than eager to join the Gehlen organization he promised, as a former Party comrade, that I would obtain speedy employment in a senior capacity in the organization.

I contacted Max, who immediately arranged another rendezvous, and we met at Dresden. He was delighted with the development and impressed on me that I should keep him informed on every step.

On November 15th, 1951, I officially became an officer of General Gehlen's Federal Intelligence Service, and celebrated the event with Hans Clemens in an inn at Munich-Stachus. Using a cover address, we both sent Max a picture-postcard on which we wrote "It's settled", then signed the card.

My career in General Gehlen's organization began with intelligence research activities at the Regional Sub-division in Karlsruhe. Later I created with Hans the Department Rhein-Ruhr in Düsseldorf, but was eventually transferred to the Gehlen H.Q. in Munich-Pullach. From my arrival there to the moment of my arrest on November 6th, 1961, I was in charge of the Department of Counter-Intelligence against Russia—a position that also enabled me to be in command of Gehlen spies in Soviet territories.

Max was naturally happy with the set-up and paid generously. He made it plain that he regarded me as his "most important master spy in the Federal Intelligence Service".

In all, I received from the Soviet Secret Service some 300,000 West German Marks. My salary was about 1660 West German Marks per month.

During the first two years of my service in General Gehlen's organization I passed the Russians top-secret documents, reports, and highly confidential material—all by means of couriers. Then, when the West German security was improved and there was increasing danger of my couriers being detected, I received orders from Max to use more modern methods, and was supplied with photographic and other equipment. From the autumn of 1952 I microfilmed every worthwhile document I could; concealed the copies and transported them safely to my Russian superior. For my personal reports to Max I used microdots affixed under postage-stamps of harmless-looking picture postcards, and dispatched them via cover addresses to Max.

How important the Soviet considered me to be can be judged from the fact that on two occasions Moscow headquarters sent a Secret Service *general* to see me and discuss future tasks. We met first in Vienna, and then in the Soviet stronghold of Berlin-Karlshorst. Apart from these high-level conferences, I travelled on some twenty other occasions to Berlin, where I submitted verbal reports to Russian intelligence chiefs. I was in their highest espionage category.

They gave me all the aid they could. To enable me to be highly regarded by my superiors in General Gehlen's Federal Intelligence Service, they supplied me with genuine State secrets which I, on my Soviet superiors' orders, presented to my West German spy chiefs. It worked, and the controllers of the Federal Intelligence Service praised me as "a man who knows how to get hold of Russian top secrets, and scores better results than anyone else".

East German policeman
threatening a photographer
at a frontier post

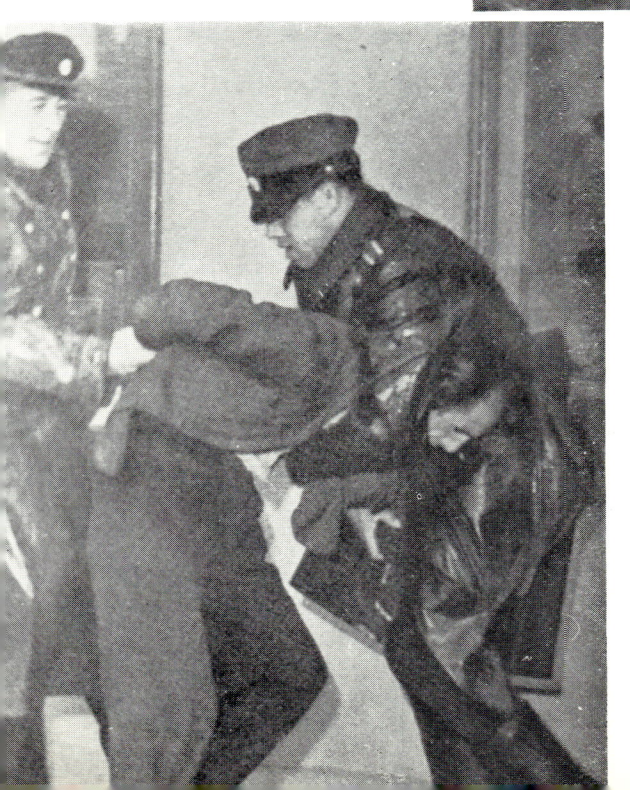

East German
Security Police
arresting a 'suspect'
in Berlin

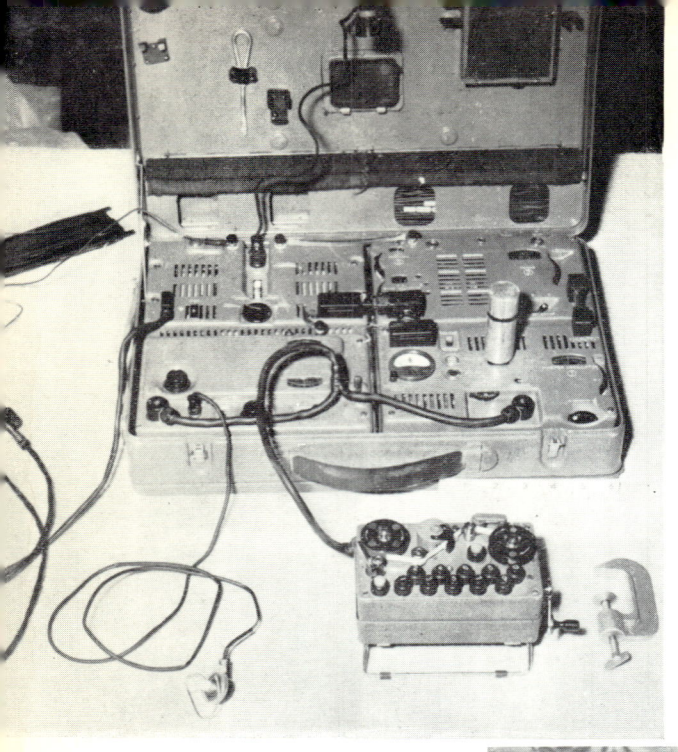

A radio transmitter powerful enough to se[nd] coded espionage messages to Moscow Secret Service head-quarters

A tape keying device (*right*)

An electronic listening device (*below*), disguised as a piece of wood, which Czechoslovak agents attempted to place in the U.S. State Department

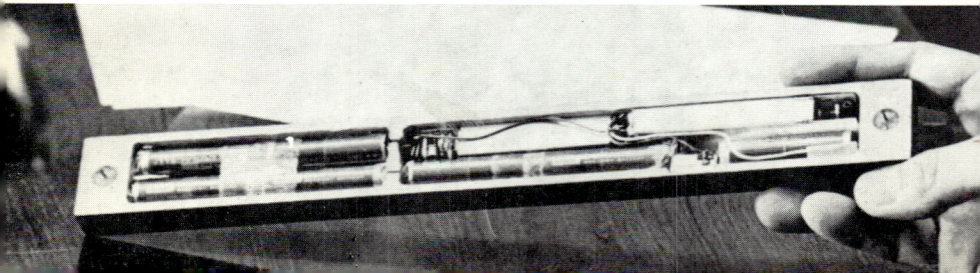

To show their appreciation of the extraordinary successes Hans and I had achieved, the Gehlen organization invested us with the Order for Devoted Service—the medal showing St George slaying the Dragon! Moscow also honoured our efforts: we received letters of praise from no less a person than Soviet espionage chief Shelyepin, supplemented by a special premium of two thousand West German Marks for each of us.

I did not make the mistake other spies sometimes do: I did not use my normal office hours for espionage activities for the Soviet. I photographed top-secret documents *after* office hours at the Munich-Pullach headquarters, when there was no danger of any other officer suddenly coming into my office and catching me. Internal security didn't suspect anything.

The precaution of working this way had another advantage. I was able to tape-record commentaries to supplement the information revealed by the photographs.

Every six to eight weeks I pretended to be obliged to travel to Berlin to attend to Gehlen business, and on each occasion I met my Soviet leader officer, Alfred, and sometimes my superior, Max. I usually used an American car for my excursions to Berlin.

Tiebel regularly took microfilms and other espionage matter to the Russians in the secret compartment of his suitcase, while ostensibly travelling on official Gehlen business.

[When Felfe was caught the indictment charged him, Hans Clemens, and Erwin Tiebel with having transmitted information to the Soviets regarding operational plans and tactics in the West German Federal Intelligence Service; with photographing for the Russians secret documents affecting the existence of the Federal Republic and the safety of foreign armed forces in West Germany.]

For some inexplicable reason I was not remanded in custody in the Durlach Prison, which is specially used for the Federal Court. Instead I was taken to the Remand Prison in Reifstahlstrasse, Karlsruhe. To my surprise, I was allowed many privileges. The Investigation Judge of the Federal Court, von Engelbrechten, allowed me to leave my cell almost at will in order to play chess in the library. My chess partner was an ex-Government official and chairman of a food factory, Jürgen Ziebell. I couldn't have found a more convenient companion, for, during World War II, Ziebell had been an intelligence officer and a friend of mine.

I used my freedom in the Remand Prison to continue my espionage activities for the Soviet. I compiled detailed reports on West German interrogation methods, using as a code a current best-seller. I smuggled my communications out of the prison inside journals which remand prisoners prepared for dispatch for a Karlsruhe publishing firm. With Ziebell's help, it was easy for me

I

to address a journal to a cover address. Every one of the coded reports reached my Russian superiors.

I employed another communication method, using my mother, who lived in the East German town of Leipzig. Investigation Judge von Engelbrechten read all my letters and found the texts harmless. But these letters contained additional text, written with invisible ink. The authorities didn't allow for invisible-ink supplies reaching me in prison.

I also attempted to obtain means to saw through the iron grille of my cell window, but the tools I requested couldn't be got in, so, through my mother, I requested the Russians to provide me with a pass key. This, too, proved impracticable. I then prepared a plan for the Soviet Secret Service to free me from prison by force, but this also failed.

The Felfe-Clemens-Tiebel trial, which opened on July 8th, 1963, before the Federal Court in Karlsruhe, became known as the greatest espionage trial in the Federal Republic of West Germany. During the two weeks' hearings most of the Felfe-Clemens-Tiebel espionage activities for the Soviet Secret Service were proved.

Chief State Prosecutor Fischer said:

"Dealing with Felfe and Clemens, people rightly call this high-treason trial the greatest since the end of the War. The Federal Court has not been able to unearth every single detail of the espionage activities of the three accused, which covered a period of ten years, but it has nevertheless been possible to draw open the curtain sufficiently to recognize the seriousness of the damage inflicted on the Federal Republic." Chief State Prosecutor Fischer underlined that Felfe even continued his espionage activities while on remand in custody.

Sentencing the accused on July 23rd, 1963, Federal Judge Werner made it plain that the material which Felfe and Clemens betrayed to the Soviet Secret Service consisted of important State secrets. There was no doubt that Felfe had been a top agent for the Soviet Secret Service whilst in the very centre of the West German counter-intelligence, and that he had inflicted very considerable damage to West Germany and her allies.

"Lust for gain has been the motive for Felfe's and Clemens's treacherous activities," declared the Judge. "Even Tiebel, who was only a courier, must be sentenced as if he had been an executive, and not merely an assistant, because he was well aware of the importance of his activities."

Felfe was found guilty of high treason; treacherous connections with the Soviet Secret Service; breach of the Official Secrets Act; breach of professional conduct; and bribery. He was sentenced to fourteen years' imprisonment with hard labour, with loss of civil rights for an additional eight years, and only one year of the period he had been remanded in custody was deducted from the prison term. He was also ordered to pay a fine of seventy thousand West German Marks.

Clemens was found guilty of the same crimes, and was sentenced to ten years' imprisonment with hard labour and loss of civil rights for an additional five years. But the full two years of his remand in custody were deducted from the prison term. He too was fined seventy thousand West German Marks.

Tiebel was sentenced to three years' imprisonment with hard labour, and the full time he was remanded in custody was deducted from his prison term. He was fined four thousand West German Marks.

17

Hotbed West Germany

WEST GERMANY as a whole is a natural objective for Soviet espionage efforts, and the spy school of Prakhovka annually turns out between 200 and 250 "genuine German" resident spy operators who are able to pose as citizens of West Germany.

Because the Soviet Secret Service is considerably strengthened by East German, Czechoslovak, Polish, and other Communist 'sister' organizations, the Communist espionage networks in West Germany are powerful, dangerous forces.

Official West German figures, released in Bonn in December 1962, disclosed that some 16,000 Communist spies are known to operate in the Federal Republic of West Germany. The same statement also revealed the efficiency of the West German and Allied counter-intelligence and security forces in the Federal Republic. It declared:

> While 566 people have been arrested for espionage in the year of 1958, in 1959 the number has already grown to 2325; in 1960 the Eastern Bloc [West German official description for Russia and her satellite countries] has lost 3585 spy operators. In 1961 and 1962 the figure of arrests of Eastern Bloc spies amounted to from 6 to 10 every day.

For the Soviet and the six other Red satellite espionage systems it is an enormous task to replace the spy operators annually exposed or arrested in the Federal Republic. But let us see exactly how the individuals work.

Willi Knipp was born in 1927 in the West German industrial city of Düsseldorf, where he worked as a baker. In the fifties his health deteriorated, and, unable to follow his occupation, he found employment with the Federal Government. But Knipp was discontented. He considered himself too good to be simply a messenger carrying documents from one office to another, and frequently voiced his resentment at being kept in low-grade service category. It was, he said, "because I didn't come from the right family and didn't know anyone in a leading position who could secure me promotion". When his application for financial aid, which he claimed he needed for medical treatment, was turned down, hatred against his superiors developed into obsession.

Knipp's friend Josef Paul was a chauffeur who secretly worked as a courier for the East German resident spy operator in the Federal Republic. Paul informed his espionage chief about the messenger's mood and suggested he could be a valuable recruit, as he had direct access to files and documents.

Despite his grudge, Willi Knipp did not hold any Communist sympathies, and when his friend Josef Paul suggested he should be a spy Knipp refused.

The resident spy operator was a typical East German Secret Service officer, and defeat had no place in his vocabulary. Knowing that Willi Knipp could supply valuable documents, he was determined to recruit him.

Introduced to Knipp by Paul, the master spy filled Willi with plenty of Schnapps, but even when semi-drunk Willi refused to turn. The Secret Service officer then said:

"You're a fool, Willi. Your Government chiefs are not your friends, and you know it well. You are a capable and intelligent fellow, but they make you work for a miserable salary, and you know you won't ever have the chance of being more than a low-grade messenger who carries bundles of paper from one office to another.

"You know full well that every word I am saying is what's in your own mind. Why did they not grant you the application for the requested financial aid which you need so urgently to restore your health? Because they despise a low-grade messenger, because they don't consider it necessary to help you in any way. If you can't do your job any longer they'll find plenty of others who will gladly do it. So, think, Willi. Are they your friends? They don't care about you, but, like a fool, *you* think you must be loyal to them. . . ."

He then took a wad of 150 West German Marks out of his wallet and handed the money to the almost drunk Knipp, saying:

"Your real friends are on the other side of Germany, Willi. Take this money; it's something towards your medical bills. It is a present to you, and doesn't put you under any obligation to work for me. But, if you aren't a fool, you'll let me have photographs of certain documents which are on the secret list. I'll give you a suitable camera for this purpose, and I'll pay you 150

Marks per month, and I'll increase the amount if your work is worth it. Think, Willi, and let me know your answer, when you have considered everything and when you have made up your mind."

Willi Knipp finally agreed to become an agent in the West German Federal Ministry, and was supplied with a Minox camera and a small clothes-brush which was the container for the spy camera—small and inconspicuous enough to be carried without causing suspicion.

From then on Willi Knipp carried the clothes-brush on him whenever he took confidential documents from one office of the Federal Ministry to another. On many occasions he locked himself in his duty room, took the camera from the clothes-brush, and photographed all the documents in his case. Thanks to this the Berlin-Pankow espionage directors were well informed of what was happening in the Federal Ministry from 1956 until 1960.

At first the East German resident spy operator complained that the documents marked "top secret" and "strictly confidential" were comparatively unimportant for Berlin-Pankow headquarters, because "they did not contain anything new". He told Knipp to get top-secret documents not carried along the Ministry corridors —the kind usually transported in locked courier cases.

Knipp smuggled one of these leather courier cases out of the Ministry and took it home. He cut out the lock and sent it to East Berlin, where a master key for all courier cases was made.

Almost by return, Berlin-Pankow headquarters supplied the skeleton key, hidden in a propelling pencil. But when Knipp tried to open a courier case with it—it didn't work! He decided to act on his own initiative. He stole a key from the duty room, and found it would unlock every courier case. He left as replacement for the stolen key the useless key which Berlin-Pankow had supplied.

According to his confession, Willi Knipp received from the East German resident spy operator about 13,000 West German Marks during the last two years of his espionage career. And for this money he supplied the East German Secret Service between the years 1958 and 1959 alone with approximately 3600 photographs —containing confidential reports on the West German Federal Security Service, and also instructions for security measures safeguarding the country from air attacks, and precautions against sabotage.

Willi Knipp and his friend Josef Paul were sentenced to terms of imprisonment, but great damage had been caused to the Federal Republic of West Germany. The East German resident spy operator escaped prosecution by fleeing to the other side of the Iron Curtain. His place was at once filled by a new spy who carried on where his colleague had left off.

Naturally, Soviet and other Communist Secret Services concentrate on West German Ministries, institutions, research centres, etc. But with West Germany still containing American, British, and French forces, and with many West German industrial concerns also working so very close with their Allies, an equal amount of attention is devoted to them by Soviet espionage sources.

An illustration is the case of the forty-two-year-old U.S. citizen Harold Noah Borger, sentenced to imprisonment in 1962 by the Federal Court in Karlsruhe for having attempted to supply the East German Secret Service with intelligence reports on military secrets. Borger was the first American tried by a West German court.

He had been a major in the U.S. Army, and first came in contact with Communist espionage agents during his military service. On his discharge from the U.S. Armed Forces he established himself as a New York businessman, and travelled about not only in the United States, but also throughout Europe.

At the beginning of 1960 Borger, complying with orders from East German Secret Service headquarters, established himself in West Germany. He was to obtain intelligence information on the exact structure of the U.S. Armed Forces stationed in West Germany; on manoeuvres of the American Army in the Federal Republic; on instructions from U.S. Armed Forces H.Q. regarding nuclear and chemical warfare; and on all other U.S. military secrets. When finally arrested he confessed that he had passed this important information, including microfilms of numerous documents, to the headquarters of the East German Secret Service.

Borger acted as a resident spy operator, and directed a network of agents and informers. His fall came when he attempted to recruit a U.S. soldier. The man reported the fact to the authorities, and Borger was shadowed and caught.

This was the end of an agent who worked so hard and with such success for the East German Secret Service that the U.S. Army Command was forced to make considerable changes in its strategic organization and plans.

The court proceedings against the thirty-four-year-old Second Lieutenant of the East German Secret Service Gerhard Block and his wife, Inge, which opened before the Third Senate of the Federal Court at Karlsruhe on August 7th, 1963, prove what painstaking care Red spy chiefs take in disguising their agents who have managed to slip into West Germany.

Up to the time of his arrest in November 1962 in Mannheim, Gerhard Block had been known only under his 'cover' name of Herbert Pfeiffer. His 'cover' occupation was a job in the warehouse of an industrial concern in Mannheim, but his real occupation was "spy leader" of Waldemar Jende, who operated in one of the largest U.S. ammunition depots in Europe; and also of Christa Gotter, who was employed in an American bank in Heidelberg. His wife, Inge, who posed under the 'cover' name of Annemarie Pfeiffer, helped him in monitoring and decoding radio messages.

In the spring of 1957, when Block worked as a post-office employee in East Berlin, an officer of the East German Secret Service headquarters proposed to him that he should change his post-office career to that of an agent of the Secret Service. "At first I wasn't enthusiastic about it," Block stated in evidence to the Federal Court, "but after some consideration I decided that working for the Secret Service would not be contrary to my political convictions. Now, too, it is my firm conviction that Communism alone is right. . . ."

Having been trained as a spy in the East German espionage school at Gransee, and afterwards in East Berlin, Block was ordered to "change into the welder Herbert Pfeiffer" (who, incidentally, lived in Halle and had no idea that his identity was being used for espionage cover purposes). East German Secret Service headquarters considered Pfeiffer's identity a perfect one because the man had worked after World War II for several years in the South of France; apart from this, Halle was in East Germany, and consequently the real Pfeiffer would be unlikely to prove a danger as a possible leak source.

In order to make Block's new identity as foolproof as possible he was sent to a place near Marseille where Pfeiffer had worked. Block travelled in October 1959 from France to West Germany, using Pfeiffer's documents and his pay-book. He had been ordered to find some sort of occupation in Mannheim so as to be able to acclimatize himself.

At Easter 1960 Block-"Pfeiffer" was summoned to East Berlin, where he was informed that he had been promoted to Second Lieutenant of the East German Ministry for State Security, and his monthly salary would be 700 German Marks. In July 1960 he married in his real name of Block, but a few months later both appeared once again at a registry office: this time the marriage certificate was issued to Herbert and Annemarie Pfeiffer.

Block's main espionage activities concentrated on the information which he obtained from the spy Jende about American military transports, and which he prepared and transmitted to Secret Service headquarters in East Berlin. His and his wife's career in West Germany earned them well-deserved prison sentences.

The British and French sectors of West Germany are also important objectives for Communist espionage. Maria Knuth's case is an example of the Soviet Secret Service using the "beautiful woman spy" method.

Maria Knuth was a thoroughly trained Russian master spy who posed as a German actress, and who almost continuously entertained British and American officers at her luxurious flat in a suburb of Cologne. For several years the numerous agents and informers of her espionage ring regularly supplied her with secret reports, plans, and documents on military dispositions, airfield construction, the organization of the West German police and frontier forces, and full details of the West German Army, which she passed on for transmission to Moscow.

One of her major agents was Inspector Hermann Westbold of the Frankfurt-am-Main police—an officer whom the Allies considered particularly trustworthy. When arrested Westbold confessed that he had been a Soviet agent for several years and had been paid at least £45 per month for his services.

Maria Knuth herself was caught by M.I.5 agents in the Central Post Office, Cologne, and documents in her possession at the time were said to have greatly shocked Allied commanders. Four other members of the network were arrested, and a powerful short-wave radio receiver-transmitter, together with valuable espionage equipment, was found. But the rest of the spy ring, including Maria Knuth's superior, were never caught.

In the French zone of West Germany many Russians and other Communist resident spy operators, and their espionage networks, have been detected and destroyed during recent years, but the French military authorities and the West German counterintelligence consider this little consolation because of the serious damage caused by spies before they are apprehended.

Yet another example of concentrated Soviet espionage in West Germany is the case of the former U.S. intelligence agent Michael R. Rothkrug, who was accused of having stolen top-secret documents and was tried before Judge Dewitt White of the American Control Commission.

Rothkrug, who came from Westport, Connecticut, had an excellent record with the U.S. Central Intelligence Agency during World War II. After he resigned in 1952 he went to Berlin, where he established a business with a German partner.

His apparently respectable business was a cover for his activities as a Soviet master spy. His outstanding successes were of such importance that evidence had to be given *in camera* at his trial, and for security reasons details were never released.

The next example is equally revealing.

United States authorities both in Washington and in West Germany were stunned when it was found out that a Russian agent had managed to photograph the private diary of Major-General Robert Grow, the U.S. Military Attaché in Moscow, when he visited the U.S. headquarters in Frankfurt-am-Main. No-one ever suspected that the diary had been in other hands, until half a year later the book *On the Path of War* was published in East Berlin, and it was stated that the British Major Richard Squires, who vanished in Germany in 1947, had written it. The Russian agent who photographed the diary many years after Major Squires's disappearance was never found. . . .

These are but a few samples of Red espionage in West Germany. Russian and other Iron Curtain intelligence activities in this part of the free world are so numerous that it would require many volumes to record all the cases. Since the first Soviet Secret Service network in the Allied zones of Germany, which was directed by operators Sedov and Shulkyn, was discovered in 1946 there has not been a single month without a new spy case in the area, right up to the present day.

18

Filling the Gaps

THE West German Government in Bonn state that the Communist espionage networks in the Federal Republic lost between six and ten master spies and agents every single day of the year 1962, and afterwards. And the supreme chief of the Soviet Secret Service, Vladimir Semichastny, revealed in his address to the Kremlin's Party Presidium in January 1963 that, "during the 'black year of 1962' over eight thousand resident operators and their assistants have been lost to the service" in all countries of the free world.

These losses represent colossal setbacks to the Communists, but, although substantial numbers of spy losses are due to the efficiency of Western counter-intelligence and security forces, it must be realized that these account for only a minor part of the *total* Communist losses. According to General Abel—now not only the Commander-in-Chief of the entire Soviet Secret Service activities in the English-speaking world, but also chief adviser and consultant to all other foreign divisions of the First Directorate at Moscow headquarters—the picture of the Russian Intelligence Foreign Service was explained as follows when he addressed the Kremlin's Party Presidium in January 1963:

"The reference to losses in the Foreign Service does not, in fact, mean that all these men and women are a complete write-off. The year 1962 shows that only 19·8 per cent of the total losses are cases where resident operators and agents of all categories have been arrested by Imperialist security. The remaining 80·2 per cent are men and women who come within the following categories:

"(a) Resident operators and agents of all categories warned by their Control Agents that Imperialist security is likely to discover them and who consequently left their country of assignment before detention.

"(b) Network agents of all categories, whose resident operators were either under Imperialist security surveillance or already under arrest, who felt that they could become involved and left the country of assignment.

"(c) Resident operators and agents of all categories betrayed, but who succeeded in escaping.

"All the three categories show that these 80·2 per cent have been lost to the Service only as far as their operations in the countries of assignment are concerned. But they are not a write-off. They are of immense value as instructors in specialized training centres and schools, because of their important field experience. Some are also of considerable value in the divisions of the Foreign Directorate, being experts on various countries. Some can be issued with new identities and returned for operational duties in different districts of the countries from which they succeeded in escaping."

The five major Soviet spy schools, Gaczyna, Prakhovka, Soyuznaya, Vostochnaya, and Novaya, now turn out over two thousand master spies of the Gordon Lonsdale, William Arthur Mortimer, Dr Geoffrey Noble class—i.e. men and women fully converted into 'genuine' citizens of the country of their assignment, who are able to work under perfect covers. But as the supreme chief of the Soviet Secret Service revealed that over eight thousand resident operators and their assistants of various categories were lost in 1962 alone, it means that, apart from the two thousand-odd resident spy operators from the five main spy schools, Moscow Secret Service headquarters must find more than six thousand additional agents yearly to make good their losses and keep their world-wide espionage system at full strength.

Communist East Berlin and East Germany play a leading rôle in the recruitment of agents and informers for the intelligence services, because of the favourable geographical position. There are so-called 'set pattern' methods which have produced consistent successes—especially among refugees from Iron Curtain countries who have sought asylum in the West, but who still have close relatives living in a Communist East European country.

Max Eckstein, a metal-worker, managed to escape from East to West Berlin and found employment in an important Allied-controlled concern manufacturing components on the secret list. His parents and his brother still lived in the Red part of Germany, and the East German Secret Service H.Q. in Berlin-Pankow decided to use this fact to force him to work as an informer.

One day an East German recruitment agent came to Eckstein and handed him a piece of paper with the following message: "You can unburden your conscience and save the livelihood of your brother, which means that your old parents will be able to live comfortably in their old age." The agent explained: Eckstein was requested to carry out industrial espionage in the plant in which he worked. He was told he would receive from the East German Secret Service considerable sums of money as reward for his services; his brother would be given a well-paid job in East Germany. But, the agent threatened, if Eckstein refused his brother and parents would be prosecuted and imprisoned.

West Berlin counter-intelligence had the East German Secret Service recruitment agent under surveillance and arrested him when he tried to hand espionage equipment over to Eckstein.

This method is widely employed not only in West Germany, but in most other countries with refugees from Communism. Only a small number of refugees report espionage recruitment approaches to the authorities because of their fear of being deprived of asylum and deported.

Another successful method of espionage recruitment is the use of fake telegrams and letters.

A nursemaid, for instance, who was classed by the Berlin-Karlshorst branch headquarters of the Soviet Secret Service as "a useful informer", unexpectedly received a telegram from her mother who lived in the East German town of Glauchau. The mother wired that she was "seriously ill" and asked the daughter to come at once.

The nursemaid left and, when she arrived in East Berlin, was taken to Berlin-Karlshorst branch headquarters of the Soviet Secret Service and asked to work as a spy in West Germany. The telegram from her mother had been a Soviet ruse to induce the girl to come to East Berlin. The nursemaid was warned that she and her mother would be sent to a slave-labour camp if she refused to "give patriotic assistance" to the Soviet Secret Service, but that she would receive generous payment for services.

The frightened girl agreed to co-operate, and received a short training course in East Berlin. She was then sent back to West Germany, with orders to report to a contact-man. But she was intercepted by West German security officers and, when questioned, broke down and confessed.

An official report by the West German security forces' investigator on the interrogation of one Herr Miehlke discloses the following:

> The interrogated's brother, Günther Miehlke, born May 21st, 1929, and living in the D.D.R. [East Germany] in Ribnitz Meklenburg, Bahnhofstrasse 26, repeatedly requested his brother to come for a visit to the East Zone.
>
> This spring Günther Miehlke, who is a citizen of the D.D.R., came for a fortnight into the Federal Republic and visited the interrogated. He informed the interrogated that his father was seriously ill and would like to see the interrogated before he

died. The East German brother stressed that the father's death could be expected at any time and added that, when the sad occurrence happened, the question of the legacy would need to be gone into.

Shortly after his return to the East Zone Günther Miehlke sent the interrogated a telegram in which he informed him that his father was dying. By registered letter he sent the permit for his brother to enter the East Zone. The interrogated then travelled to Ribnitz on May 15th. He found his father in excellent health. The father did not know anything of what had been going on.

When the interrogated challenged his brother Günther about the matter he was told that he had been under instructions to lure him into the East Zone so that he could be recruited as an agent for the Communist Secret Service.

At first the interrogated was forced to live with his brother, because the parents lived in a small room and could not accommodate him. The interrogated had been living in a well-furnished self-contained apartment in the Federal Republic, and grumbled about the poor living accommodation. His brother told him that shortly he would be getting an apartment in Ribnitz which would be even better furnished than the one he had left behind.

The interrogated found work in the Energy Supply Distribution Centre and earned during three weeks 218 D-Marks. His brother helped him repeatedly with additional sums of money. He was given an apartment.

At the end of May he was summoned to the District Council. There a member of the Secret Service told him that, due to the fact that he earned so little, he would give him the possibility to make much more money. He explained: Being a West German citizen, the interrogated could work for the Communist Secret Service in the Federal Republic. The interrogated refused.

A few days later he was summoned again. The same proposition was made. But the Secret Service officer added that, if need be, he could be forced to do as he was told. Despite this threat, the interrogated again refused.

A few days later he was sacked. The following day he was summoned to appear at State Security H.Q. There it was made clear to him that he was unlikely to find a new job, and that his precarious financial position would ultimately force him to accept the Secret Service offer.

The officer then told him that he was to travel to Wiesbaden, where he was to keep under continuous observation four buildings in which American forces headquarters, as well as the U.S. Commander-in-Chief, were billeted. He was also to visit places which American officers frequented and was to try to involve them in conversations which might provide him with valuable information. He was shown a map on which the buildings were marked, and the officer repeatedly made it clear to him that he had no other alternative but to accept the Secret Service offer. . . .

Due to the fact that the interrogated refused the latest offer, a few days later he received an official notice to vacate his apartment.

He was evicted and succeeded in finding a small furnished room. He and his family lived on the money they got from selling their clothes. On July 2nd the interrogated and his family managed to escape across the frontier into West Berlin.

During 1962 in the Federal Republic of West Germany alone 293 cases were discovered of people who had sought freedom in the West being forced into espionage work for the Soviet; in other Western countries in which refugees from Communist countries have found asylum 118 more such cases were recorded in the same period.

Citizens of the Communist bloc, who live and work in Russia or any of her satellites, are constantly being recruited as agents and informers. 'Suitable' citizens are chosen from lists and taken to Secret Police or Secret Service headquarters.

How these men and women are 'persuaded' to become Communist Secret Service agents and informers is shown in the following report which a West German security forces' interrogator submitted to the *Staatsanwaltschaft* (Office of the Director of Public Prosecutions) to decide whether the interrogated woman should be prosecuted. This report states:

Fräulein B. worked in the leather works in Ludwigslust (East Germany). At the end of June or at the beginning of July a member of the Communist Secret Service, who introduced himself as Ernst Sens, called at her place of work and requested her to become an agent of the intelligence network operating in the Federal Republic. She was eventually forced to undertake in writing that she was willing to carry out any order. . . .

Her first assignment was to become friendly with a man suspected by the State Security, and she was given the cover-name of "Amsel". But the interrogated woman did not carry out her orders and instead applied for an inter-zonal passport, which, strangely enough, was granted. She moved into the Federal Republic.

She kept in touch with her parents by post. Her letters were, however, intercepted by the State Security, and were answered by Sens. After her disappearance Sens had visited her parents and asked about the daughter. When told that she had gone to West Germany he did not ask further questions.

A fortnight later Fräulein B. received a letter from Sens, in which she was threatened that the *Kriminalpolizei* [C.I.D.] would be informed about her undertaking to work as an agent for the Communist intelligence network in the Federal Republic if she did not reply to him without fail.

Fräulein B. then went to an official bureau in Düsseldorf, near Graf Adolf Platz. Fräulein B. cannot remember the name under which the office was listed, or the name of the street or the building number. She claims that German and English people have been working there together. She produced a letter to a Mr Gilbert. Later Mr Gilbert told her that his real name was Reuter. Reuter requested Fräulein B. to return. At first Mr Reuter agreed that she should go, but later he ordered Fräulein B. not to write any more letters. He discouraged her from travelling back.

Fräulein B. discontinued writing to Sens, but received two letters from him, which she produced at the above-mentioned official bureau.

In one (from her parents) was a permit to enter East Germany; on May 1 she travelled to Ludwigslust. She registered with the police, and the following day Herr Sens called. He questioned her as to whether she had said anything in West Germany about her undertaking to carry out espionage, and also about the exchange of letters. Fräulein B. replied in the negative. When Fräulein B. told him that she intended to return to West Germany he ordered her not to go to Düsseldorf, but to travel instead to Bonn. There she was to engage in intimate relations with Ministry officials. But first there would be training at a "school for agents". Sens told her that she would not be allowed to return to Communist East Germany for at least six months, and during this time she was to write down everything and take photographs.

The senior office at Schwerin, however, considered it to be wiser if Fräulein B. remained for some time in East Germany on probation.

She was consequently ordered to approach the twenty-seven-year-old chaplain Kegelbein, in Schloss-Strasse, Ludwigslust. She was to tell him that she had returned from West Germany and that she wanted to become a Catholic. During the conversation instructions she was to attempt to seduce the chaplain, and was to report to State Security what happened. Fräulein B. went to the chaplain; he gave her a number of books to read for instruction purposes. Before the lessons commenced she slipped away to West Berlin.

She had been ordered to apply to the manager of the Station Restaurant in Ludwigslust, a Herr Beyer, for a job as a saleswoman. State Security knew that Herr Beyer had a weakness for young girls, so if necessary she was to have an affair with him, and worm out of him information about his connections with the Federal Republic.

She was also required, if necessary, to have intimate relations with a Herr Behn who had come from West Berlin into Communist Germany. Her orders were to find out from him whom he would meet in West Berlin if he travelled there. If it

Alexander Rado (*top left*)—one
of the greatest spies

Photo United Press

Lieutenant-Colonel Siegfried
Dombrowski (*top right*)—the
East German Secret Service
chief who defected to the West

Bogdan Nikolayevich Stashynsky

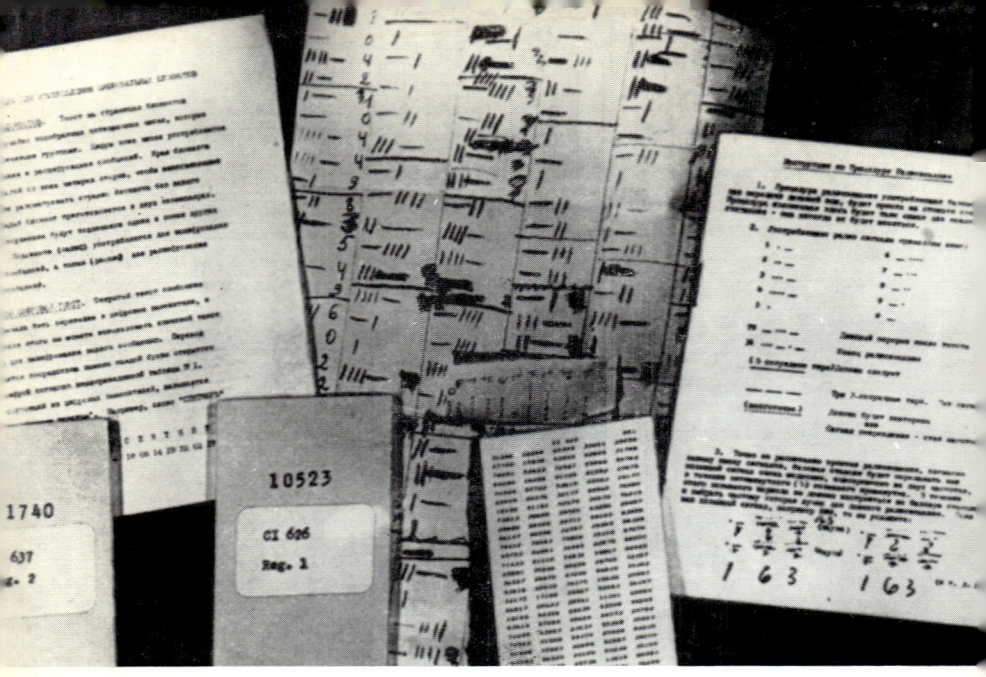

Codes, notebooks, instructions for using them, etc.

Photos United Press

The secret instructions which Skripov wrote to the woman agent
on the back of an innocuous letter

4. 2. 63

PLEASE COME HERE ON
SATURDAY 9TH FEBRUARY
(NINE) AT USUAL TIME
AND BRING THE PARCEL
(PARCEL) YOU WERE ASKED
TO HAND OVER TO MY FRIEND
THE END

turned out that Herr Behn worked with Western "agent centres" she should pretend to be interested in working in these same places.

On June 17th Fräulein B. was also ordered to visit certain restaurants and eavesdrop on conversations.

None of these orders were carried out because Fräulein B. went to West Berlin after she had gone to chaplain Kegelbein and before she could be forced to comply with her instructions from State Security.

The West German and other Western files are full of records of this method of recruitment. During the past two years several hundred residents in West Berlin and West Germany received letters from Communist Secret Service recruitment agents, threatening them to disclose incriminating material to West German security forces and judicial authorities if the recipients were unwilling to engage in espionage activities in the Federal Republic.

In an effort to emphasize the threats, these letters in many cases contain photostats of enrolment forms, which the individual forcibly signed when being 'persuaded' to join the Communist Secret Service. They sometimes contain photostats of parts of reports which the individual had sent from West Berlin or from the Federal Republic to his Secret Service superiors before he broke off relations.

A lathe operator, for example, was requested by the State Security Command in Brandenburg that he should immediately report to Berlin-Pankow H.Q. if he wished to avoid the West Berlin police being notified of his past collaboration with the East German Ministry for State Security, and of his intelligence reports on a number of people.

A soldier who managed to escape from the Communist People's Army in East Germany and had been granted asylum in the Federal Republic received the following letter:

> It was with astonishment that we learned of your unexpected change of address. We are, however, still interested in maintaining contact with you under the present circumstances.
>
> We must impress upon you that, should you disagree with us, several authorities in West Germany would be interested in the reports which you previously sent to us. We attach a sample of the material we are referring to, so as to refresh your memory.
>
> You may reach us under the following address. . . .

Berlin-Pankow headquarters of the East German Secret Service, usually acting on direct orders from the Soviet Berlin-Karlshorst branch headquarters, frequently advertise 'jobs' in West German

K

newspapers. These advertisements are always cloaked with "respectable cover" addresses.

Advertisements appeared in the *Bonner Generalanzeiger*, offering jobs as a waiter in a hotel and as a chauffeur to a diplomat.

A twenty-five-year-old West German waiter applied for the hotel job. He received a letter from the employment agency *Vermittlungsbüro Ruschkamp* at 44 Helmholzer Strasse, Berlin-Oberschoeneweide, offering a good position with "excellent prospects" at a beach hotel. He was invited to travel to East Berlin at the agency's expense.

The unsuspecting waiter accepted the invitation. In East Berlin the *Vermittlungsbüro Ruschkamp*, instead of arranging the promised job at the beach hotel for him, took him to the Recruiting Division of the East German Secret Service in Berlin-Pankow, where he was 'persuaded' to engage in intelligence activities for East Germany against military targets in the Federal Republic. The job at the beach hotel, which the waiter had wanted, was never mentioned.

A thirty-two-year-old Bremen journalist saw an inconspicuous advertisement in *Die Welt* and applied to the alleged Interpress Newspaper Agency in East Berlin for the advertised position. On his first appearance at the office of the Interpress Newspaper Agency the supposed editor commissioned him to write a report on the development of Bremen. He was told that this was to test his writing abilities and to help assess the financial basis for his proposed employment. He was told that he would be paid for his 'test' report, because the Interpress Newspaper Agency wanted his confidence. The Bremen journalist wrote the report. When he presented it to the editor he was persuaded to carry out intelligence work for the Soviet Secret Service.

Despite continued warnings to beware of jobs connected with East Berlin or East German addresses, many still disregard the cautions because they consider them 'propaganda'. Some of these job-seekers return to the West and, in fact, engage in espionage activities for the Soviet and other Iron Curtain Secret Services, because of fear.

It is estimated that during 1966 alone between fourteen and seventeen hundred recruitment attempts were made in East Berlin by combined Communist Secret Services.

The Soviet Secret Service agent Epp was ordered to start a love affair with Fräulein K., who was a confidential secretary in a West German Ministry with access to strictly confidential and top-secret documents of value to Moscow headquarters. Epp was successful, and Fräulein K. became his mistress. Arrangements were made for compromising photographs, suitable for future blackmail, to be taken by secretly installed cameras.

In due course Epp requested the girl to let him photograph top-secret documents and to supply him with any other confidential information she could collect. When she refused Epp showed her photographs which pictured her in compromising circumstances, and threatened that copies would even be scattered from an aeroplane over Bonn if she did not "come to her senses".

Fräulein K. came to her senses—but not in the way Epp had meant it. She confided to her superior, and the result was that the work of Epp, and some of his comrades, was stopped.

East German Secret Service agent Engelmann started love affairs with four confidential secretaries of the West German Ministry of Defence and succeeded in blackmailing them into working for his spy ring. A Soviet Secret Service agent succeeded in seducing another confidential secretary of the same Ministry, and while on a winter holiday with his mistress, in a mountain resort, he recruited her for espionage work.

In most cases secretly taken photographs showing women in compromising circumstances prove to be very effective blackmail material. Few women have the courage of Fräulein K. to confess to the authorities. Records prove that most women yield to blackmail, and their weakness is revealed only when they are eventually arrested on charges of espionage for Communist Secret Services.

Continually on the look-out for new agents and informers, Soviet and other Iron Curtain espionage directors bind every single operator to report to his or her superior anyone potentially useful for Secret Service work. If the possible future recruit is considered by the Secret Service security officers to be a likely *Novator* (Russian Secret Service description for a newly recruited agent abroad) another agent is instructed to collect information on the possible candidate—concentrating in the first place on hobbies, financial status, loyalty to country, sexual abnormalities, drinking habits, preference for women, etc. The agent entrusted with this task is required to 'comb' even the distant past of the possible candidate, in the hope of discovering something hidden which could make recruitment easy.

It was discovered that the Soviet Secret Service agent Oumard was paid 300 German Marks per month, in addition to other payments received for intelligence work, for collecting "background material on possible candidates". Another Communist Secret Service agent was paid still more for 'combing' the private lives of fourteen officials of the U.S. Embassy in Bonn. Still another agent was ordered to provide the Polish Secret Service with "all background information suitable for recruitment of Poles living in West Germany", and received for his part-time work 500 German Marks per month.

Apart from the above recruitment methods, the combined Communist Secret Service also believes very much in the so-called 'economic' method. The Secret Service recruitment officers, who are ordered to follow this pattern, concentrate on individuals who are hopelessly in debt, or who are known to be willing to do anything for a substantial amount of money.

The Danish diplomat Blechinberg was recruited some years ago for Communist espionage. It was also the temptation of money which Herr Otto, who was sentenced for espionage by a Federal Court, could not resist. The photographer Cassell also fell for the temptation to make money by photographing from an aircraft Army installations in the Federal Republic—until he was arrested by West German counter-intelligence.

In West Germany 12,994 men and women have confessed during the past eight years that they were recruited as sub-agents or informers for the Soviet or other Iron Curtain Secret Services. Only a minority of these recruits confess, however; the majority work on undetected.

19

Recruiting Agents Overseas

INVESTIGATION by the Committee on Un-American Activities of the House of Representatives reveals that the Secret Police in Communist countries gather information on potential recruits, employing a system that involves checking mail to and from the U.S.A., including the names of senders of food parcels to Iron Curtain countries. A check is then made to see if the occupations of potentially useful people can be determined by means other than direct approach. When the person's occupation cannot be learned in any other way direct contact is made.

Oddly enough, results beneficial to Communism sometimes flow from contacts which originally appear to be useless. The procedure is for an Iron Curtain representative in the United States to telephone someone he wishes to contact, and explain that he has heard of him from a business friend known to them both. He will add that he is passing through the city and would like to meet for a talk. He then spends an hour or so in friendly conversation. If it is obvious that the person is likely to be useless as a source of information he is never contacted again.

A large number of cases investigated by the committee reveal that in their recruiting operations Communist Secret Police devote special efforts to Americans with relatives behind the Iron Curtain. Often, but not always, these people are naturalized U.S. citizens.

Typical cases reveal the pattern of current Soviet espionage recruiting operations in the U.S.A. They fall into two general categories:

First, those involving the espionage recruiting operations of Iron Curtain diplomatic officials in the U.S.A.

Second, cases revealing the activities of the Soviet Secret Police in attempting to discover potential sources of information among

Americans visiting Iron Curtain countries with the object of persuading or forcing people to co-operate with the Kremlin's spy rings after they have returned to the United States.

For obvious reasons the real names of the persons involved in these cases are not used, and certain of the details in each case have been altered to protect the identities of the parties concerned. But each case given here is based on facts uncovered by the committee's investigations.

Maria Zetko, naturalized U.S. citizen, is an employee of a Government Defense Agency. Some time ago she went to the Embassy of the country of her birth—which is now controlled by a Communist régime—to inquire about some of her relatives still in her native country.

Shortly afterwards she was contacted by an official of the Embassy, who, in a series of meetings, tried to recruit her into the Soviet espionage network. He asked for information on policies and plans relating to the U.S.A. in the Agency for which she worked. He interrogated her regarding persons who could be useful for Communist intelligence and infiltration activity, and who were employed by other Government agencies in some way connected with defence—the Central Intelligence Agency, certain intelligence schools of the Armed Forces, the Voice of America, and the Department of State.

He tried to persuade Miss Zetko to invite influential employees of the Agency for which she worked to lunch at her home with him so that he could procure from them information about policy trends.

Miss Zetko was assured by the Communist diplomat that if she ever ran into trouble for co-operating with him he would take care of her, see that she would immediately receive a passport, be transported safely out of the country, and be given a new and better position in her native land.

At the time that this diplomat was trying to recruit Miss Zetko into espionage for Moscow he was also contacting American educational institutions to promote student group visits to the U.S.A. He told officials of institutions that the purpose of such visits was to improve the chances of "peace" and to bring about "better understanding" between the people of the United States and his own Government. . . .

John Feltan is a naturalized American citizen active in refugee and anti-Communist exile groups comprising people from his native land, which is now under Red control. Through his association with these organizations he developed a considerable number of contacts with U.S. Information Agencies.

He was approached by an official of a satellite Embassy in Washington, D.C., which represents his homeland. The official tried to persuade Mr Feltan to gather certain types of information and turn it over to him—on the clear understanding that it was for the use of the Kremlin.

In his talks with Mr Feltan the Iron Curtain Embassy official revealed a surprising amount of knowledge on the case histories of many persons prominent in anti-Communist émigré organizations in the U.S.A., and also on a number of key employees in U.S. Information Agencies, their assignments and backgrounds, etc. He asked Mr Feltan why certain employees had been shifted from positions they had formerly held. He inquired about duties, salaries, financial and material status of others, and asked Mr Feltan to obtain the names of employees of this Agency who had relatives behind the Iron Curtain.

He offered to pay for any information passed on, and said he had been ordered by his superior to "enforce" co-operation. He reminded Mr Feltan that he still had relatives behind the Iron Curtain, and that, if he refused to co-operate, something "could happen to them". . . .

Years ago Stanislaw Salowski came to the U.S.A. from a country since taken over by the Communists. He worked hard, became an American citizen, married, succeeded in business, had a large family, and, like most immigrants, became completely devoted to his adopted country. At the same time he naturally retained affection for the land of his birth and its people. In the city where he lived he joined a club for men of his national origin, and frequently attended meetings and social affairs. Discussion and business at these gatherings for the most part concerned the United States and community matters, but there was also considerable talk of the old country and its affairs.

A number of years ago the club formed a committee to help refugees from, and natives of, this country who had come to the U.S.A. Mr Salowski was appointed to the committee and supported it financially. The committee experienced difficulty, however, in securing exit permits from the Communist Government for people it wanted to bring to the United States.

Mr Salowski, on behalf of the immigrant committee, agreed to go to New York to talk to representatives of the satellite consulate to see what could be done to overcome obstacles. When he discussed the problem with a consulate official he was informed that the consulate would be happy to help the committee if Mr Salowski, in turn, would do some favours for its personnel. He was told that consular employees could not leave New York without a permit, and that, for this and other reasons, they found it difficult to get around the country as much as they would like. They wanted him to assist them in obtaining articles from other cities. Mr Salowski agreed to help.

A few weeks later he received a telephone call from the consulate official. He was asked if he would be coming to New York in the near future. When he said yes he was requested to call in at a store in Boston to pick up a package and deliver it to the New York consulate. He did this. At the consulate he was asked to wait. A few moments later he was ushered into the office of one of the consular officials. The official was unfriendly. He told Mr Salowski that the package he had just delivered contained espionage material. He also told him that he could be jailed or even killed for this, and that the only thing to be done was to continue working for the network. Or face exposure. He was reminded that he had a fine family with many children and grand-children, and that he should think of them if he had any ideas of going to the police. From time to time, the consular official said, he would be given the names of "refugees" who had to be helped into the United States.

Mr Salowski left the consulate and returned home. For months he worried and kept his fears to himself. He started drinking. Finally, he could bear it no longer and told his wife.

He continued to receive telephone calls from the consular official in New York. When the first call came he said he was sick. At the second call he said his shop needed remodelling and that he couldn't make any trips until the work was complete. During a third call the consular official advised him to remember what he had been told, that it would be tragic if one of his grandchildren were to disappear.

Mr Salowski turned to his parish priest for help. Government Security Agencies were brought in. The result was the expulsion of the Iron Curtain diplomat from the United States. . . .

Mr and Mrs Josef Zent are both naturalized citizens of the U.S.A. Mr Zent came from one Central European nation now under Red domination, his wife from another.

Some time ago Mrs Zent heard that one of her relatives, who still lives in the country where she was born, was seriously ill and in need of medicines unobtainable there. She discussed the prob-lem with her husband. They decided to go to the Washington Embassy of the Iron Curtain country in question to discover if they could send medicines to Mrs Zent's sick relative. When he visited and spoke to an Embassy official Mr Zent was informed that the matter would be investigated and that he would receive an answer shortly.

Mr Zent was later contacted by the Embassy official, who asked a series of personal questions about himself, his wife, and her sick relative. After he had answered Mr Zent was told that the only way the medical supplies could be sent was through the Embassy. Mr and Mrs Zent bought a supply of the medicines needed by the sick relative and gave them to the Embassy for shipment.

Mr Zent is employed by a United States Defense Agency in a position that gives him access to a considerable amount of classified information. Several times after he and his wife gave the medicines to the Embassy the official with whom he had talked contacted him and questioned him about the defence establishment in which he was employed. Practically all the questions concerned classified matters.

The Iron Curtain diplomat also tried to persuade Mrs Zent to return to her native land to visit her sick relative. Concerned to learn all she could about her relative's progress, Mrs Zent was tempted to make the trip, but on the advice of her husband and representatives of the United States Security Agencies, she decided against the idea. It was pointed out that if she made the trip she might be held as a hostage, and her husband would then be faced with the choice of betraying the U.S.A. in return for a guarantee of her safety or of causing injury or possible death to her by refusing to do so. . . .

Mrs Rose Bartin, a resident of an industrial city in the northeastern United States, is a naturalized American citizen. She had already been thirteen years in the country when she heard that an aunt who had brought her up when she was a child was seriously ill. Her aunt's illness was said to be such that recovery was unlikely, so she decided that, if possible, she would visit her.

She applied for a visa through the Washington Embassy of the Iron Curtain country in which her aunt lived. She was informed that she would be able to make the trip, and was advised that if she made travel arrangements through a certain tourist agency the issue of her visa would be expedited. She did as advised, received the visa, and went to her aunt.

She was shocked by what she saw when she reached her native village. Conditions were bad. The people worked from sunrise to sunset and didn't earn enough to feed or clothe themselves decently. The local minister was paid by the State and forced to hold Sunday services in the evening because he, as well as all the people in the village, had to work all the daylight hours on Sundays. Her cousins, who had been her playmates when she was a young girl, were avid Communists, completely lacking in morals and religious belief.

After her return to the United States Mrs Bartin, in conversations with friends and acquaintances, was strongly critical of the country she had visited, its Government, and the condition of its people.

Some time later, although she lived many miles from Washington, she received a visit from a diplomat attached to the Washington Embassy of the country she had visited. The man talked to her for hours. He asked her if she had taken pictures during her stay abroad and questioned her about her conversations there with the people of her village. He also asked her about her own life, and work in the U.S.A.

Shortly afterwards she heard from relatives that some time before she was visited by the diplomat the Secret Police had seen her aunt. They had asked her aunt if Mrs Bartin planned to come again. They also indicated that they knew the nature of the remarks Mrs Bartin had been making after her return to the United States, and that they would probably take action against her if she ever went behind the Iron Curtain again.

Mrs Bartin's employment is such that she learns nothing from it that would be of any use to the Kremlin's intelligence service. For that reason and because of her strong anti-Communism she has not been approached to do anything in the nature of espionage work. She has received no further visits from the Iron Curtain diplomat, but, for fear of what may happen to her relatives, she no longer makes any critical remarks about their Government.

The Communist diplomat did not find a potential agent when he visited her, but an American voice that had learned the truth about conditions in an Iron Curtain country was effectively stilled by threats. . . .

Mr Rudowski is a native-born American of Middle-European descent. He works for one of the major aircraft-manufacturing companies in the U.S.A. His parents are American-born, but his aged grandparents, as far as he knows, still live in the country where they were born. For years he had no word from them, and did not know whether they were ill or well, alive or dead.

Some time ago Mr Rudowski received a letter from the country of his grandmother. The writer of the letter claimed to be a nurse who was taking care of her. She said that as a result of treatment received from the Nazis his grandmother had had a mental breakdown and was under constant care.

Mr Rudowski wrote two letters to his grandmother, both of which were answered, allegedly by the nurse. His third letter was returned unopened, marked "addressee unknown".

Mr Rudowski went to the Washington Embassy of the country in which, he believed, his grandmother was still living. He talked to one of the staff members and asked for the assistance of the Embassy in obtaining definite information on her whereabouts and condition. He was told that the Embassy would investigate the matter.

A few weeks later an Embassy official contacted him and said that his grandmother had been arrested and was to be tried for making pro-Western statements. Several weeks passed, and a representative of the Embassy contacted him again. He was told that the Embassy would definitely help his grandmother, but only if he reciprocated. Mr Rudowski asked what form the 'reciprocation' would take. He was told the Embassy wanted information about the aircraft company for which he worked. There were additional meetings between Mr Rudowski and the representative of the Embassy. At each one Mr Rudowski was told that if he expected the Embassy to do anything for his grandmother he would have to co-operate. Each time he refused. Eventually the meetings stopped.

Mr Rudowski has not received any further word from the Embassy about his grandmother. He does not know if she was tried, and, if so, whether she was convicted or acquitted. He does not know if she is alive now, or even if she was actually alive when he received the first letter from her 'nurse'.

John Tentil is a naturalized American citizen who emigrated to the United States from an Iron Curtain state in 1935. He married an American-born woman, and is the father of three children.

John Tentil's parents still lived in his native land, which was taken over by the Communists in the late 1940s. He obtained only sparse news about them and other relatives from the time their country fell under Communist domination.

Like many Americans of similar background, John Tentil could not help welcoming the apparent thaw in relations between the Communist and Western nations that took place after the death of Stalin. Not only did this hold out the promise of reliable news from and about his relatives, it also brought a feeling of relief. There might be some chance that his parents and other relatives would have a better life and be safer from arrest, imprisonment, deportation to slave-labour camps, or death, for some political offence. In addition, the improved atmosphere held out hope of visits to see their family again.

In 1956 John Tentil obtained a passport and visa to visit his parents. He took his daughter with him; she was the eldest of his three children.

Shortly after arriving at his parents' home they were visited by the Secret Police. He was interrogated, and the police showed a special interest in his friends and acquaintances in the United States, who, like him, had been born in countries now controlled by Communists. They questioned him, too, about a number of his neighbours in the U.S.A. of Middle-European background who were suspected of opposing Communist régimes.

The Secret Police continued to visit Mr Tentil during his stay. They indicated in all their sessions that if he failed to co-operate by answering all questions his parents might be arrested and imprisoned.

John Tentil knew nothing of United States security or defence that would be of value to Soviet intelligence. But the police did obtain from him information useful for approaching others in the United States for espionage purposes, and for bringing pressure on anti-Communist exiles to halt anti-Soviet activity. . . .

Mrs Helen Frosch is the American-born daughter of a Russian couple who emigrated to the U.S.A. several years before the Bolshevik revolution. When she was in her teens her parents decided to return to Russia and took her with them. Some years later, dissatisfied with life there, she made repeated attempts to obtain a visa to return to see her sister and other relatives who had remained in America. Despite her claim that she was a U.S. citizen, all requests were denied by the Soviet Government.

She gave up hope, and eventually married a Russian without benefit of formal ceremony—as was commonly done in the Soviet Union at the time. They had a daughter.

Years later she renewed her efforts to obtain a visa to go to the U.S.A. She was granted one on condition that she sang the praises of the Soviet Union wherever she went.

Following her arrival in America, she started work to support herself and to raise money with which she hoped to bring her child to the United States. She secured a position in a defence plant, and then asked the Soviet authorities to let her daughter and husband come to the U.S.A. to live. All her pleas were denied. After several years, with no apparent chance of seeing them again, she met, fell in love with, and married an American.

More years passed, and then she received a letter from her daughter, asking her to come back to see her and her father. Soon afterwards Mrs Frosch received word from Soviet authorities that if she returned she would be able to bring her daughter back to the United States with her.

With the developing 'thaw' in U.S.-Soviet relations, it was now possible for her to get a passport and visa to visit the U.S.S.R. She went in 1956, taking with her her ten-year-old son, the eldest of the three children of her American family. As soon as she arrived in Moscow she went straight to the U.S. Embassy to make her presence known, as she had been advised to do by United States Government authorities before she left.

When Mrs Frosch reached the village in which she had lived she found that her former husband and her daughter (who was now twenty years of age) were both fanatical Communists. During her stay at the village she was seen repeatedly by Soviet intelligence officers, and also by others who were obviously working for the Secret Police. She was questioned about the defence plant where her present husband was employed and where she had worked. She was also asked about a large U.S.

air base located near her home. When she refused to answer she was accused of being an American spy.

Soviet authorities delayed her departure until her entry permit had expired, and then delayed granting her an exit visa for several months. She was forced to sell her jewellery to buy food for her son and herself during their enforced stay. When she finally got an exit visa she was sure it was only because she had registered with the U.S. Embassy at the time of her arrival and had kept in touch with it regularly during her visit, and because her son was an American-born citizen. . . .

Mrs Mary Harshkin came to America in 1945. Her husband had been killed in World War II. She left behind her parents, a brother, and a young daughter. In the years that followed she had little news of her family, and rejoiced at the easing of tensions that enabled her to obtain a passport to visit her homeland. She hoped to make arrangements to bring her daughter, her mother (her father had since died), and her brother to the United States.

On arrival she went to officials of the Communist Government and asked them to help obtain exit permits for the members of her family. Later she was called to a Government office and informed that she could take her family to the U.S.A. if she co-operated. There was information they wanted, and if she would obtain it there would be no trouble in getting to America with all her family. Mrs Harshkin agreed to the deal, and subsequently carried out a number of espionage assignments in Western Europe for the Secret Police of her native land. She then returned to the United States.

Shortly afterwards a Communist diplomat contacted her and paid her a large sum of money for the information she had obtained in Europe. He also asked her to continue her espionage activity in the United States. She agreed to do this when promised that her daughter, brother, and mother would be sent there in the near future.

None of them ever arrived. Her mother and daughter were held as hostages by the Communist Government to guarantee Mrs Harshkin's co-operation with the Soviet espionage in the United States. Her brother, she learned, was sent to an intelligence training school behind the Iron Curtain. After completing his training he was sent to a Middle-Eastern country, where he has been serving as an espionage agent. . . .

Charles Schmidt lives and works in a New England industrial town, where he is employed on a defence project which gives him working knowledge of certain restricted and confidential information. He was born in what is now a Communist-controlled country, and is the eldest son of a large family. A number of his brothers and sisters also left their country at various times in the last twenty years and settled in the U.S.A. or in free Europe. Some members of his family are still behind the Iron Curtain.

Mr Schmidt corresponded with his sisters and brothers, including those in the Communist countries. Through this correspondence the Secret Police learned the nature of his employment in the United States. They visited one of his sisters to interrogate her about him, his position, and everything she knew of his life. They forced her to write, urging him to visit her and take up residence in the old country. Her letter promised that if he did so he could get a far more profitable position than he had in the United States. She wrote several letters in this vein.

Mr Schmidt then received a letter from a brother in Europe who had managed to make contact with members of the family still behind the Iron Curtain. The letter from his brother warned that his sister's letters were a ruse used by the Secret Police to get him back so that he could be taken into custody and subjected to treatment aimed at extracting all he knew of the defence project on which he worked.

In addition to the officially documented cases I have just related, another should be included in this chapter, because, although different in pattern from those already given, it illustrates how the Kremlin works through all possible channels to recruit espionage agents. The case is based on facts obtained from the U.S. Department of State.

Early in 1957 a Washington newspaper reported the investigation of the case of a former employee of the Central Intelligence Agency who, shortly before committing suicide, had reportedly held several secret meetings with a Soviet military attaché in Washington.

Actually, the Committee on Un-American Activities had, by then, completed its investigation of the case, having inquired into it from the time that the person concerned had taken his life, almost a year earlier, on April 25th, 1956. Only a brief report of the suicide had appeared in the Press.

These were the facts:

In 1954 a man who, for the purposes of this report, will be called Thomas Jones, and who had been an Army Air Force captain in World War II, applied for a position with the Central Intelligence Agency. He was cleared for assignment with the C.I.A. on January 17th, 1955. As a foreign-documents officer with the C.I.A., it was Jones's job to scan foreign-language publications of possible interest to U.S. Intelligence. He did not hold a high position.

On December 12th, 1955, Jones resigned from the C.I.A. for

personal reasons. His resignation was not requested, and he was under no suspicion of any kind.

On January 6th, 1956, Jones delivered to the Embassy of the U.S.S.R. in Washington a communication saying that he was a former employee of the C.I.A. and that he had information of interest to the Soviet Union.

On Jaunary 24th, the Assistant Military Attaché of the Soviet Embassy visited Jones at his apartment in a Washington suburb. Jones gave the Soviet attaché general information on his background, and arranged a further meeting, which took place on February 1st—again in Jones's apartment. On this occasion the attaché suggested that Jones get a job with another Government agency to give him the opportunity to handle classified information. He also told Jones he would receive pay commensurate with the value of any information he turned over.

There was a third meeting on February 10th. The Soviet attaché again stressed the desirability of Jones securing a post with the Department of Defense and listed specific types of information he particularly wanted. Meanwhile, on February 1st, Jones had written a registered letter to Allen W. Dulles, Director of the C.I.A., informing him of the communication he had sent to the Soviet Embassy and explaining that he had taken this step because he wished to serve as a "double agent" for the United States Government.

A fourth meeting between Jones and the attaché was arranged for February 16th. Jones, for some unknown reason, did not keep the appointment. When the attaché called him the next day Jones informed him that he did not wish to see him again.

Two months later Jones committed suicide. A note left to his wife revealed that he was in a state of extreme depression and was taking this way out because he felt he was a failure. No foul play was suspected. His death was recorded as suicide.

Available evidence indicated that Jones had lost all interest in living and in carrying out his self-appointed mission of becoming a counter-agent.

A week after the suicide the Soviet Military Attaché was recalled to the U.S.S.R. at the request of the State Department.

It was not until almost a year later, when the story broke in the Washington newspaper, that the American public had any indication of a relationship between Jones and Soviet espionage. That Jones must have realized the futility of his trying to meet, and beat, Communist diplomats at their espionage game was indicated in his suicide note, which said:

"I seemed to have been caught in a chain of circumstances over which I had no control, and after a while I lost interest in the purpose and causes for which I was working."

20

Perfect Identities

MOST Iron Curtain master spies in the free world have been converted during training in special schools into 'genuine' citizens of the countries in which they direct their espionage webs. The conversion is usually so perfect that these master spies are rarely suspected of having come from a foreign country. They are provided with foolproof documents that enable them to establish their 'cover' identities.

For Aleksandr Karyn, who was chosen for the function of Russian resident spy operator in Switzerland, the espionage directors at Moscow headquarters decided to utilize the following details which they had on file.

At the beginning of the century the daughter of a well-to-do Swiss couple had gone to Tsarist Russia for a holiday, and had met and married there a young Russian teacher. In 1903 she gave birth to a boy, but she died in 1910. After their daughter's death the parents in Switzerland continued to show great interest in their little grandson and kept in touch with their son-in-law. But when the 1917 revolution and the civil war swept Russia and caused a mass migration of people the Swiss couple lost touch with their son-in-law.

Aleksandr Karyn was ordered to impersonate the grandson, to enter into correspondence with his 'grandparents' and tell them he would like to emigrate to Switzerland. He received an answer to his first letter from his 'grandmother'. He learned that his 'grandfather' had died, and that his two 'uncles' were wealthy businessmen with respectable standing in Swiss society. He was then provided with photographs of his 'mother' from the Secret Service archives and ordered to send these to his 'grandmother'. He repeated that he would like to emigrate to Switzerland to be with his 'family'.

The Swiss family immediately contacted all their influential friends in Switzerland and other European countries, requesting them to use their influence to ask the Soviet authorities to allow their 'grandson' to leave Russia. The Soviet authorities pretended to consider the application favourably, and after some 'obstacles' the exit visas for the 'grandson', his wife, and his little daughter were eventually granted and the three were permitted to leave for Switzerland.

The fake 'grandson' was received by the Swiss family and, in due course, obtained a genuine Swiss passport.

Two months after the reunion the frail old lady, for whom the excitement had been too great, died peacefully. She left her 'grandson' her house and all her estate, and, had it not been for Karyn's conscience, which eventually induced him to reveal all the facts, the truth might never have been discovered.

Another illustration of how ingeniously Russian Secret Service directors provide their spies with perfect identities is the case of Gordon Lonsdale, the Russian master spy, sentenced to a long term of imprisonment at the Old Bailey in March 1961.

When the twenty-one-year-old Russian lieutenant Vasilyi Vasilyevich Pakhomov was transferred from his Secret Police duties to Secret Service recruitment in 1943 he was better known as Molodyi, Russian for "the young one", because of his youth. And when he later entered the spy school of Gaczyna, where he was converted into a 'genuine' Anglo-Saxon to be able to work after his graduation as a resident spy operator in England, the espionage directors at Moscow headquarters chose the identity of Gordon Lonsdale for him.

A Gordon Lonsdale was born in 1924, in Canada, to a half-Cree-Indian named Jack Emmanuel Lonsdale and a Finnish immigrant to Canada, Alga Bousu. Two years after Gordon was born the parents separated, and six years later Mrs Alga Lonsdale took her son home to her native Finland. In the winter of 1939–40 both the mother and her sixteen-year-old son were swallowed up in the Russian-Finnish war, and they were never heard of again. Gordon Lonsdale's identity was, therefore, perfect because Moscow Secret Service headquarters were in possession of all the necessary data and documents.

When the fake Gordon Lonsdale was smuggled ashore at Vancouver from a Russian grain ship he was under strict orders from Moscow to do nothing, but to assimilate himself into the background of the man whose identity he had now taken. His first move in Canada was to rent a $15-a-week room in Vancouver, pretending to his landlady that he was a salesman. As soon as he had a respectable address he took out a driving licence to secure some sort of Canadian identification document.

One month in Vancouver was enough for him to acclimatize himself to his new country of birth. He moved to Toronto, and, when he thought the time ripe for his next move, he applied

L

for a Canadian passport—an easy task for anyone in possession of a genuine birth certificate. As soon as he had all the documents he required, and his identity was complete, he left Canada.

For almost six years Gordon Lonsdale managed to work as a Soviet resident spy operator in London, and, throughout this time, no-one discovered a clue to indicate that he was not the Canadian he claimed to be.

These are but a few examples of the care and thoroughness of Moscow's espionage directors when deciding cover for spies. From the archives of the Third Division of the Foreign Directorate at Moscow Secret Service headquarters Russian master spies can be provided with perfect identities for practically every country of the globe.

In cases when a fake 'native' of a country is provided with a genuine birth certificate entitling him to obtain a passport from the country's consulate, Soviet spy operators are ordered to proceed by conventional means to their destinations, because it is natural that they should embark from the country in which their passport was issued by the respective consulate. But in cases where they receive genuine birth certificates from Moscow Secret Service headquarters, as in the example of Gordon Lonsdale, they are usually smuggled into 'their' country, as they must claim passport and documents in their native country.

Records reveal that the number of spies in the Gordon Lonsdale category is much greater than any other type. Records also disclose how other Soviet spies smuggled into countries set about obtaining genuine identification documents.

Mark Borisovich Zagorsky, for example, a Soviet resident spy operator in London who directed his spy ring under the 'cover' of Dr Geoffrey Noble, was dispatched to England in a somewhat unconventional way. The Transport Division at Moscow Secret Service headquarters decided that no suitable conventional and safe transport was available, so Dr Noble was put on board a special Red Navy submarine and slipped, in November 1952, into the United Kingdom.

When the Russian submarine reached the British coast at night Dr Noble was ordered to swim ashore. Under his waterproof frogman's suit he wore warm woollies, and his typical English suitcase was protected by a specially designed waterproof container blown up with compressed air for buoyancy to enable the lone swimmer to carry it easily.

Dr Noble managed to reach the coast without difficulty or detection. While he changed into English-made clothes the submarine—with the use of a thin rope attached to the container—hauled back the spy's swimming outfit.

Dr Geoffrey Noble succeeded in establishing his 'cover' in the Pimlico district and in directing his espionage network—until he was later detected by Scotland Yard's Special Branch.

The use of Russian submarines for secret landings of resident spy operators in some countries of the free world is not very common, but the example of Dr Geoffrey Noble is by no means an isolated one. Official records reveal that since the beginning of 1950 Russian and other Communist spies have been landed by submarine on the Belgian, Dutch, French, West German, Norwegian, Spanish, and United States coasts. Some of them were caught, others were arrested later.

Another unconventional landing in a Western country was made by Tanya Markovna Radyonska, who posed under the 'cover' of "Eileen"—a quiet, unassuming English miss who emigrated from England to Canada and became a spy.

In May 1958 Eileen travelled from Russia aboard a Soviet fishing trawler to the British coast and was, during the night, taken by rubber dinghy to Scotland. She reached London eventually, and succeeded in establishing her 'cover' of a quiet, shy spinster. Nine months after her secret arrival in Scotland she left her 'country of birth' and sailed as an immigrant to Canada, where she operated as an extremely successful spy until March 1961.

The case of Gennadyi Maksimovich Glazunov, who chose the 'cover' of a respectable Australian businessman, Reginald Kenneth Osborne, and who worked for over seven years as a spy in London, is an illustration of what "conventional landings" means in Soviet Secret Service language.

When Osborne's schooling at the Soviet spy school of Gaczyna came to an end in December 1949 he passed his final examination which classed him "fit for foreign service". He left Russia on a Soviet merchant vessel, sailing to the Far East. True to the precautions the Soviet Secret Service always takes, he was smuggled aboard ship to ensure that no member of the crew saw him. He was confined to his cabin throughout the long journey. The only people he met were two State Security officers who brought his food and who made sure he remained out of sight.

By the end of January 1950 the Russians managed to smuggle him into Australia, where he was to undergo an acclimatization period, and where he was then to claim an Australian passport against a birth certificate showing he was born in Sydney—before finally reporting at his real destination, London. He operated as an extremely cunning spy.

21

Efficiency and Safety
Precautions

I N our modern scientific age technical devices of many descriptions play a substantial part in espionage. It is, therefore, not surprising that the Soviet Secret Service, and their Iron Curtain counterparts, maintain special Workshop Departments.

The most commonly known technical spy device, which has played an important rôle in world espionage for decades, is the camera. But spy cameras should not be confused with even the most efficient and reliable microfilm cameras that many well-known manufacturers produce and market throughout the world.

The "FD-3" camera, for instance, which the Workshop Department of the Soviet Secret Service produces for their agents and informers, is concealed in a man's sports wrist-watch. And the "FD-3" is not only so disguised that even fully trained and experienced security officers fail to notice it, but it is also so efficient and powerful that the spy is able to microfilm any sort of material accurately even under unusually difficult light conditions.

Those who doubt that a highly efficient microfilm spy camera can be concealed in a man's sports wrist-watch are referred to officially disclosed cases, which revealed that security officers overlooked such hidden spy cameras.

Another equally efficient microfilm spy camera, also produced by the Workshop Department, is the Russian "F-1". This camera, which is as efficient and powerful as the "FD-3", is concealed in a lighter of a design commonly used in the West. This lighter contains only a small tank which holds just enough petrol to enable the lighter to work for a day or so; the remaining space houses the ingeniously concealed microfilm spy camera. When the agent needs to take microfilm photographs all he does is unfasten the 'filling' screw, and this enables him to gain access to the hidden camera.

The East German Secret Service produce in their Berlin-Hohenschoenhausen Workshop Department microfilm spy cameras very similar to the Russian "FD-3" and "F-1", but they conceal them in hearing-aids and pocket transistor radios. The Czecho-slovak Secret Service Workshop Department in Prague-Zbraslav conceal their microfilm spy cameras in ladies' compacts, in men's spectacle-holders, and in clothes-brushes.

All these microfilm spy cameras are known to the combined Allied counter-intelligence and security forces. But this fact does not deter numerous Red agents and informers operating throughout the free world from using their well-concealed equipment, for they are fully aware that microfilm spy cameras look so much like everyday articles people carry about that they cannot be spotted by security officers in Government and military establishments, research institutes, and other places from where secret information and documents can be obtained. They therefore have little fear of being caught.

Apart from the microfilm spy camera, which can be classified as traditional basic technical espionage equipment, our modern technological age has also produced a number of equally important gadgets. One of these is the so-called 'limpet' microphone which, according to official records, has been used widely and successfully by Soviet and other Communist agents since the mid-fifties.

'Limpet' microphones are ingenious electronic devices that can easily and unobtrusively be fixed outside a building, and are constructed to pick up very clearly every sound from inside a room. These marvels are smaller than a matchbox, and can simultaneously transmit by means of ultra-short-wave radio communication up to a radius of five miles. They thus enable a monitoring station in some safe hide-out inside this radius to record every sound on tape. Then every item of importance is coded, typed out, photographed, reduced to microdot size, safely affixed under a postage-stamp of a harmless-looking picture post-card or letter, and dispatched to Moscow or any other Communist Secret Service headquarters.

Between 1949 and 1960, 130 clandestine listening devices had been removed from United States Embassies.

In 1945 Soviet diplomats in Moscow presented Mr W. Averell Harriman, the United States Ambassador to the Soviet Union, with a carved replica of the Great Seal of the United States, which was immediately accorded a place of honour in the Ambassador's study in the U.S. Embassy. But the Soviet gift was a very special ornament. The shield was made of wood and within the thickness of the wood was a hollowed-out cavity inside which Soviet intelligence agents had concealed a U-shaped piece of metal with a spring-steel vibrator fastened to it.

Once the shield was hung in the Embassy the spring vibrated from sound waves generated by conversations held in the Ambassador's study. Across the street from the Embassy, Soviet intelligence agents installed a highly sensitive continuous-wave radar set aimed right at the spring-steel vibrator. The receiver could pick up the smallest motion of the vibrator and translate its movements into intelligible speech, enabling the Russians to overhear every word spoken in the Ambassador's study. State Department security officers discovered this sad fact in 1952.

Investigation of the decorative shield revealed that Soviet intelligence agents had also developed methods for listening-in on conversations by reading the vibrations of window-panes—vibrations set up by voices within a room. This was done by focusing a beam of ultrasonic energy on the window-pane and using a sonar-like apparatus to detect slight motions of the glass and convert these vibrations into intelligible speech.

Another way of interpreting vibrations on the window-panes was to replace a pane of a window with electrically conductive glass—a special leaded glass with a thin transparent film of tin oxide on its surface. A highly sensitive continuous-wave radar was then able to detect the motion of the electrically conductive glass and convert its vibrations to intelligible speech. State Department security officers also discovered that where a window was guarded by a conventional metal-foil burglar-alarm strip the eavesdropper had the hardest part of the job done for him because the vibrations of the metal-foil strip could be picked up by radar, and the agents didn't have to go near the building.

According to official records, the 'limpet' microphone was first discovered in 1954 under a window-sill of the Iranian Embassy in Moscow, where presumably a window-cleaner had, without being noticed, placed it outside the first-floor office of the Ambassador. It was realized that some of the Iranian secrets, which the Russians had discovered and used for political and other purposes, had been obtained by means of the 'limpet' microphones while the Ambassador had discussed confidential matters with top-ranking staff members in his private office.

Between 1956 and 1960, Russian 'limpet' microphones were also found on the outside of important Allied buildings in West Berlin, the Federal Republic of West Germany, France, and many other countries of the free world. It was also disclosed that even in the British and United States Embassies in Moscow electronic listening devices were found. In turn, Russia and other Iron Curtain countries also revealed that 'limpets' and other electronic spy listening devices had been discovered inside and outside important Soviet buildings.

In the spring of 1964 security officers at the U.S. Embassy in Moscow became suspicious of a security leak from the Embassy. On May 19th, 1964, U.S. experts discovered a plot that shocked State Department security officers.

The thick interior walls of the eighth, ninth, and tenth floors of the Embassy concealed a network of wires leading to forty microphones which, presumably, informed Soviet Secret Service officers at their headquarters of conversations in the Embassy. Security officers recalled that before the Embassy moved into its quarters in Tchaikovsky Street in 1953 the building had been seven storeys high and that Soviet workmen had added the three top storeys—and secretly wired them for sound. Each microphone was fastened to a wooden peg that extended through the walls almost to the surface of the plaster. The Russian microphones had eluded repeated searches by U.S. State Department security experts, and for more than a decade conversations held in the U.S. Embassy in Moscow had clearly been piped directly to Soviet intelligence headquarters.

This was not an isolated case. In May 1965 the United States dispatched nine Navy Seebees to Warsaw, to debug the U.S. Embassy there. In the same month the State Department asked Congress for $1,644,600 to debug other U.S. Embassies.

'Limpet' microphones are still being used by Russian and other Communist spies in almost every country of the globe. But, due to the fact that during the past few years Allied counter-intelligence and security forces in West Berlin and other Western lands have succeeded in tracing the 'limpet' microphones and their monitoring stations by means of special electronic detection devices, Moscow Secret Service headquarters now warn spies to "use this gadget only in cases where information cannot be obtained by other means".

This does not mean that Russia's espionage directors are abandoning the widespread use of electronic listening devices. A new, much better and safer electronic device, the "K-9", is now being mass-produced by the Workshop Department, and now, to a certain extent, replaces the 'limpet' microphone.

The Soviet Secret Service's "K-9" is, in fact, a slightly improved copy of the 'miniature microphone' which the Workshop Department of the East German Secret Service in Berlin-Hohenschoen-hausen perfected in 1957. Their experts succeeded in producing an "electronic miniature listening device" measuring only half an inch in diameter, but which, despite its small size, was so highly selective that it could clearly pick up every sound anywhere in a room, even if concealed in a hollowed-out table-leg, or if placed in furniture upholstery, or any other place that muffled sound. Then, in mid-1958, the size was reduced, to a mere five-sixteenths of an inch, and the selectiveness improved.

Soviet Secret Service directors were, of course, interested in the East German "electronic miniature listening device" and were quick to spot the many possibilities which this new tiny 'hidden ear' offered. There was, of course, a slight handicap, because the ultra-short-wave broadcasting radius of the gadget was limited to only "within a quarter of a mile". But experts soon solved this problem. A miniature gadget was constructed—a radio receiver that picked up the transmission from the miniature microphone and automatically recorded everything on wire. This gadget, which is known as "K-9-R", is only a fraction larger than the 'limpet' microphone, which makes it easy for it to be concealed in the same building from which the secret information is picked up.

Western counter-intelligence and security officers have, during the past two years, discovered and seized many Soviet-manufactured "K-9" and "K-9-R" gadgets, in West Berlin, Bonn, Frankfurt-am-Main, Geneva, and also at the United Nations headquarters in New York. Some of the gadgets were placed in private offices of important executives, in living-rooms and bedrooms, even in motor-cars.

During his last address to the Kremlin's Party Presidium, in January 1967, General Rudolf Ivanovich Abel spoke in detail of the "excellent results which have been achieved in the English-speaking world and other Imperialist countries by extensively using the 'K-9' and 'K-9-R'." Other reports from Russia, which have been corroborated by Communist Secret Service defectors to the West, divulge that the Workshop Department has greatly increased the output of these instruments.

Still another electronic listening device is the East German Secret Service Workshop Department invention "F-2". The function of this is to monitor confidential telephone conversations. The "F-2" is unobtrusively placed at a suitable point of the telephone-line which the Soviet or other Iron Curtain spy wishes to intercept, and the confidential conversation is then obtained for headquarters in the same manner as above.

The gadget has been discovered and seized on many occasions. But it is impossible to detect *all* gadgets placed on the many V.I.P. telephone private lines throughout the free world, and the danger from these electronic 'secret ears' is considerable.

Every possible precaution is taken to prevent hostile eavesdroppers listening in. A number of telephone communication security methods have been devised for the protection of Resident Network Operators and their agents working in foreign countries, and one of these is known as the 'black box'. This works as follows:

The Resident Network Operator finds a suitable apartment or office, then orders the telephone company to provide him with two different numbers. He gives one number to his agents and informers for phoning through messages, but keeps the second number secret. The two telephones are linked with the 'black box' device, and when the network operator expects the agent to call him he dials from outside the number. The agent dials the number of the other telephone and establishes contact through the 'black box', which has an automatic timer that disconnects the call after a few minutes. This precaution prevents counter-intelligence agents from tracing the telephone call, for it takes approximately seven minutes to trace a call even if security agents are forewarned.

The 'black box' has also another value: it instantly disconnects the telephones if anyone attempts to enter the room in which they are installed. The network operator never, of course, visits the premises in which the two telephones and the 'black box' operate. He (or she) always calls the secret number from a public callbox at different locations.

Still another ultra-modern spy gadget which the Workshop Departments of the combined Communist Secret Services produce is an electronic television camera, used for visual observation. Western intelligence and counter-intelligence also use this particular device.

The Communist-manufactured transistorized television cameras are operated by tiny batteries, are as small as a lady's handbag, and can be hidden in walls and ceilings. Light pipes of optical fibres, which bend light around corners, make it possible for these cameras to be installed in an adjoining room with only the optic fibre bundle of thin flexible glass rods penetrating into the room under observation.

Visual surveillance can be carried out in darkness as well as light by using transistorized devices with pick-ups which convert the infra-red heat waves emitted by human beings, motor-cars, or other warm objects into visible light which is then fed into optical telescopes for magnification. These devices are powered by tiny batteries. Even in absolute darkness these infra-red surveillance devices can locate a moving object at five hundred feet and establish positive identification of individuals a hundred feet away.

The Workshop Departments of the Soviet and other Iron Curtain Secret Services produce, apart from photographic and electronic espionage devices, other aids for agents. One of these is what is commonly described as 'invisible' ink and the necessary chemical for 'developing' the unseen writing.

Invisible ink no longer plays such an important rôle in world espionage as it did before microfilm, microdots, and electronic spy devices were perfected. It would be unsafe to dispatch messages written in invisible ink: the risk of interception would be too great.

Invisible ink has, therefore, now been down-graded for use as an "internal communications means", as the *Manual of the Soviet Secret Service Orgburo* (Moscow, 1963) describes it. In plain English this means that an informer is permitted to write top-secret details in invisible ink between the lines of a letter written in ordinary ink, and then pass it through the established link of go-betweens to the resident spy operator in control of the espionage network. But, as soon as the master spy has developed and coded the received secret information, and transformed it into microdot size, the communication written in invisible ink must be destroyed.

These rules are not always observed by operators in Communist satellite Secret Service networks. Franz König, for instance, an East German agent in Austria, was discovered because one of his reports to Berlin-Pankow headquarters was intercepted, and the invisible-ink message developed. Alois Vinar, Czechoslovak resident spy operator in West Berlin, was arrested because he made the same mistake.

A Rumanian agent operating in Switzerland obtained some important secret information and, fearing he might forget some details, decided to record everything in invisible ink. He complied with the orders from Bucharest H.Q. and did not, in fact, write the message on paper. But he wrote notes on his shirt, which he then placed among some dirty linen in his suitcase, believing that it would never be found. He was, however, under surveillance, and, as he boarded the Basle-Vienna express, he was stopped and detained. All his belongings were subjected to thorough examination. The invisible-ink message on the shirt was discovered, and the spy jailed.

The availability of almost detection-proof microfilm spy cameras and all manner of highly efficient electronic devices makes the use of invisible ink seem old-fashioned—at least as far as the Soviet and other Iron Curtain Secret Services are concerned. There is, however, a brand of invisible ink which appears to be foolproof, but it is unknown to Communist intelligence and counter-intelligence directors and is successfully used by Western operators working behind the Iron Curtain.

Apart from providing their world espionage networks with technical aid gadgets, Soviet Secret Service headquarters also take every possible precaution to safeguard the security of their agents. To save master spies, their agents, and informers from arrest when Allied counter-intelligence and security forces start to pay them too much attention, the Control Agents in every country of the free world can arrange immediate transport facilities to enable endangered operators to escape.

Any time it is feared that spies might be detected by Western counter-intelligence the Control Agent at once contacts Moscow, who, in turn, notify the Transport Department to make arrangements for immediate escape.

Control Agents are never reprimanded for having made unnecessary escape arrangements, for, although the Russian Secret Service directors know that in the majority of cases a detected spy will not talk, they nevertheless believe in the "safety first" motto and take every precaution to prevent any spy being broken and revealing more than he should.

The better or lesser known cases of Communist spies being helped by Control Agents in collaboration with the Transport Department to reach Russia in safety are numerous. Among those rescued there are, however, some who made front-page headlines in the international Press—as much as the public trials of spies have done.

There is, for instance, the sudden disappearance of the British scientist Dr Bruno Pontecorvo, who had supplied the Russians with atomic secrets. He vanished in 1950 and, helped by the Control Agent, who made the necessary arrangements with the Transport Department, reached Moscow safely.

There is also the mysterious disappearance from Britain in 1951 of the Foreign Office diplomats Guy Burgess and Donald Maclean—recruits of Rudolf Ivanovich Abel's espionage organization. Their Control Agent arranged their escape with the Transport Department, and they were smuggled out of Europe to Moscow before the F.B.I. could request Scotland Yard's Special Branch or M.I.5 to take steps against them.

Every year considerable numbers of Russian and other Communist spies are helped by their Control Agents to escape arrest and prosecution. A more recent example of how Control Agents and the Transport Department work is the case of William H. Martin and Bernon F. Mitchell—the former employees of the United States National Security Agency, who operated in this organization as Soviet spies since the beginning of 1959. They escaped from America at the end of June 1960, and reached Moscow safely.

Some six months later, around Christmas 1960, the Soviet resident spy operator in the United Kingdom, who had posed under the 'cover' of Reginald Kenneth Osborne for over seven years, fled to Russia, because the Control Agent received warning

that the Special Branch were secretly investigating the activities
of a Russian master spy in London. The tip-off did not make it
sufficiently clear that the investigation concerned Gordon Lonsdale
alias Pakhomiv alias Molodyi, so the Control Agent believed the
Special Branch men were after Osborne, and whisked him out
of the country before disaster. Yet, although the wrong master
spy had been transported to Moscow and the Lonsdale spy ring
was arrested and sentenced at the Old Bailey in March 1961 to
a long prison sentence, the Control Agent was not reprimanded
for his hastily made safety arrangements.

William Arthur Mortimer, whose widespread spy webs operated
successfully in many parts of the U.S.A. for nearly eight years,
escaped to Russia in February 1961. A month later the successful
Soviet resident spy operator in Canada fled to Moscow. In
October 1962 the Russian spy operator in Italy, who posed under
the 'cover' of Luigi Soma, and who successfully directed a number
of espionage networks for nine years, escaped to Russia just
before the Italian counter-intelligence could arrest him.

Perhaps the most daring 'rescue operation' of this sort is the
recent case of George Blake, the forty-four-year-old double agent
who was sentenced to forty-two years' imprisonment in 1961.

True to their promise to "look after Soviet Secret Service agents
in danger or peril", the Transport Department made the necessary
elaborate preparations to free Blake from prison on Christmas
night 1964, when only a few warders were on duty and the escape
could be carried out comparatively easily. This plot was foiled
by a fellow-prisoner. The Transport Department did not give up
their rescue efforts, and elaborate steps were taken to ensure that
the next effort would be a success. A nylon ladder of twenty
rungs, each reinforced by a plastic-covered knitting needle, was
smuggled into Wormwood Scrubs prison. A device with which
the bars of a window could be smashed from inside the prison
found its way to Blake. And some time before the escape a pink
chrysanthemum plant was placed at the foot of the wall at the
exact point Blake would be coming over, to serve as a marker
for the escape car.

Every single stage of the rescue operation was planned with
great skill by the Transport Department. Blake, not usually a
talkative man, went out of his way to talk to warders and establish
his presence in the prison shortly before his escape. He was in
the central hall where the prisoners were eating at 5.30 P.M. on
Saturday, October 22nd, 1966. He had ninety minutes to carry
out his escape—during the recreation period before the next
check at 7 P.M. At this check he was missed.

The first stage of the escape was for Blake to break the bars
of the landing window which was his route to freedom.

The next step was to drop a short distance and sprint to the nylon ladder. This too was comparatively easy, and he reached the foot of the wall where he was to be picked up by the escape car.

The last task was getting away from Wormwood Scrubs prison in London and out of the country. This was the easiest part of the rescue operation. It was no more than a routine job for the Transport Department specialists, and despite the fact that British security started a full-scale alert as soon as the escape was discovered, the double agent was not found.

Every recruit for the Soviet Secret Service is assured by his superiors on his (or her) enrolment that every possible assistance of any sort will always be given from Moscow headquarters throughout the term of duty abroad; he is also promised that all the necessary precautions for his safety will be taken. The numerous rescue operations by the Transport Department seem to confirm that the Communist Secret Service directors do everything possible to keep their promises.

22

Diplomatic Spies

APART from the network of resident spy operators and their espionage organizations, there is another kind of Red spy ring in each country—the Diplomatic Corps of the Soviet and their satellites, the second and third Embassy secretaries, the air, military, naval and other attachés, the vice-consuls, and others. Although I am not implying that *all* Communist diplomats engage in active espionage, they are nevertheless all trained as spies and frequently direct military, naval, and other intelligence operations.

Diplomatic spies rely on the very fact of their being diplomats to impress people and persuade them to assist in obtaining valuable information. They openly risk approaching people because they recognize that the worst possibility is their being ordered to leave the country.

The greater the international tension, the more Russian and other Red diplomats step up their activities to supply Secret Service headquarters with any information useful for stoking up crisis heat.

The Committee of Foreign Relations, U.S. Senate, in a report on Soviet espionage in the free world, stated :

> The manner in which the Soviet espionage system with its various interlocking parts functions abroad has been clearly set forth in the findings of the Royal Commissions in Canada and Australia which were set up as a result of the Guzenko and Petrov defections. The Commissions established that there were not one but at least three parallel Soviet intelligence networks operating in Soviet missions abroad : Military, State Security, and Party. To these may also be added naval and commercial intelligence networks. Sometimes these operate under the control and direction of a Soviet Embassy. On the other hand, many of their operatives, bearing nominal diplomatic titles and attached to the Embassy, report directly to their separate headquarters in Moscow, and the Embassy has no control over them.

The work of Communist diplomat spies differs so greatly from the activities of the normal espionage agent that it is important to give some indication of how they operate.

Officially, Commander Igor Aleksandrovich Amosov was Assistant Naval Attaché at the Soviet Embassy in Washington, D.C. In reality he was a Russian diplomatic espionage director operating extensive spy networks. He ordered agents and informers to supply him with details on radar development, constructions of the latest cargo ships, highly confidential manuals giving details of new electronic developments. He passed countless important U.S. secrets to Moscow. When he was finally exposed he was simply declared *persona non grata* and forced to return to Russia.

Major Yuryi Pavlovich Krylov, Assistant Military Attaché at the Soviet Embassy in Washington, D.C., engaged in espionage activities in the U.S.A. for almost two years. He contacted an employee of the Atomic Energy Commission, in search of classified information concerning the technical aspects of nuclear power. When finally discovered Krylov was declared *persona non grata* for "having improperly purchased quantities of electronic equipment through American intermediaries and having attempted to purchase classified military information". He also went home to Russia.

Soviet Secret Service agent Anatoliy Yakovlyevich used the cover of Soviet Vice-Consul in New York to become the chief organizer of atomic espionage in the eastern part of the United States. Yakovlyevich, together with Semyon Semyonov, another Soviet diplomat in the U.S.A., succeeded in working undetected for five years. When the United States became too hot for the two spy chiefs they left.

The Russian spy operator in Australia, Ivan Skrypov, who was cloaked by diplomatic immunity because he held the post of First Secretary at the Soviet Embassy in Canberra, was declared *persona non grata* and was forced to leave Australia in February 1963, because a "beautiful woman agent" of Australian counter-intelligence succeeded in putting an end to his spy activities.

When Skrypov arrived in Australia in June 1959 he was under orders from Moscow Secret Service headquarters to set up an elaborate spy web which would supply him with secret information, documents, photographs, and other data about the rocket experimental station in Woomera, as well as about the American radio station that keeps in continuous contact with the Polaris submarine fleet operating in Southern waters. But Australian counter-intelligence were aware of Skrypov's mission and took effective counter-measures in planting the "beautiful woman agent" on the Russian diplomat spy.

The Australian woman agent found it comparatively easy to meet the Russian master spy and to play a cat-and-mouse game with him right from the start. At their first meeting she told him that the Australian Government was responsible for the death of her lover and pretended to feel such great hatred against her own country that she was ready to support the Soviet Union. Skrypov believed her story and—was tricked.

Every meeting between the woman agent and the Russian diplomat spy was secretly photographed and recorded for Australian counter-intelligence. And when at last conclusive proof was obtained, establishing Skrypov's espionage activities, his unsuccessful spying career in Australia was terminated.

The New Zealand Government declared the Soviet Commercial Counsellor W. S. Andreyev—second highest in rank at the Soviet Embassy in Wellington—no longer acceptable and expelled him from the country. The Second Secretary of the Soviet Embassy in Wellington was also requested to leave, because of spying.

The Turkish Government expelled Corner Rizu, Third Secretary at the Rumanian Embassy in Ankara for eight years, because Turkish police caught him attempting to copy a highly classified N.A.T.O. document. He was given twenty-four hours to depart.

The list of Communist diplomats banished from free countries during this decade could continue almost indefinitely. There is scarcely a month in which a Russian or other Iron Curtain diplomat spy is not declared *persona non grata*, but during the past years the discovery of Communist diplomat spies has become so common that such cases rarely hit the headlines.

Further links in the chain of Soviet espionage are the numerous 'semi-official' missions and delegations. Many of these also hide behind diplomatic immunity. 'Semi-official' espionage in almost every country of the globe is considered in Moscow "of utmost importance".

Next to the Soviet Embassies, consulates, and trade missions, official delegations to the United Nations Organization are of great value to the Communist Secret Service, because a considerable number of their spies can work under the diplomatic immunity which U.N.O. affords to some of its delegates.

In the course of his stay in the United States Aleksandr Petrovich Kovalyev, a Second Secretary of the Soviet Delegation to the United Nations Organization, arranged to receive undeveloped microfilms of materials of intelligence significance at a 'drop area' in New York City.

The recruited agent was told to park his car in a designated area in New York City at a specified time and to place a package wrapped in red paper in the rear window of his car so that it could be seen. The red paper indicated that he was in possession of material which he was going to deposit in the 'dead drop'. To notify the agent that his material had been picked up from the 'dead drop' a telephone directory in a New York restaurant was marked on a prearranged page.

Material of intelligence significance was frequently left by the recruited agent in the New York 'dead drop' area and was retrieved every time by Kovalyev. It was established that the agent was given $500 to purchase an electronic device for delivery to the Soviets, and an additional $500 in payment for delivery of microfilm reproduction of portions of a manual dealing with an automatic steering device for ships.

Kovalyev was ordered to leave the U.S.A.

Colonel Maksim Grigoryevich Martynov, a member of the Soviet Representation to the United Nations Organization Military Staff Committee, approached a U.S. Army officer to obtain for him military manuals from the Army Command and General Staff School at Leavenworth, Kansas. The U.S. Army officer reported the approach and a special agent of the Federal Bureau of Investigation, made up to resemble the Army officer, was contacted by Martynov at the agreed time and place in New York City. Martynov asked for the proposed assistance and paid an advance of $250. Another meeting was fixed. Martynov kept the appointment, but this time the F.B.I. agents got him. The U.N.O. official identified himself and claimed diplomatic immunity. He was expelled.

Viktor Ivanovich Petrov, a translator at the United Nations Secretariat, New York, responded to an advertisement which an aviation draughtsman, seeking part-time employment, placed in a New York newspaper. The draughtsman was an employee of one of the largest American factories, so Petrov offered him a part-time job.

At first Petrov requested insignificant drafting work, for which he paid well. Later he asked the draughtsman to order brochures on aviation and, when he received them, requested information concerning United States military aircraft. The information Petrov sought concerned the state of U.S. aircraft development. The draughtsman became suspicious. The Secretary-General of the United Nations Organization was informed and Petrov's employment at U.N.O. at once terminated.

The *Exposé of Soviet Espionage,* prepared by the Federal Bureau of Investigation and the United States Department of Justice, commenting on the misuse of the United Nations Organization for Communist espionage purposes, states :

> Soviet employees of the United Nations are guests of the United States and are supposedly dedicated to the cause of

M

international peace, but they are, in fact, carefully selected envoys of international Communist conspiracy, trained in trickery and deceit and dedicated to the concept of fully exploiting the freedom of the countries they seek to destroy. It is too much to expect that they would not prostitute the United Nations.

23

He wanted to save Mankind

WHENEVER a high-ranking Communist spy defects sensational headlines appear, and people in the free world are naturally intensely interested to read of defectors bringing with them information and documents of extreme importance to the West.

From time to time other espionage cases hit the headlines—Western agents being discovered by Soviet and other Communist Secret Police forces.

Public reaction to reported arrests of spies is always one of satisfaction at the destruction of an opposition espionage network. The arrest of Western spies behind the Iron Curtain is disturbing, of course, but feelings are somewhat overshadowed by the comforting and satisfactory revelation that "we too have well-established intelligence organizations in Russia. . . ." But have our spies been as effective as, say, Colonel Abel, Gordon Lonsdale, Colonel Wennerström, and many other Soviet master spies?

The most important of all Western spies to have operated in Soviet Russia was Colonel Oleg Penkovsky. From the start of the Cold War to the day of his arrest in Moscow—eighteen years—he kept the West informed on important strategic, scientific, and political developments and moves in the U.S.S.R.

A highly placed Western intelligence officer said this of Penkovsky:

"What Penkovsky managed to tell the West during the time he was in active operation as a spy against Russia amounted to an intelligence agency's dream. Penkovsky was far and away the most outstanding man with whom we have dealt since 1945.

"He was an artillery colonel at the age of thirty. It scarcely needs adding that he was in the K.G.B. (Soviet Committee for State Security) and a very highly placed intelligence officer.

"Penkovsky poured out to us the most vital information on

every sort of military subject of which he had any knowledge.
It was a sort of compulsive necessity to tell—to withhold nothing.
He seemed to be genuinely convinced that what he was doing
would help to save mankind."

Oleg Penkovsky was a thoroughbred Soviet product, a man who
had passed all the Secret Police scrutinies, and was consequently
allowed to become an artillery commander and Soviet Secret
Service colonel, a scientific worker with access to Russia's top-
secret research stations, and organizer of exchanges of delegations
between the Soviet Union and Britain and the U.S.A. How was
it possible for a Soviet citizen of such calibre to be willing to
spy for the West?

Penkovsky explained it as follows:

When the atomic bomb was exploded at Hiroshima I became
more determined than ever to do everything I possibly could
to save mankind from destruction.

My determination was strengthened when we [the U.S.S.R.]
started the race for nuclear research and development and
nuclear weapons production on the largest possible scale
immediately after the end of World War II. I imagined that
. . . we could not only catch up with America in the nuclear
weapons race, but would probably overtake them, . . . and
thus gain nuclear supremacy.

But where would this lead to? To still greater destruction
—and destruction of our country and people too. . . . It was
quite obvious to me that we could never stop the Americans
dropping some of their atom bombs on our territory, and
even if they dropped only a few bombs of the Hiroshima type
the destruction would be so terrible that I shuddered at the
mere thought of it. . . .

Here you have the explanation why I began to pass on to
the West vital information. . . . You see, I firmly believe that
a nuclear war can only be prevented if all the main world
powers have nuclear weapons and thus deter anyone from using
these weapons. And by letting the West have the vital information about our top-secret research, development, etc., I do not
consider that I am betraying my country. On the contrary, I
am doing everything I can to save my people—and my own
country—from the destructive horrors of a threatening nuclear
war. . . .

This was the motive that led this man to become one of the
most important spies the West has ever had.

"In terms of hard military intelligence, probably the most
important information passed on by Penkovsky to the West concerned the 'secret weapon' with which Khrushchev planned to
intimidate and paralyse the free world," said a Western intelligence officer. "This weapon on which Soviet scientists were

working, Khrushchev announced at the beginning of 1960 as 'even more perfect, more terrible' than the most powerful existing weapons. It was an 'unbelievable' weapon, Khrushchev claimed. Of course, we needed to know what sort of new secret weapons Soviet scientists were working on—or whether Khrushchev's announcement was just one of his 'we have done it again' announcements—so the man who could provide us with the answer—Penkovsky—was requested to oblige."

And Penkovsky did oblige. As Penkovsky revealed:

> Marshal Varentsov [the commander of Russia's tactical missile forces, who was demoted in 1963 for his close friendship with Penkovsky, though he was not accused, or even suspected, of having helped his spy friend] told me: "We are only thinking about these things, only planning. Even if we have actually achieved some successes here and there, we still have a long way to go before we actually achieve the things about which Khrushchev keeps talking and boasting."

Khrushchev felt somehow uneasy at having announced the terrible new secret weapon, yet being unable to prove its existence, so he pressed the scientists to produce the missile of his dreams— a missile powered by a nuclear propellant.

In the autumn of 1960 Penkovsky gave Western intelligence the following information:

> The laboratory tests are completed, and the people in charge of the project hope to be able to make K. a present of the new weapon on the occasion of the Great October Revolution's anniversary. Preparations for a test firing are being made, and the test is to be attended by most important men in the military missile programme.

His next report continued:

> The count-down went according to plan, but the new missile failed to leave the ground. The observers waited for some twenty minutes, then came out of the shelter. At this time the missile exploded. Over three hundred people were killed, among them Marshal Nedelin [Commander-in-Chief of Russia's Strategic Rocket Forces].

The Soviet Press announced that "Marshal Nedelin and a number of other officers have been killed in an aircraft accident."

A West German Government foreign affairs specialist said this of Penkovsky:

"On the diplomatic side the most important service rendered by Penkovsky was to warn the West of the exact nature of Soviet intentions during the Berlin crisis of 1961, so that it was possible in good time to take the measures necessary to compel a Russian climb-down. In repeated messages Penkovsky kept telling the political leadership of the West that Khrushchev's bark was worse than his bite, that Russia did not have the military force, especially in inter-continental ballistic missiles, to back up its threats."

Penkovsky kept the West informed of military movements that were disguised as training manœuvres, but were actually designed to bring troops and weapons into Germany. He also reported:

> K.'s plan "to win without a fight, but to be ready to fight if it comes", is opposed by some of his closest associates in the Soviet leadership, particularly by Anastas Mikoyan. Marshal Varentsov told me: "We are taking a risk, a big risk".

The West German official commented:

"This information was clearly of the greatest importance in reassuring President Kennedy that the firm line he was taking over Berlin was right, and in helping him to rally some of his more reluctant allies. Faced with Kennedy's response, Khrushchev announced that there was no hurry after all about arriving at a final solution of the German problem, that there was still plenty of room and time for negotiations. The crisis was over."

Four days before the Berlin Wall went up in August 1961 Penkovsky is said to have supplied Western intelligence with its exact planned dimensions.

In October 1962, when a horrified world held its breath, fearful that the ordeal of nuclear war was about to start through the menacing Russian presence in Cuba, the late President John Kennedy of the United States and Nikita Khrushchev, the head of Soviet Russia, were in direct confrontation. The two statesmen were, as was remarked at the time, "eyeball to eyeball—but then someone blinked." Fortunately, the one who blinked was not Kennedy, and the world breathed again.

"President Kennedy was widely applauded for his dauntless courage and coolness during those almost unbearable days of tension," a Washington official stated. "But there were people in many lands who murmured, 'What a gamble he took!' It was no gamble. President Kennedy was ordering his policy and making his moves because he was aware of certain vital facts, and thus knew that America's was a position of unassailable strength! How? The answer lies in two words—the name of *Oleg Penkovsky*."

It was Oleg Penkovsky who supplied information of such importance that it was at once passed to President Kennedy, and it was Penkovsky's information that turned the crisis over Cuba. Penkovsky told President Kennedy that the United States—in that disturbed October of 1962—*had a lead in nuclear weapons over the Soviet Union of about three to one.*

But in the same month Penkovsky was arrested in Moscow by Soviet Secret Police, and eighteen days later one of his contacts, the British businessman Greville Wynne, was arrested in Budapest by the Hungarian Secret Police on November 4th, 1962, and brought to Moscow for interrogation and trial before a Soviet court with Penkovsky.

The indictment against Penkovsky and Greville Wynne was published on May 7th, 1963—the day their joint trial opened in Moscow before the Military Collegium of the Supreme Court of the U.S.S.R., presided over by Lieutenant-General Viktor Borisoglebsky.

Penkovsky was charged with having been an agent of the British and American intelligence services and with espionage against the Soviet Union. The indictment stated that he had pleaded guilty to all charges, had given "detailed evidence about his criminal activities", and had said during interrogation in January 1963: "I had many defects—I was envious, selfish, vain, career-minded. I liked to court women and had several mistresses. I frequented restaurants and in general liked an easy life. All these vices corrupted me and I fell . . . I became a worthless man and traitor."

The indictment said that Penkovsky, while in London in April-May 1961, had given a written undertaking to co-operate with the British and American intelligence services, and had given away information constituting a State secret of the Soviet Union. While on official missions to London in July and August 1961, and to Paris in September and October of the same year, he had repeatedly met British and American agents at secret addresses, disclosed top-secret economic, political, and military information, and received instruction in espionage techniques.

The indictment continued that, in the course of his co-operation with the British and American intelligence services, and up to the day of his arrest, Penkovsky had received coded radio messages from the espionage headquarters and had regularly met "representatives of the British and American intelligence services", including Mr Roderick Chisholm (Second Secretary at the British Embassy from May 1960 to August 1961) and Mr Rodney Carlson, in Moscow streets and hotels and at diplomatic receptions at the British and U.S. Embassies. He had received instructions and espionage equipment from these 'agents' and had conveyed secret information to them verbally, in written reports, and on film.

The indictment alleged that Greville Wynne met Penkovsky during the latter's visits to London and Paris in 1961, had received espionage materials from him, had passed them to British agents, and had taken part in arranging secret meetings between Penkovsky and representatives of the British and American intelligence services.

While in Moscow in May-June 1961 and in July 1962, Greville Wynne was alleged to have delivered packages with espionage information collected by Penkovsky to "the British agent Chisholm", and to have taken from Chisholm and delivered to Penkovsky "packages with instructions from the espionage head-quarters, photographs of agents, a Minox camera and films, and containers for the delivery of espionage material."

The indictment said that Penkovsky's activities were confirmed by material evidence, reports of experts, investigation experi-ments, the testimony of Greville Wynne, a confrontation with Wynne, the evidence of witnesses, and documents. It went on to say that Wynne's activities were confirmed by the testimony of Penkovsky, a confrontation with him, the evidence of witnesses, material evidence, and documents.

In the course of frequent meetings with Wynne in Moscow, London, and Paris, the indictment went on, Penkovsky had handed over top-secret information. Among the espionage tasks given to Penkovsky had been that of collecting information about rocket troops, about Soviet troops stationed in East Germany, about preparations for a Peace Treaty with the German Demo-cratic Republic, about Soviet-Chinese relations, and other information of political, military, and economic nature.

Penkovsky, while in Britain and France, had repeatedly met representatives of the British and American intelligence services. He had been given an assurance that after completing espionage activities in the U.S.S.R. he would be given a responsible post in a British or American military establishment, at his own choice, with a salary of $2000 (over £700) a month. He would also be paid a lump sum for his past espionage activities on the basis of $1000 (about £350) a month.

In the course of his co-operation with the British and American intelligence services Penkovsky had supplied them verbally, and also by written reports and films, with extensive information which, according to experts' findings, were of a secret or top-secret nature and constituted a State and military secret of the U.S.S.R.

It was stated that searches of Penkovsky's apartment had revealed a forged passport, code-books, paper for sending invisible messages, miniature cameras, a radio which was alleged to have received coded messages, and other espionage equipment, found in a secret compartment of his desk.

The indictment said that while in Moscow between April 1961 and July 1962, Greville Wynne had met Penkovsky on several occasions and received from him packages for British agents containing rolls of film with secret information and reports. On August 23rd, 1961, while in Moscow, Wynne was alleged to have received from Penkovsky a package containing a "military instrument" and to have delivered it to British intelligence.

The following members of the British and U.S. Embassies in Moscow were alleged to have acted as Penkovsky's contacts—"the former U.S. Embassy official Richmond C. Jacob"; Mr Roderick Chisholm; his wife, Mrs Janet Anne Chisholm ("Anna"), described as a "British agent" and alleged to have been one of Penkovsky's principal contacts; "the American Embassy official Rodney C. Carlson"; and Mr Gervace Cowell, Mr Chisholm's successor as Second Secretary at the British Embassy.

For the purpose of espionage communication Penkovsky had used various telephones and a cache (the letter-box) in Pushkin Street, Moscow. One of the telephones was said to have been in the apartment in which the U.S. Assistant Air Attaché, Captain Alexis Davison, had been living since May 1961, and another in the apartment occupied from 1960 to February 1962 by a Second Secretary at the U.S. Embassy, Mr William C. Jones, and now occupied by an attaché at the U.S. Embassy, Mr Hugh Montgomery.

To check Penkovsky's testimony, the indictment continued, an experiment had been carried out in which all prearranged signals were observed. As a result, a man who proved to be Mr Jacob of the U.S. Embassy had come to retrieve documents inserted in the cache in Pushkin Street. Investigations had also established that a telephone number given to Penkovsky in Paris was in the apartment where the former Assistant Naval Attaché Lieutenant-Commander John Varley had lived until June 1962, and which was subsequently occupied by Mr Ivor Rowsell, Transport Officer at the British Embassy. On returning from Paris, Penkovsky had informed British agents through a telephone call to an apartment then occupied by Miss Felicity Stuart, a former member of the British Embassy staff.

Finally, the indictment said, Penkovsky had been caught *in flagrante delicto* on October 22nd, 1962, and arrested. Wynne had been arrested on November 4th, 1962.

The trial took place from May 7th to 11th, 1963. And, testifying on the first day of the court hearing, Penkovsky gave a detailed account of his espionage activities, and also said he had been in charge of organizing exchanges and delegations between the Soviet Union and Britain and the United States of America, and had first met Wynne in Moscow in December 1960.

Understandably, not very much attention was paid to

Penkovsky in the West at the time of the trial, because it was overshadowed by that of Greville Wynne. In the widespread sympathy which the Englishman Wynne and his wife attracted, Penkovsky tended to be overlooked.

Greville Wynne was sentenced to eight years' detention—three years in prison and five in a labour camp. Oleg Penkovsky was sentenced to death. On May 16th, 1963, they shot him. The sentence was carried out speedily to avoid the possibility of Penkovsky becoming an exchange for a Soviet master spy imprisoned in a Western gaol.

A U.S. Government diplomat admitted:

"I describe Penkovsky as an almost priceless contributor to world peace and human rights."

When asked to detail Penkovsky's espionage activities for the West he said he couldn't divulge such secret matters. When asked to comment on whether it was Penkovsky's information that enabled President Kennedy to score his victory in the Cuba crisis of October 1962 he replied:

"I cannot answer your question. I am not aware of the fact that any information of this sort has been released officially, but when you ask me whether I deny that this information was correct I must say that I am not denying or confirming it. I have neither *personal* nor *official* knowledge of it."

Typical official diplomatic talk, but another diplomat, a West German, wasn't so guarded as his American colleague. He said:

"Penkovsky was a Soviet artillery general, a Soviet Secret Service colonel, with open access to the best-guarded Soviet secrets—you don't often find people of this standing, although, it is no secret, there are some very valuable undetected agents working for the West in the Soviet.

"Penkovsky supplied accurate information on secret weapons, strategy, political moves, economy, and everything of vital importance to the free world, and it is no longer a secret that it was Penkovsky who, with his invaluable information, enabled the West, and particularly President Kennedy, to score fundamental victories by enabling him to adhere to his firm stand over Berlin, and especially during the even greater world tension during the Cuba crisis."

This then is the case of Oleg Penkovsky—the Communist whose sole reason for becoming a master spy was to save mankind from disaster.

The affair ended with the usual totalitarian State moves. The Soviet Government newspaper *Izvestiya* announced on May 29th, 1963, that several Soviet Army officers and a scientific worker, who had been friends of Oleg Penkovsky, had been given "severe disciplinary punishment" because of their "negligence" over

Penkovsky's activities. The officers named were Chief Marshal of Artillery Sergei Varentsov, Major-General A. Pozovny, and Colonel V. Buzinov; the civilian was V. Petrochenko, a colleague of Penkovsky in the State Committee for the Co-ordination of Scientific Research.

We have a lot to thank Oleg Penkovsky for.

24

West goes East

ALTHOUGH this book is an exposé of Soviet Russian and other Communist espionage strategy and tactics, it would not be complete if some of the activities of Western intelligence networks operating behind the Iron Curtain were not mentioned. For after the Penkovsky trial many people in most countries of the free world asked the questions: "Was this outstanding master spy the only one we ever had? Are there any Western agents behind the Iron Curtain? Do we have any agents behind the Iron Curtain who work as excellently as the Red spies do in our country? Do we manage to get as many top secrets from Russia as the Russians seem to get from us?"

It will be appreciated that exact details cannot be disclosed because it would endanger the Western intelligence operators and networks working in Soviet Russia and other Communist countries, but some information can be divulged.

The most appropriate answer to the questions "How are our agents getting on in Russia?" and "Are our spies as good as the Russian master spies?" is given by quoting a recent case of a British agent in Moscow—Mr "X".

Mr "X" had been in charge of a successful intelligence network which supplied top secrets over a long period. When Mr "X" was about to make a routine visit to London—camouflaging the journey by saying he was taking a short holiday in Britain—he decided to carry a microfilm one of his agents had just obtained, containing valuable documents and data. He decided to use his pipe for transporting the top-secret material from Moscow to London.

On arrival at the airport he went through the usual 'formalities', but sensed that a security officer had his eyes fixed on his unlit pipe stuck between his teeth. He took out his lighter and lit the pipe, aware that he risked damaging the microfilm with the smoke and heat. He hoped that the special protective packing would save it from destruction.

"Can I see your lighter, please?" said the security officer.

"With pleasure," Mr "X" said and handed it over.

The security officer, accompanied by another, left the airport hall and went into one of the small rooms. They were busy searching the lighter! It was just an ordinary one.

Mr "X" knew that the counter-intelligence men might subject him and his belongings to a thorough search, regardless of whether this entailed missing the departure of the airliner. So when they reappeared and returned his lighter he said, "Would you like to take my pipe now?"

"It's a nice pipe," said the officer who had been looking at it earlier.

Mr "X" said, "If you like it so much you can have it. I can always get another one in London."

The officer was obviously undecided what to do. Mr "X" took the pipe from between his teeth, held it in front of the Russian, and said, "Take it. As I said, I can easily get another one in London."

The Russian behaved typically: unwilling to admit that the West produced better goods than his own country, he said gruffly, "I don't want it. I don't smoke a pipe." He cleared Mr "X" and requested him to put out his pipe, as "smoking is not permitted on the tarmac."

Soon afterwards Mr "X" boarded the London-bound airliner.

"When the microfilm was eventually taken out of the pipe it was in perfect order and not at all affected by the smoke or heat," Mr "X" confirmed. "But if I had been obliged to smoke my pipe to the end I dare say the film might have perished."

An American operator of an extensive espionage network in Prague was able to work undetected for many years and regularly passed information of vital importance to his superiors. As soon as he recruited agents and informers he broke off all personal contact with them and kept in touch merely by using 'dead drops' —prearranged places where agents and informers were to deposit microfilms, or where they would recover payment for their services, together with further instructions.

This spy operator had a large number of agents and informers. Then one of his agents became suspect and was shadowed by plain-clothes State Security officers. As arranged, he phoned his spy leader and spoke the identification sentence. The spy leader went next day to collect the deposited material from the 'dead drop'.

This particular 'dead drop' was behind a bench in Letna Park on a path which went through open countryside. And at this time of the morning this area is usually deserted.

The American walked along the path as if taking a stroll. As he came nearer the bench he observed men seated on near-by benches, and, although they all seemed to be reading newspapers, it was possible that the 'dead drop' bench was under observation. He suspected a trap, and as the 'dead drop' bench was the only one unoccupied in this part of the park, he sat down on it and started reading his book, more than ever certain they were waiting for him to make the wrong move. When he tired of sitting in the park he continued his leisurely walk, without having even glanced in the direction of the 'dead drop'. None of the men on the benches followed: they were still waiting for someone to collect the incriminating material.

The spy-ring operator remained undetected and was able to continue his work.

Then there was a certain British resident network operator in Moscow.

As private advertisements in Soviet newspapers cannot be inserted as easily as in Western countries, he devised a system of radio and telephone signals so ingenious that the alert Soviet counter-intelligence and State Security officers never suspected. For obvious reasons this particular signal method, which was a working code for numerous British spy-web agents and informers in various parts of the U.S.S.R., cannot be revealed. But it can be said that it enabled the British resident network operator to pass on instructions and requirements to agents and informers, and it also served as a communication method for them to advise him whether or not his instructions and requests had been carried out.

The passing by agents and informers of microfilms was equally ingenious.

Travelling about in the Soviet Union is not as easy as it is in the countries of the free world. So travelling for the purpose of collecting espionage material left at 'dead drops' is impractical, and resident network operators must use all their imagination and inventiveness to achieve efficiency.

This particular spy leader found the answer to his problem by the simple method of using the Soviet postal service. Micro-dotted messages, reports, and even blueprints and documents were secreted under postage-stamps, and microfilms concealed in small Russian-made commonly used articles and posted in the ordinary way. This method entailed the resident network operator establishing a chain of accommodation addresses.

A Western resident network operator in an important Soviet city—working for the U.S. Central Intelligence Agency—devised another means of receiving microfilms of blueprints, documents, and other reports. Her contact worked in a Soviet establishment dealing with books published in the U.S.S.R. This contact concealed microfilms in books so expertly that even the most searching eyes would not suspect. All that remained was to pass the books to the spy leader.

Still another method for passing microfilms to the spy leader was devised by a resident network operator, working in Moscow for the West German Secret Service. His contact was a shoeblack. The spy leader went to have his shoes polished regularly by the same shoeblack. He was careful to keep a reserved attitude towards the shoeblack, and usually read a copy of *Pravda* while his shoes were polished. But whenever a microfilm was passed the shoeblack slipped it into the shoe while putting on polish or treating the leather with his brushes. This method was used successfully for years, and neither the Secret Police nor the network of Soviet spy-catchers suspected. The channel closed only when the shoeblack was given the "honourable opportunity" to be trained as a toolmaker at a factory in the Soviet Far East, and had, of course, to comply with the trade union's orders.

A resident network operator working for French intelligence in Prague was extremely inventive in obtaining regularly and safely microfilms on progress in the Skoda Works and other important Czechoslovak factories; information on Soviet and Iron Curtain strategic developments; and reports on secret political, economical, and production meetings. This was one of his methods:

His contact was an aircrew member of C.S.A.—the Czechoslovak Airline—a fully trusted member and actually in the employ of the Czechoslovak Secret Police and Secret Service. He had been assigned to report on other crew members, airport personnel, and to try to pick up any scrap of valuable information while landing in foreign countries. He was particularly valuable to the French spy-web operator in Prague because he was so trusted by his own people.

How this particular aircrew member was selected as a likely double agent and eventually recruited it would be unwise to reveal, but I can describe how he worked. He secured microfilms concealed in harmless-looking containers, and took them out on flights to Paris, Brussels, London, Rome, Zurich. But when he landed at any of the Western airports he did not pass the microfilm to anyone. He was always more than careful not to come into close contact with any 'foreigners'.

Being himself a Czechoslovak Secret Service agent, he knew only too well that many agents working in foreign countries are planted at airports and seaports. So when he landed at a foreign airport he would go to a toilet and affix microfilms in a hiding-place, then return to the rest of the crew. His French spy leader knew of the flights to the particular airports, and, when signalled that the agent would be carrying microfilm on the journey, would contact another agent of the French Secret Service to recover the microfilm.

Direct electronic recorders play a very substantial rôle in espionage. A tiny hair-wire recorder, housed in the shoe of an American agent who had access to confidential meetings of the Soviet Russian Party Presidium, was successfully used in Moscow. This particular recording instrument could operate many hours non-stop, and was so designed that hair-wire cartridges could be swiftly and simply inserted to permit the agent to keep his 'secret ear' operational whenever required. Its invaluable service was terminated when the U.S. agent in Moscow was promoted and was no longer concerned with intelligence activities. To prevent accidental discovery of the instrument, which could not be returned to the resident network operator, the agent was instructed to destroy it.

A similar hair-wire recorder was used by a British spy ring in Moscow. An agent with access to a research department for nuclear guided missiles and task-force weapons was able to hide it in a room in which scientists and technologists discussed their progress and research problems. It was in continuous use for well over a year, during which time the agent was able to pass on cartridges containing the recorded information. This 'secret ear' was never discovered—not even after the Penkovsky case, when the Soviet counter-intelligence and State Security officers probed everyone in this particular establishment and thoroughly searched the place for concealed espionage instruments.

Electronic 'ears' are also used by counter-intelligence and security agents for keeping a check on the movements of suspect agents and informers. A resident network operator working for the West German Secret Service in Soviet Russia reported the following:

"I found a little gadget about the size of an aspirin fixed under the collar of my overcoat, and I consequently knew I was suspect. It meant I had to be more than careful not to give them any proof to support their suspicion. If I succeeded they might eventually cross me off the suspect list.

"The first thing was to signal my superiors and my agents and informers to cut off communications until further notice. Next was to pretend I hadn't located the instrument. They might get fed up with shadowing me and assume there was nothing suspicious about me after all.

"Two days after finding the gadget under my collar I discovered it had been removed; but by chance I found the same kind of device in the briefcase I always carry about, so I knew I was still under surveillance.

"As weeks passed I found more of the same type fixed to different personal belongings. If I hadn't been on the lookout and not checked all sorts of places I wouldn't have found them.

"I began to worry. I couldn't do anything but continue normal activities, waiting all the time for the knock on the door. Nothing happened.

"Then, after almost six weeks, I couldn't find a gadget anywhere. Did it mean they had called off electronic surveillance and had gone over to the ordinary method of trailing by teams of agents each of whom follows a suspect only a short stretch and then hands over to the next shadower? Or did they now have a trickier technical method of trailing which was unlikely to be discovered? I didn't know.

"The uncertainty lasted two weeks, by which time I concluded the watch had been called off. I risked a message to my superiors asking for guidance. I was ordered to stop operation for three months and, in the event of making any further significant discoveries, to advise them immediately. Nothing occurred, and it was clear the surveillance must have been a random security check. For three years since the day I first discovered the gadget under my coat collar I have been able to continue my activities undetected."

Drugs of a wide variety also play an important part in international espionage. They are frequently used by agents for all manner of purposes.

An agent working for the U.S. intelligence wanted to microfilm some secret documents and blueprints, but was prevented from doing so by the watchfulness of a Soviet security officer. The microfilming could not be postponed to another time because the research files were to be taken the same night to a Ministry where access would be virtually impossible.

The solution was to dope the security officer and, while he was asleep, microfilm the documents and blueprints. But the doping had to be done without causing suspicion.

The agent suggested they should have a glass of tea, to which the security officer agreed. Two glasses of tea were brought from the canteen, and the agent managed to squirt a few drops of tasteless fast-acting dope into the officer's glass without his noticing. A few minutes later, the glass still three-quarters full, the officer became drowsy and fell asleep.

The U.S. agent microfilmed the documents, then deposited the microfilm camera in a safe 'dead drop' where it could be collected later. Usually only the microfilm would be deposited in the 'dead drop', but on this occasion it was considered wiser to dispose of the camera as well in case of any search. His task completed, the agent squeezed some of the dope into his own glass of tea,

N

poured the rest of the drug down the toilet, and sipped the tea, which put him to sleep, too.

The security officer and the agent were discovered by the men who came to collect the secret files. Laboratory tests established the drug in both glasses, and questioning of the two men and the canteen staff followed. Assuming that a member of the canteen staff had doped the two for some purpose, but unable to detect a particular culprit, the security directors removed the entire canteen staff and installed hand-picked replacements.

The microfilm camera and its photographs were safely picked up from the 'dead drop' and passed to the spy leader for ultimate transmission to his intelligence headquarters. The U.S. agent working in the closely guarded research establishment remained unsuspected, and was able to continue his activities.

"Self-defence and unarmed attack is as important for an intelligence agent as microfilm and electronic equipment," said Sir Percy Sillitoe, K.B.E., former head of Britain's M.I.5. "Case histories from all over the world contain information that proves conclusively how imperative self-defence and unarmed-attack training is for a spy working in a foreign country, and especially in a country where rough-handling is common procedure applied by counter-intelligence and security men. Many an Allied agent escaped disaster by mastering the techniques of sophisticated self-defence, and many an agent . . . was only able to obtain important secret information by having been able to render harmless security men by using silent but effective unarmed-attack methods."

An appropriate illustration to Sir Percy's words is the following case.

An American agent who operated successfully in Berlin and was known under the identification name of "Marie" escaped kidnapping by Soviet security officers and being dragged behind the Iron Curtain through effectively using a combination of judo and karate.

Marie was a slim-built woman in her thirties, and more of an office type than a sportswoman. She returned one night to her apartment in a quiet side-street, and, as she inserted the key to open the front door of the block of flats, two men detached themselves from the adjoining house entrance, cornered her, and demanded that she accompany them. Although taken by surprise, Marie remained master of the situation.

From the accent of the man who addressed her she concluded he was a Russian State Security officer, and, creating the impression that she would go without fuss, she accompanied her two captors. But as they walked towards a car waiting at the corner of the street she acted. She knocked unconscious the man walking half a step in front of her and, a second later, 'dealt' with the other. Marie's fight for survival lasted a minute or two. The Russian State Security officer was also well trained in ju-jitsu, but Marie managed to hurl him through the air, and she knocked him unconscious with a karate blow.

The two men were later picked up by a police squad car, and it was established that they were Soviet special-task officers.

These cases of Western intelligence agents working successfully in Soviet Russia and other Iron Curtain countries are only a fraction of case histories contained in Allied intelligence head-quarters. However, they provide a definitive answer to the crucial question about whether we too have successful master spies behind the Iron Curtain.

It is a comfort to know that we have, and it is in their existence, and in our awareness of the dangers that surround us, that our main hopes for the future must lie.

Appendix

IN August 1958 the East German Secret Service chief, Lieutenant-Colonel Siegfried Dombrowski, who was also a senior officer of the Soviet Secret Service Berlin-Karlshorst branch head-quarters, defected to the West. His comprehensive knowledge, acquired during years as a Communist Secret Service top man, made it possible for the Western intelligence services to gain most valuable information on the Soviet and other Russian satellite espionage systems.

Lieutenant-Colonel Dombrowski was not the only Communist Secret Service executive to defect to the West. Among those Soviet and other Iron Curtain top espionage officers who sought asylum in the free world between 1945 and 1966 were Igor Guzenko, Nikolai Khokhlov, Vladimir Petrov, Bogdan Stashynsky, Günther Maennel, Klimov, Mikhail Goloniewski, and many others.

The defections of all these Communist Secret Service chiefs to the West, together with the information gained from various other Red spies arrested, helped Western intelligence services to check and corroborate the information obtained from their own agents, and to fill in missing details. It is therefore now possible to expose the exact structure and tactics of all the Red Secret Service organizations and the branch headquarters in East Berlin.

Apart from the dangerous Berlin-Karlshorst Soviet Secret Service branch headquarters, the most important espionage net-work of Russia's satellites is the intelligence service of the East German Democratic Republic. It is largely organized on the pat-tern of the Soviet Secret Service and consists of two separate but fully synchronized organizations—Mfs, the Ministry for State Security, and Vfk, the Military Intelligence Service.

The Ministry for State Security (which calls its equivalent of Moscow headquarters' Foreign Directorate, the Main Intelligence Administration) is the larger of the two East German organizations. Since February 1st, 1950, its Berlin H.Q. has been located in the huge building which is merely known as 22 Normannen Strasse, Berlin-Lichtenberg. But during the past fifteen years this intelligence organization has grown so rapidly that further extensive accommodation had to be found for the nearly 3000 officers who work round-the-clock duties in the twenty-two departments.

The Main Intelligence Administration, which to a very large extent carries out orders received from Soviet Secret Service branch headquarters in Berlin-Karlshorst, is headed by Major-General Markus Wolf, and his deputies Major-General Hans Fruck, Colonel Herbert Hentschke, Colonel Alfred Scholz, Colonel Erwin Koletzki, Lieutenant-Colonel Hans Morgenthal, and Lieutenant-Colonel Willi Woehl. It is housed at Gross-Berliner Damm, Berlin-Johannisthal. Its main task is to penetrate important Ministries, authorities, and offices in the West German Federal Republic and other Western countries, and to obtain "secret political directives of governments hostile to the East German Democratic Republic", as well as top secrets on scientific, technological, and other developments.

Due to the East German Government's continuous fight for reunification of the country in an effort to impose Communist rule throughout Germany, the Main Administration intelligence has chosen as its most important target West Germany. But Major-General Markus Wolf's department also operates against almost every N.A.T.O. Power and, in recent times, has concentrated espionage activities in Austria and Scandinavia.

Department II, also called the Counter-Intelligence Department, headed by Colonel Josef Kiefel, is housed in the Berlin headquarters of the Ministry for State Security—at 22 Normannen Strasse, Berlin-Lichtenberg. Its function is to penetrate Western intelligence services and obtain information on organization, personnel, and missions of these services. One of the tactics of Colonel Kiefel's Counter-Intelligence Department is to send large numbers of often insufficiently trained agents to West Berlin and the West German Federal Republic for assignments which could be carried out by simple observation. The motive for this mass-employment of low-standard agents is deliberately to divert Western counter-intelligence from the activities of the highly trained and efficient Communist spies, and so disrupt to a considerable extent Western security.

Colonel Kiefel's Counter-Intelligence Department is divided into the following sections:

Section I, which is headed by Lieutenant-Colonel Walther Koenig and works against the U.S. intelligence service.

Section II, which is headed by Lieutenant-Colonel Werner Gruenert and works against British intelligence.

Section III, which is headed by Lieutenant-Colonel Heine and works against the French intelligence.

Section IV, which is headed by Lieutenant-Colonel Werner Kubelski and works against the West German intelligence service and the offices of the West German Agency for the Protection of the Constitution.

Section V, which is headed by Lieutenant-Colonel Boede and works against refugee organizations in Western countries.

The other nineteen departments of the East German intelligence service headquarters in Berlin engage in transport and abduction, coding and decoding, radio communication, and in all the other espionage activities which every intelligence service carries out. The Technical Departments of the East German Ministry for State Security are, however, typical Communist institutions and deserve to be exposed.

Department K, also known as the technical Workshops Department, for instance, is headed by Major Rudi Weber and has its mechanical and technical workshops in the closely guarded Freiwalder Strasse, Berlin-Hohenschönhausen. There all the electronic, photographic, etc., equipment for intelligence operations is manufactured. And the men and women who manufacture the equipment are specialists who have been jailed for all sorts of crimes and were released from prisons all over East Germany to work in Department K under the strict direction and supervision of State Security officers.

Other sections of Department K manufacture forged documents of every description; turn out unobtrusive containers for the safe transport of microfilm; and provide many other gadgets which are of substantial assistance to master spies and their networks in Western countries.

The East German Secret Service headquarters also maintain no fewer than forty-nine 'cover establishments' in East Berlin to carry out systematic deceptive recruitment of agents and informers.

The Main Intelligence Administration's military counterpart, the Administration for Co-ordination, began life as a separate intelligence network in 1953, and was then known as Administration 19. For four years it was housed at 42–45 Behrens-Strasse, Berlin, and worked with considerable success under the personal command of Major-General Karl Linke. Then, in late July 1957, the Major-General, charged with "loss of official documents and neglect of duty", was demoted to the rank of colonel, and sacked from his post as chief of the East German Military Intelligence.

His successor, Colonel Willi Saegebrecht, was appointed on September 1st, 1957, and his deputies were Colonel Erich Ripperger—in charge of operations; Lieutenant-Colonel Siegfried

Dombrowski—in charge of organization; and Lieutenant-Colonel Werner Schmutzler—in charge of political affairs, and holding the position of political deputy. Five years after its creation Administration 19 was renamed Administration for Co-ordination, and moved its offices to 25–29 Regatta-Strasse, Berlin-Grünau.

The newly born Administration for Co-ordination was destined to undergo numerous substantial changes and reorganizations during its first year. For, in August 1958, Lieutenant-Colonel Dombrowski defected to the West, and "his treacherous and unpatriotic act" created a great upheaval within the Soviet and Russian-controlled intelligence networks.

The Administration for Co-ordination, which is much smaller than the Main Intelligence Administration, and employs only some 500 officers on round-the-clock duties at Berlin H.Q., consists of over twenty departments dealing with the military intelligence organization. But, as far as active military espionage in the West is concerned, only the following three main divisions are engaged in this task:

Division A, also known as Tactical Intelligence Division, which is headed by Major Gerhard Kunze. At first this division engaged in spying on military units and military supply installations of the West German Armed Forces, the West German border police, the West German uniformed police—city, country, and riot police—and on all Allied forces stationed in West Germany. But, as the division grew and gained experience, its activities extended to spying on N.A.T.O. military units and military installations anywhere in the free world.

Division C, also known as Strategic Intelligence Division, which is headed by Lieutenant-Colonel Helmut Apelt, engages in collecting military information, and information relating to armaments and new weapons development, anywhere in the West. Of primary importance is information on troop units and N.A.T.O. installations in Western Europe, including air forces and naval bases, and Division C's main targets are Great Britain, France, Belgium, the Netherlands, Luxembourg, Denmark, Norway, Italy, and Spain. To be in complete charge of all the East German strategic intelligence the Administration for Co-ordination's Berlin headquarters' Division C is also responsible for directing the operational bases of the military intelligence services in Schwerin, Magdeburg, Erfurt, and Leipzig.

Division T, which is headed by Lieutenant-Colonel Buechel, is the last of the three main centres for carrying out East German military espionage abroad. This division, which is also known as Secret Weapons Division, engages in obtaining secret information about strategic devices, armaments factories and supplies, and chemical plants in the Western world.

The next-best Communist intelligence network which, like the Soviet and East German Secret Services, constantly launches large-scale spy operations from East Berlin against the West is the Polish espionage system. It is largely patterned on the Soviet Secret Service, and consequently consists of two entirely separate but fully synchronized institutions—the Polish Ministry of the Interior and the Defence Ministry—one controlling general espionage and the other military intelligence throughout the free world.

Unlike the Russians and East Germans, who maintain huge and independent branch headquarters in East Berlin for directing their extensive espionage networks, the Poles have no fully independent intelligence headquarters in Berlin. Their master spies and spy networks in the West are directed from their Embassy at 120 Berliner-Strasse, Berlin-Pankow; from their consular section at 15 Tal-Strasse, Berlin-Pankow; from the Polish Information Bureau at 3 Neustädtische-Kirch-Strasse, Berlin, N.W.7; from the House of Polish Culture at 103 Friedrich-Strasse, Berlin, W.8; and from the branch offices of P.A.P.-Press Agency; from Orbis, the Polish travel agency; from L.O.T., the Polish airline; and from the Polish merchant marine.

All the above Polish institutions are in continuous contact with Warsaw Secret Service headquarters and receive their directives from there.

As far as general espionage is concerned, this is headed by the Polish Ministry of the Interior. Polish military intelligence is, however, to a considerable degree, directed from the Polish Military Mission in West Berlin—under the cloak of diplomatic immunity.

The West Berlin Polish Military Mission at 19–21 Lassen-Strasse, Berlin-Grunewald, which is officially recognized by the Allied Control Council, employs, at present, some thirty officials, officers, and clerical staff, including eight persons protected by their diplomatic immunity.

Military Attaché Hirszowicz, for instance, was identified as the employer of the notorious Polish spies Maria Knuth, Klaus Wensien, and Bronislaw Sniegowski, who were sentenced to prison terms of four, three and a half, and five years respectively. These sentences for Hirszowicz's agents underline the dangerous character of this espionage group, especially when they are compared with other far shorter prison sentences passed on Communist spies during the post-War era by West Berlin courts.

The arrest of Hirszowicz's spy ring did not deter the Polish Military Mission in West Berlin from espionage in the West. But eventually Embassy Secretary Kalinski, who was a 'diplomat' with the Polish Military Mission, was caught red-handed in West Berlin and arrested on charges of espionage.

The widely publicized spy cases of Knuth, Wenzien, Sniegowski, and Kalinski were responsible for the Polish Military Mission in West Berlin reducing its espionage activities and, from then, working more cautiously. And although much of the direction has been shifted to the Polish Embassy in East Berlin, and the Polish Military Mission in West Berlin acts only as a liaison office to spy directors in East Berlin in the recruitment of agents for their Secret Service, the Polish Military Mission in West Berlin is, nevertheless, actively engaged with espionage rings in West Germany and Western Europe.

East Berlin is also the branch centre of operations for the rest of Russia's satellite countries—Czechoslovakia, Hungary, Bulgaria, and Rumania—and it has been established that about 30 per cent of all Red satellite espionage centres and master spies in the free world (in West Germany about 70 per cent) receive direct, or indirect, orders from the masterminds of the Iron Curtain Secret Services in East Berlin.

The Czechoslovak Secret Service maintains well-organized and dangerous espionage directorates in both zones of Berlin.

Josef Cermak, an officer of the West Berlin Czechoslovak Military Mission at 54 Podielski Allee, Berlin-Dahlem, was arrested on charges of having recruited a West Berlin citizen for espionage activities. The authorities were satisfied that Cermak was one of the most dangerous Czechoslovak espionage directors. They knew he directed a large number of master spies and their espionage rings in West Berlin, West Germany, and many other Western countries. He did not belong to the ten officials of the Military Mission who were covered by diplomatic immunity, and could, therefore, be dealt with like any other espionage executive in the West.

The case of Karel Andres, who, together with a number of other Czechoslovak spies operating in West Germany, was arrested and sentenced by the Supreme Court of the Federal Republic to four years in prison, is another striking illustration, because it reveals how the Czechoslovak Embassy in East Berlin manipulates master spies and their networks in the West. Andres had established a number of spy webs in West Berlin, West Germany, and other countries of the free world, and, once these widespread and dangerous networks operated efficiently, he confined himself to directing them from the Czechoslovak Embassy at 10–11 Schönhauser Allee, Berlin, N.54. His undoing was, however, that he believed he was beyond suspicion of Western counter-intelligence, and dared to cross the border into West Berlin, where he intended to supervise an espionage venture of great importance. He was caught red-handed.

The case of Tibor Benedek, an intelligence director of the Hungarian Secret Service, is an example of how the East Berlin Hungarian Embassy at 48–49 Pushkin Allee, Treptow, co-operates with the Hungarian Trade Mission in Frankfurt-am-Main—the centre of the American zone of West Germany.

Benedek went from East Berlin to Frankfurt-am-Main, where he established a number of master spies who commanded several elaborate espionage networks. These agents and informers swiftly succeeded in spreading their webs to almost all parts of the Federal Republic of West Germany, and to a number of Western countries. For a few months Benedek stayed in Frankfurt-am-Main and, being on the spot, supervised the activities of his networks. When the Soviet Control Agent tipped him off that counter-intelligence had started to notice him he hurriedly returned to East Berlin and continued his activities from the safety of Pushkin Allee.

The arrests of the two Bulgarian Secret Service directors Maslenkoff and Petrounoff, who were members of the Bulgarian Trade Mission at 62 Friedrich-Strasse, Berlin, and who were caught red-handed by Western spy-catchers, and the arrest and conviction of Tanegaru, who had been an espionage executive of the Rumanian Embassy at 23 Park-Strasse, Berlin-Pankow, sufficiently illustrate that the Bulgarian and Rumanian Secret Service headquarters in Sofia and Bucharest also maintain efficient world espionage directorates in East Berlin.

In a report to the Kremlin Party Presidium on Soviet and Russian satellite espionage activities and successes in the free world, delivered in January 1967, the Chairman of Russia's Committee for State Security, Vladimir Semichastny, declared: "As far as Soviet and all the combined Communist Secret Service operations in foreign countries are concerned, East Berlin branch headquarters are almost as important as Moscow and all other headquarters."

Index